Integrated Series in Information Systems

Volume 39

Series Editors
Ramesh Sharda
Oklahoma State University, Stillwater, OK, USA

Stefan Voß
University of Hamburg, Hamburg, Germany

More information about this series at http://www.springer.com/series/6157

Saqib Saeed • T. Ramayah • Zaigham Mahmood
Editors

User Centric E-Government

Challenges and Opportunities

 Springer

Editors
Saqib Saeed
Department of Computer
  Information Systems
Imam Abdulrahman Bin Faisal University
Dammam, Saudi Arabia

Zaigham Mahmood
School of Computing
University of Derby
Derby, UK

Shijiazhuang Tiedao University
Hebei, China

T. Ramayah
School of Management
University Sains Malaysia
Penang, Malaysia

UTM International Business School
  (UTM-IBS)
Universiti Teknologi Malaysia
Kuala Lumpur, Malaysia

ISSN 1571-0270   ISSN 2197-7968 (electronic)
Integrated Series in Information Systems
ISBN 978-3-319-86625-3   ISBN 978-3-319-59442-2 (eBook)
DOI 10.1007/978-3-319-59442-2

Printed on acid-free paper

This Springer imprint is published by Springer Nature
The registered company is Springer International Publishing AG
The registered company address is: Gewerbestrasse 11, 6330 Cham, Switzerland

To
My Sweet Kids
Rameen, Eshaal and Huzaifa

Preface

Electronic Government, or E-Government, is about harnessing the information revolution to improve the efficiency of government processes and the lives of citizens. If appropriately implemented, it promotes transparency and effectiveness of a government's processes as well as citizens' participation (e-participation) in the affairs of the government. An effective E-Government aims at a citizen-oriented user-centred approach to governance through the effective deployment of information, communication and social media technologies. After all, a government works for the benefit of its citizens.

E-government projects require solid commitment of the political leadership as well as effective planning and availability of financial resources. Whereas provision of effective E-Government is a government's responsibility, it is important that citizens have the knowledge and skills to consume the available technology to exercise positive commitment to affect the governments' strategies. Thus, a government's responsibility also extends to ensuring the availability and accessibility of necessary technological infrastructure and the training demands from the general public.

Developing countries are often at the initial stages of E-Government development, where they offer a portal providing 'one-way' Government-to-Citizen information via a website; however, the technologically developed nations have successfully progressed to the 'interactive' stages of open governments, sometimes, also referred to as Government 2.0 or Connected Government. Whereas the benefits of transparent and user-centric Connected Government, or C-Government, are tremendous, there are numerous inherent issues that hinder the satisfactory adoption and provision of E-Government. These include lack of a number of necessarily required factors including will and commitment of political leaders; clear vision and long-term workable strategy; political stability of the nation and its government; economic and governmental structures; financial resources and support; regulatory and legal frameworks and procedural controls; easy availability of ICT technologies to general public; as well as technical expertise. Additionally, there is often a lack of technological familiarity that may result in the unwillingness of the citizens to engage with the governments using innovative technologies and methodologies.

In this context, this book, *User Centric E-Government: Challenges and Opportunities,* considers the various dimensions of the Connected E-Governance and presents the prevailing situation in the form of status reports, development methodologies, practical examples, best practices, case studies and the latest research. The present volume is a collection of 13 chapters authored by academics of international fame and reputed industry practitioners from around the world. Hopefully, the book will serve as a reference text in the subject areas of E-Government and electronic governance for the provision of an open and transparent government.

Dammam, Saudi Arabia   Saqib Saeed
Penang, Malaysia   T. Ramayah
Derby, UK   Zaigham Mahmood

Contents

List of Contributors and Editors

Contributors

Asiya Abdus Salam Imam Abdur Rahman Bin Faisal University, Dammam, Saudi Arabia

Michaela Black School of Computing and Intelligent Systems, Ulster University, Northern Ireland, UK

Brian Cleland School of Computing and Maths, Ulster University, Northern Ireland, UK

Hüsna İrem Coşkun Turkish Airlines, İstanbul, Turkey

Robert Cropf Department of Political Science, Saint Louis University, Saint Louis, MO, USA

Emmanuel Eilu School of Computing and Informatics Technology, Makerere University Kampala, Kampala, Uganda

Titiana Ertiö Technology Experience Center, Austrian Institute of Technology GmbH, Vienna, Austria

Department of Social Research, University of Turku, Turku, Finland

Luz Maria Garcia-Garcia Universidad de la Sierra Sur, Oaxaca, Mexico

Bogdan Ghilic-Micu Department of Economic Informatics and Cybernetics, The Bucharest University of Economic Studies, Bucharest, Romania

J. Ramon Gil-Garcia University at Albany, State University of New York, Albany, NY, USA

Md. Abir Hasan Khan School of Management, University of Tampere, Tampere, Finland

Bastiaan van Loenen Knowledge Centre Open Data, Delft University of Technology, Delft, The Netherlands

Marinela Mircea Department of Economic Informatics and Cybernetics, The Bucharest University of Economic Studies, Bucharest, Romania

Mohammad Anwar Rahman Central Connecticut State University, New Britain, CT, USA

T. Ramayah School of Management, Universiti Sains Malaysia, Penang, Malaysia

UTM International Business School (UTM-IBS), Universiti Teknologi Malaysia, Kuala Lumpur, Malaysia

Manuel Pedro Rodríguez Bolívar Faculty of Business Studies, Department of Accounting and Finance, University of Granada, Granada, Spain

T. Santhanamery Faculty of Business Management, University Teknologi MARA, Penang, Malaysia

Madeeha Saqib Abasyn University, Islamabad, Pakistan

Marian Stoica Department of Economic Informatics and Cybernetics, The Bucharest University of Economic Studies, Bucharest, Romania

Buket Taşkın Hacettepe University, Ankara, Turkey

Sarah-Kristin Thiel Technology Experience Center, Austrian Institute of Technology GmbH, Vienna, Austria

Department of Social Research, University of Turku, Turku, Finland

Hakan Tüzün Hacettepe University, Ankara, Turkey

Glenn Vancauwenberghe Knowledge Centre Open Data, Delft University of Technology, Delft, The Netherlands

Jonathan Wallace School of Computing and Maths, Ulster University, Northern Ireland, UK

Editors

Saqib Saeed is an assistant professor in the Computer Science Department at Imam AbdulRahman Bin Faisal University, Dammam, KSA. He has a Ph.D. in Information Systems from the University of Siegen, Germany, and a master's degree in Software Technology from Stuttgart University of Applied Sciences, Germany.

Dr. Saeed is also a certified software quality engineer from American Society of Quality. He is a member of advisory boards of several international journals besides being guest editor of several special issues. Dr. Saeed's research interests lie in the areas of human-centred computing, computer-supported cooperative work, empirical software engineering and ICT4D, and he has more than 50 publications to his credit.

T. Ramayah is currently a professor at the School of Management in USM. He teaches mainly courses in Research Methodology and Business Statistics and has also conducted training courses for the local government (Research Methods for candidates departing overseas for higher degree, Jabatan Perkhidmatan Awam). Apart from teaching, he is an avid researcher, especially in the areas of technology management and adoption in business and education. His publications have appeared in *Computers in Human Behavior, Resources, Conservation and Recycling, Journal of Educational Technology & Society, Direct Marketing: An International Journal, Information Development, Journal of Project Management* (JoPM), *Management Research News* (MRN), *International Journal of Information Management, International Journal of Services and Operations Management* (IJSOM), *Engineering, Construction and Architectural Management* (ECAM) and *North American Journal of Psychology*. Having his contributions in research acknowledged, he is constantly invited to serve on the editorial boards and programme committees of several international journals and conferences of repute. In addition, T. Ramayah has collaborated with noted companies from various disciplines of business through multiple consultancy projects. To date, his consulting experience includes research conducted for companies such as Tesco, World Fish Center and MIMOS. Next to consultancy projects, T. Ramayah is also actively involved in short-term research grants. He has completed two research grants, one in the area of organizational behaviour and the other in the validation of a new methodology and has another ongoing research grant concerning the preservation of batik among Malaysians. As a person who believes in a well-balanced life, T. Ramayah is an active sportsman, playing hockey in the varsity team since his freshman years. He enjoys spending time with his wife, Sally, and their children and travelling to new places.

Zaigham Mahmood is a researcher and author. He is the author or editor of 14 books, six of which, focusing on the subject of Cloud Computing, are published by Springer. Formally, a *Reader in Applied Computing* and *Assistant Head* of a Research Group in the School of Computing at the University of Derby, UK, he now supports the research activity in the School. Dr. Mahmood is also a *Technology Consultant* at Debesis Education, Derby, UK, a Foreign Professor at NUST and IIUI Universities in Pakistan and Professor Extraordinaire at NW University in South Africa. Dr. Mahmood has published over 100 articles in proceedings of international conferences and referred journals. Professor Mahmood is also the *Editor-in-Chief of the Journal of e-government Studies and Best Practices (JEGSBP)*, Associate Editor of IBIMA Conference proceedings as well as a member of editorial boards of several international conferences, journals and books. He has also organized conference tracks, special sessions and workshops and given numerous guest lectures on Cloud Computing, emerging technologies and E-Government.

Part I
Introduction

Chapter 1
The Challenges in Implementing E-Democracy in the United States

Robert Cropf

Abstract Early predictions for information communication technology foresaw a transformation of the way that civil society interacts with government, but the implementation of that technology has thus far failed to transform the democratic process. Technology has changed certain aspects of government administration, particularly for governments in technology-rich areas, but a full synthesis of public participation and technology has yet to occur. This chapter discusses the prerequisites for full implementation of e-democracy, which includes but is not limited to the internal government implementation of technology. Beyond effective implementation of technology, e-democracy also requires a virtually engaged civil society willing and able to utilize an electronic public sphere. Great care must be taken in the event of the rise of true e-democracy to prevent marginalization of those who lack the ability to connect for reasons of income, infrastructure, or privacy concerns. Technology has the potential to foster a more inclusive public sphere and a more inclusive democracy, but great care must be taken to ensure that unnecessary censorship does not occur, that the virtual public sphere is not abused by corporations, that e-democracy is accessible, that the privacy of participants is protected, and that participants in the virtual public sphere are acting in good faith.

Keywords E-government • E-democracy • Public sphere • Path dependency • Digital divide • Full internet access • Civil society • Government information policy • Political inclusion

1 Introduction

It was not until nearly 30 years after the birth of the personal computer that information-communication technology (ICT) finally began playing the important role in the political process that early net-activists had predicted. Obama's two successful bids for the United States presidency in 2008 and 2012, the Arab Spring

R. Cropf (✉)
Department of Political Science, Saint Louis University, Saint Louis, MO, USA
e-mail: cropfra@slu.edu

© Springer International Publishing AG 2018
S. Saeed et al. (eds.), *User Centric E-Government*, Integrated Series in Information Systems 39, DOI 10.1007/978-3-319-59442-2_1

in 2011, and the Black Lives Matter movement starting in 2013, were examples of the heavy and effective use of ICT, particularly social media, to mobilize supporters to effect fundamental political change; which led to widespread acceptance of ICT by the mainstream as a powerful mobilizing and organizing tool. Add to this the many other instances of using ICT to widely transmit a political message and to rapidly start mass movements, and it is unsurprising that the mass media and academics now credit social media and the Web in general for sparking an increase of citizen interest and participation in politics (e.g., the 2016 Bernie Sanders for President campaign). There have been, however, few attempts to establish theoretically and empirically the conditions and prerequisites for successful implementation of e-democracy in the United States. In this chapter, a set of conditions, or opportunities and challenges, if you will, are described and analyzed as the means by which ICT can serve as a catalyst for the development of e-democracy in the United States. These technologies have proven to be effective tools for empowering millions of politically disenfranchised people and giving them a greater voice in the political process. The rise of these ICT-fueled movements, however, begs the question: Can ICT help update (or essentially, "reboot") antiquated political structures and institutions for effective governing in the twenty-first century? In other words, can a tool that plays a pivotal role in the creation, spread, evolution, and sustainability of modern political and social movements also play a central part in the more prosaic institutional aspects of modern democracy? Part of the answer to this question involves an examination of some of the constraints on technology's ability to construct the virtual public sphere as a means to revitalize traditional political institutions.

This chapter examines first the connection between e-government and e-democracy, making the argument that the latter requires the former, but also noting that e-government only provides some of the necessary preconditions for e-democracy. The next section examines the transition of traditional public spheres to virtual public spheres as a result of new technologies including social media, as well as drawing a contrast between the virtual public sphere and the traditional public sphere, as conceptualized by Habermas [1] and others. In this section, the argument is made that governments can help to facilitate the transition to e-democracy but the task of creating and maintaining e-democracy falls mainly to civil society. In the third section, the challenges the path to e-democracy faces are analyzed. One of the most difficult of the current challenges is the persistence of a digital divide, separating the haves and the have-nots in the virtual realm. Part of the third section therefore is devoted to an analysis of the new digital divide and how universal Internet access does not necessarily bridge the gap between haves and have-nots in society.

2   E-Government a Necessary Condition for E-Democracy

In the early 1980s, when personal computers were starting to catch on with the general public, a few far-sighted individuals predicted that the revolution then being unleashed by ICT would transform government and politics by increasing political participation and citizen engagement on a scale that was previously impossible. It was not until the 2000s, however, that the potentials of electronic participation (e-participation) and electronic democracy (e-democracy) have started to be fully realized. Obama's 2008 and 2012 presidential campaigns, for example, marked the first time a successful presidential candidate in the United States used social media and other ICT tools to generate, mobilize, and sustain mass political support. Similarly, the Arab Spring in 2010–2011 depended largely on Facebook, YouTube, and other social media outlets to build and maintain popular support in the face of intense government opposition. In 2014, the shooting of Michael Brown by a white police officer in Ferguson, Missouri, was propelled into the national and international spotlight by social media and fueled the Black Lives Matter social movement. These examples show that ICT's effects on politics are powerful and worth further scrutiny. Furthermore, insofar as the impact of ICT on civil society and politics can be explained, this will provide the insight necessary to understand the possible role of technology in politics in the future.

One of the Internet's important strengths is its ability to connect people from anywhere in the world in virtual communities without regard to geographical proximity. At the dawn of the personal computer revolution, however, Internet access was still relatively expensive and few people owned their own computers, so that the technology's potential to spur social and political change was still very limited. Nevertheless, even then, it seemed likely that ICT would have a huge impact on the democratic process, particularly as the costs of computer technology fell and personal computers went from being large machines on a desk to small devices that could be easily carried around. The turning point came in the early years of the twenty-first century when smartphones became inexpensive enough for many people, even in developing countries, to own. This meant that ordinary people finally had inexpensive, convenient access to the Web, literally in the palms of their hands. This major technological advance, along with the rise of social media and apps, led to ICT being the favored tool of community organizers and political activists.

3   Important Terms Used in This Chapter

Terms that are used extensively in this chapter need to be defined before we can go further. It is not uncommon in the scholarly literature for different authors to employ the same or similar terms but for the terms to mean something different; for example, there is generally no agreed upon distinction between e-government and e-governance in some of the literature. Dawes [2], for instance, defines e-government as the use of information technology to support government operations, engage citizens, and provide government services. Heeks [3], on the other hand, defines e-governance as comprising three dimensions: (1) operations to improve government processes employing ICT, or e-administration; (2) connecting citizens to government via ICT; and (3) using ICT for building external interactions. On every dimension, Heeks' definition concurs with Dawes', but ostensibly they are two different concepts. In this chapter, e-government is defined as government's using ICT to exchange information with and provide services to citizens, businesses, and other units of government including different levels of government (i.e., local, state, and national) chiefly to improve either administrative efficiency or the delivery of public services. Facilitating citizen participation in government as an aspect of e-government, however, has been typically de-emphasized or simply ignored by most governments in the United States.

There are important reasons for this distinction between e-government and e-governance as well. Misuraca [4], for example, contends that governance entails more than merely the mechanics of government by also encompassing the entire political process and not only the ends of government; while government's chief focus is the foundation and regulation of institutional means of achieving public administration. He argues that governance concerns itself primarily with the manner in which governmental institutions relate to citizens and the magnitude of participation in this relationship [4]. These important conceptual differences between government and governance can be transferred to e-government and e-democracy. Thus, e-government is the use of ICT to perform the administrative functions of government including delivery of services while e-democracy is the use of ICT to facilitate those functions of government falling under Misuraca's definition of governance.

4   Importance of Civil Society in Implementing E-Democracy

In line with Misuraca's view of governance, it is not enough for government to opt for an e-government strategy that merely aims to improve administrative efficiency and to serve citizens better; government must also seek ways to actively engage with citizens and expand opportunities for their participation in the democratic process. In the context of mass media and information environments where random events can go viral, often with serious political repercussions, government must make the transition from e-government to e-democracy [5].

Using ICT as a means to help expand the citizen's role in government and the political process goes by several names such as e-participation, e-governance, e-engaging, and e-democracy. In this chapter, e-democracy is used as the catchall label to describe government's online efforts taken to encourage, facilitate, and empower citizens to play a more active role in governance of their community, to become more active in politics, and to engage more with each other in civil society, that is, the virtual public sphere [6]. It is important to consider e-government and e-democracy as separate concepts, although it is not uncommon in the literature for authors to merge the two (e.g., [7]) since many non-democratic nations, including China, have embraced e-government as a means to cut costs and administer government more efficiently [8].

The natural ally of government in seeking to develop e-democracy is civil society. According to Putnam [9], civil society is a basic requirement for "strong democracy" [10]. Put another way, a sufficient social foundation must exist before the entire democratic process can function effectively online. The virtual public sphere, that is, the myriad of ICT-mediated interactions involving government, civic organizations, and private citizens, is simply civil society translated to the online environment. E-government presumes the existence of an extensive technological infrastructure including grid, networks, training, etc. For there to be e-democracy, civil society requires a vigorous presence in cyberspace.

The rest of the discussion in this chapter focuses on two overarching issues: first, conceptual issues surrounding the transition from e-government to e-democracy; second, the issues surrounding the structural opportunities and constraints that influence participation and engagement in online political and governance processes, or virtual public spheres.

In the first set of issues, three different models of democracy are examined in order to understand some of the institutional and political constraints affecting the transition from e-government to e-democracy. In general, while the Internet does increase the amount of information that is available, it cannot be presumed that the network automatically leads to a well-informed populace that is politically engaged. In light of this, the question of what are the best means to create e-democracy is addressed. Next there is an examination of research on the institutional and technological constraints affecting the transition from e-government to e-democracy. These constraints include the effective use of ICT by civil society (the virtual public sphere). A key part of this discussion is an analysis of the institutional challenges that virtual public spheres must overcome before e-democracy can become a reality. The technological barriers to e-democracy are discussed in the following section. These mostly deal with the digital divide. Not the typical divide, however, that is based on lack of access but rather one that is created as a result of certain structural characteristics of the network.

4.1   Aggregative, Direct, and Deliberative Democracy

This analysis begins by looking at three different models explaining democracy and highlighting the distinctive features of each one. The three models of democracy are aggregative, direct, and deliberative. Each model applies a particular lens emphasizing different major aspects of the democratic process. As theoretical frameworks, the aggregative, direct, and deliberative models of democracy also illustrate the institutional variety that is possible in e-democracy.

In aggregative democracy, voting, political competition, interest group bargaining, and efficiency characterize the democratic process. Aggregation assigns to choice, within and among institutions and among constituencies, the predominant role in the democratic process rather than direct citizen engagement or deliberation. Self-interested actors pursue their preferences, develop optimal strategies for achieving their goals, and then seek out compromise positions through bargaining and negotiation with other self-interested actors. An aggregationist's view of e-democracy might focus on whether it successfully translates pluralist choices into political outcomes. The aggregationist emphasis on efficiency would lead to e-government where the main concern is enhancing the efficiency of the delivery of public goods and services. According to aggregationists, citizens benefit from the efficiency gains and expanded choices brought about by e-government efforts.

The direct democracy model stresses the importance of direct citizen participation and emphasizes the grassroots approach to the democratic process. In direct democracy, citizens are afforded "a voice" rather than merely "exit" if there is serious disagreement engendered during the process. Direct democracy proponents would approve of the way ICT provides more opportunities and venues for direct citizen participation in the political process and its ability to enhance grassroots organization and mass mobilization. In direct democracy, e-government is all about expanding everyone's access to government and political information, as well as the wide sharing of citizens' opinions and ideas through the latest technologies. The Internet makes information accessible to a greater number of people with no centralized authority (government, mass media outlets, corporations, think tanks, universities, etc.) dictating what is and is not "approved," "official", or "accepted". This lack of centralized control over content has both positives and negatives, however. On the positive side, it allows ordinary people to fully participate in creating content and influence the political debate because the most important thing is how many pairs of eyes view your blog, video, or web page and not whether you're a government official, corporate executive, TV talking head, or big-name politician. However, on the negative side, this freedom from a central authority can result in misinformation, "dis-information", and the proliferation of falsehoods masquerading as facts. Nevertheless, for direct democracy theorists, the shift from elite control over information dissemination is viewed as both empowering and transformative.

The deliberationist stresses the key role public discourse plays in the democratic process through shaping political opinions, galvanizing support for different candidates and positions, and influencing policy decisions. E-democracy efforts, according to this perspective, should focus on employing ICT to translate the offline public sphere to the online environment. Thus, new technologies and tools, such as smartphones, apps, and social media give birth to virtual communities based on shared interests, political and social causes, sense of identity, and a whole host of other factors. ICT enables new forms of self-expression and engagement with government and other citizens. According to the deliberationists, in these virtual communities, citizens directly engage with one another, debate issues and ideas of concern, and in the process, it is hoped, develop deeper understandings of ideas and positions, which then translates into larger influence in the political process.

One of these three models, or some hybrid, could describe the final shape that a particular e-democracy assumes. In some of the earlier literature, it was optimistically assumed that the deliberative democracy model would prevail [11–14]. The basis for this belief lies chiefly in an approach, which for lack of a better term, can be described as technologically determinative. In other words, the rationale goes that because of its open architecture, easy accessibility, low transaction costs, absence of central authority, and other factors, the Internet provides the optimal conditions for deliberative democracy. However, this position fails to take account of the character of the "offline" political culture that exists. It can be argued that this political culture is at least as important as the Internet's features and unique attributes in affecting the shape an e-democracy takes in a particular national context. In this regard, it is useful to turn to Douglass North and others' insights on path dependency in national economic and political systems. North, for example, stipulates the importance of formal rules, i.e. constitution, legal system, etc., and informal constraints, i.e., political culture, in shaping economic systems in both developed and developing countries. Similarly, it can be argued that formal political structures and the informal civic culture can exert a powerful influence on the success of e-democracy implementation efforts.

4.2 The Public Sphere and the Virtual Public Sphere

The virtual public sphere is merely an updating for the twenty-first century of a well-known theoretical construct from last century. The *public sphere* refers to the part of society that is separate from, and not controlled by, either government or commercial interests; this domain consists of voluntary organizations that work on behalf of a particular cause, shared interest, or for the general good, without regard for personal material profit. The German political philosopher, Jürgen Habermas [1], is credited with introducing the concept to describe political developments in eighteenth-century Europe (particularly France and England), in which the widespread popularity of coffeehouses, salons, and other public places led to people from all social classes gathering to engage in free-wheeling discussions and debates on the political events of the day. Habermas said that the public sphere promoted the core individual rights that we identify with modern democracy, including freedom of speech, the press, and assembly. A strong public sphere is therefore necessary to protect individual freedoms; otherwise a tyrannical government would be free to run roughshod over the society. The traditional public sphere, as described by Habermas, represents an ideal for deliberationists who view it as the optimal setting for the type of deliberative politics central to their theoretical position.

4.3   Decline of the Traditional Public Sphere

Habermas attributes the decline of the public sphere to the rise in the twentieth
century of mass broadcasting (first radio and then television), which offered
private entertainment that distracted people from going to cafes and other public
meeting places to socialize, engage with one another, discuss current events, and
debate politics. Television completed the public's transformation into politically
disengaged consumers of information ([15], p. 160). The advent of the Internet,
however, revitalized the idea of the public sphere for some who saw in the
worldwide computer network a new, more effective means for individuals to access
information, socialize, discuss politics, support political and social causes, and
generally, become more politically and socially engaged [16]. One could say that the
Internet helped to revive the flagging hopes of the deliberationists and civil society
activists more generally who saw the technological developments of the pre-Internet
twentieth century as threatening to the public sphere.

5   Institutional Constraints on the Virtual Public
Sphere and E-Democracy

The Internet provides the environment in which virtual public spheres can thrive and
flourish. Nevertheless, the network merely provides the necessary infrastructure for
virtual public spheres. What are the institutional, structural, and systemic factors that
explain the development of virtual public spheres and by extension, e-democracy,
and how might they be optimized? Van der Graft and Svensson [17] employ three
types of explanations for variations in a country's decision to adopt e-democracy:
(1) ones based on objective rationalization and modernization; (2) ones based on
political evaluation and discretion; and (3) ones based on the technology itself as
the driving force behind institutional change.

The first set of explanations refers to the belief that traditional democratic
procedures and processes are out-of-date and require updating to reflect the social
and political changes of the twenty-first century. As a result of these structural
and institutional deficits, investing in e-democracy efforts provides government
an opportunity to finally address long put-off needs and demands of a systemic
nature. So, for example, e-democracy could be viewed as a means to provide a
more inclusive and non-threatening space through the online environment to discuss
racism and racial politics in the United States. The development of e-democracy,
according to the second type of explanation, would be framed more as an expression
of popular political will, which can be best met through citizen participation
in online policy discussions, e-dialogue with each other and policy makers and,
through direct actions like electronic voting or electronic referenda that help to
make policy choices. Finally, the technological force explanation refers to the belief
that advances in technology ultimately drive institutional changes. As governments

implement e-government initially to improve their internal operations and produce efficiencies, this has spurred business and nonprofit organizations as well as ordinary citizens to increase their online interactions with government, which has over time driven demands for e-participation and using the mechanisms of e-government to become more engaged in the political process.

In their examination of Dutch municipalities, van der Graft and Svensson [17] subject these different explanations to an empirical test. They find the technology-as-driving-force explanation the most compelling. In other words, e-democracy efforts are more likely to occur if the municipalities possess the necessary hardware, software, trained workforce, and separate ICT departments. As this is only one study, the relationship between technology and e-democracy remains unclear. One could argue that the causal direction might actually be the reverse of what van der Graft and Svensson assert, that political reform is a necessary precondition for technological innovation. This would explain why the United States, one of the most technologically advanced countries, still lags behind other countries, including Canada and the UK, in adopting e-democracy.

Using path dependency to explain how e-democracy might be implemented offers an important advantage that is often lacking in the research—it underscores the significance of the evolutionary changes occurring in political institutions and mechanisms of governance as factors shaping the process. As North astutely points out, "We cannot understand where we are going without an understanding of where we have been" ([18], p. 51). More importantly, however, path dependency acknowledges the self-perpetuating nature of institutions and the organizations that have been spawned by those same institutions. These institutions will vigorously resist any change that is perceived as threatening their continued dominance. One therefore ignores the institutional context at one's own peril, particularly if the endeavor involves an effort to radically remake political institutions.

5.1   Governmental Institutions and E-Democracy

As a result of the important part institutions play, in the process of building e-democracy, it is imperative for national and local governments to play a major role. Takao [19], for example, examines Japan's adoption of e-government, which varies by different levels of government, with local government better able to integrate the use of ICT for public input and information dissemination in the policy process than the national government. The UK has been generally out front of other developed countries in its efforts to promote e-democracy. Wright [20] analyzes the effects of e-democracy movement in the UK after more than a decade of innovation. He views as instructive the beginning of the UK e-democracy movement, which initially was a top-down effort, led by the Prime Minister to forge "a new relationship between the individual and the state." Both national government-driven attempts at e-democracy, Citizen Space and Downing Street, performed below expectations, however, so much so that the British government has backed away from similar large-scale efforts in recent years, focusing instead on smaller efforts that can be used more effectively to facilitate consultation between the public and government [20].

A key element in any attempt to build e-democracy is the willingness of the national government to provide adequate resources to expand and enhance e-government services. Wright [21] points out that government is the only institution with the authority to command both the types and amounts of resources necessary to undertake any serious e-democracy effort. Without state intervention, in many cases, Internet access would hardly exist at all, particularly in rural areas. Effective e-government is thus a necessary but not sufficient condition for e-democracy, as was pointed out.

6 The Technology-Related Constraints on Virtual Public Spheres and E-Democracy

A robust e-democracy should guarantee free and equal online access to all participants regardless of their social or economic status. Questions of access, in general, refer to the structures, procedures, processes, and mechanisms (of a formal or informal nature) that govern who are included and excluded from society's major resources. Access refers to the means to physically connect to the Internet and to the ability to make one's voice effectively heard [22, 23]. Technology provides the means to expand entry to the political process but gaps in access, often referred to as the 'Digital Divide', must be overcome for e-government to reach its full democratic potential [24]. Internet penetration and use is notoriously asymmetric across place and socioeconomic conditions, with significant variation from one nation to another and across such demographic variables as income, education, social class, and race [24, 25]. As Habermas and others have pointed out, free and equal access to the public sphere is paramount to true public discourse, which is a prerequisite for strong democracy. Access thus plays a pivotal role in ultimately determining whether e-democracy efforts are successful or not.

6.1 Multi-dimensionality of the Digital Divide

The digital divide is well documented and consists of multiple dimensions. This gap between digital haves and have-nots is the most basic challenge facing successful e-government implementation in many countries. The digital divide presents a formidable modern barrier to full enfranchisement of the populace in technological society. Developing nations face greater challenges in providing access at rates similar to countries with more wealth and resources at their disposal. This technological division between rich and poor nations worsens the socioeconomic conditions and spatial inequalities already existing within the latter. Countries with higher socioeconomic status are better equipped to acquire technology and have urban areas that have the infrastructure for providing ICT to a broader community. The less affluent and rural dwellers are thus more likely to be without reliable access to ICT; this is true even in developed countries such as the United States.

For these reasons, several initiatives now focus on creating the infrastructure for ICT use or expanding that infrastructure to underserved areas and populations. Several cities and counties in the United States, for example, are moving toward providing Wi-Fi access at no direct cost to users. Such an approach begins to treat Internet access the same as access to public utilities such as water and electricity. Programs like the Technological Opportunities Program (TOP) provide grants to nonprofit entities to reduce disparities in low-income areas [26]. Many universities and private organizations are taking similar steps. Currently, many public libraries and schools in the United States—including the vast majority in urban areas—provide computer facilities with high-speed Internet access.

Additionally, patterns of ICT *use* vary depending on resources and other social characteristics [23]. The disabled have less access to the Internet and are online less than those who do not have a disability [27]. Generational gaps exist, as well. Adults may have greater access to ICT, but younger age groups tend to spend more time online [28]. Other characteristics, however, have shown recent improvements in narrowing this aspect of the digital divide. Evidence of this narrowing of the digital divide comes mainly from developed countries, however, as many developing countries still face a considerable gap *vis-à-vis* their more developed counterparts and within their boundaries.

6.2   Constraints on Access

Examining the manner in which countries currently provide access to all citizens reveals several serious constraints. Access can be best understood as a series of gaps or disconnects, rather than as a continuum from none to total access. These gaps currently limit the potential of e-democracy, but they are not surprising given the relative infancy of widespread ICT use around the world. By examining access, we are able to evaluate the characteristics of those who enter the online public sphere and determine ways to bridge these gaps.

A deeper issue relates to the way Internet access reproduces inequalities in the existing social structure and the way in which these inequalities restrict the ability of all citizens to engage in their country's political process. Online environments, even those sponsored by government, are often filtered and monitored, which results in keeping some people out or diminishing their contribution. Some users are more capable than others in navigating the online environment. The Internet and social media vary tremendously in their interfaces with the public, some are very "user-friendly" and others decidedly less so. These and other elements privilege those in control of online public discourse and those tech-savvy users who often engage with the online setting. The terms on which online environments operate and the ability of users to engage each other and the mediated space thus become essential to providing forums that are "free and equal" for all participants.

User restrictions are important elements of mediated public discourse. Some scholars have focused their attention on the impact of location and individual use of ICT [29]. Location limits autonomous online engagement by applying social, structural, and political constraints. DiMaggio and Hargittai [23] point out that access points at work or in public places may require monitoring and filtering of user activity. ISPs provide their own set of restrictions for users and some nations, notably China, continuously monitor online activity of their citizens. The threat of terrorism has led democratic societies to embrace e-surveillance of citizens. Beyond these issues, online environments have internal characteristics that may also impose limits on users, either intentionally or unintentionally. Forms of moderation and policies regulating online interactions can often affect whose voice gets heard. While policies and moderators may indeed be helpful in improving the quality of discourse, careful attention must be paid to the way they can limit expression. Certain digital forums, for example, may privilege abbreviated comments and expression. Though concision is not limited to online behavior and the digital environment, it plays a significant role in these situations due to the need to harness and organize large amounts of information for purposes of discussion. *Who* does the limiting and *how* they do it, however, play the key roles in online environments. These constraints, which are typically designed to help manage discussions and to keep abusive behavior at a minimum, also have the potential to restrict user autonomy. Thus, there is often a trade-off which must be made between encouraging free expression and assuring reasonable and non-antagonistic online discussions.

Users vary considerably with regard to their "Internet competence" [23]. Good language skills and the ability to effectively collect, analyze, and assimilate data are two core competencies for Internet users. Some research points out that frequent participants, or 'old hands,' in online forums tend to take control of debates, though often in positive ways [22]. To provide a more egalitarian atmosphere, online environments should be designed in a manner that is user-friendly for those who possess a range of technical abilities, from novice to expert. For example, information can be posted on websites or social media to help new users or those unfamiliar with online discussion norms and practices. In addition, links with informational websites can be included to help equalize disparities in data-gathering skills between different users.

6.3   Using ICT to Foster Greater Social Inclusiveness: Positives and Negatives

Besides the important trends noted above, which affect all of society and not just government, there are several emerging trends that have greater impact on government and therefore deserve special attention. The growth of the disability rights movement and its impact on society will continue to have a major impact on politics and public policy. One likely outcome is developing new policies to promote a more inclusive society with respect to people with disabilities and their accessibility to e-government. E-government could unintentionally exacerbate the current digital divide by ignoring or choosing to de-emphasize the significance of certain inclusivity issues relating to technology use. According to research examining the problems with the implementation of federal disability law, an accessible-for-everyone e-government still remains an extremely elusive goal [30]. Jaeger makes a strong case for federal policies to work toward a truly egalitarian e-government that is fully inclusive of individuals with disabilities. Another area where more work needs to be done is in bridging the digital divide between high- and low-income Americans with regard to e-government. As part of the modernization of social service agencies, increased networking and integration of technology have played increasingly significant roles. ICT, for example, has allowed agencies to prescreen applicants and put application forms online, which has decreased administrative costs, improved case management, and increased accessibility [31].

6.4 Structural Barriers to Inclusion

If a major goal of e-government and by extension, e-democracy, in the United States is accessibility for every citizen, then the interaction between human beings and technology needs to be better understood. Furthermore, a goal of inclusiveness is the removal of barriers, including technological ones that prevent certain groups from fully participating in the processes that directly affect them. Hetling, et al. [31] examines the relationship between the expectations and desires of the clientele and the design of technologies used by social service agencies. Many states, for example, allow people to apply online for welfare benefits but still require them to make an in-person visit to an office. Budget problems are behind efforts to put more services online because that reduces administrative costs. ICT, moreover, allows links to be made to other relevant government agencies, communication to occur in multiple languages without the need for an interpreter, and overall increased accessibility.

The research indicates that using technology to deliver some government services can result in fewer people receiving benefits. Whether this is an unintended consequence or simply another means to lower costs is a matter of conjecture. It is clear, however, that certain challenges exist to social service applicants online; they include Internet access, training on the technology, availability of call centers, complex application processes, and language and personal barriers. As a result, food stamp modernization in Florida has led to an overall decrease in the number of applications, especially among African Americans and seniors. According to advocates, this can be linked to application scheduling conflicts, difficulty of assembling eligibility documents, and expectation of denial of benefits. Presumably, once these issues are overcome, the online application process itself will not pose a barrier for those receiving the services they are eligible for.

6.5   Structural Barriers Caused by E-Government

Sometimes e-government inadvertently creates a type of barrier that cannot be fixed by technology. Making all services go completely online removes an often-ignored aspect of welfare services: human interaction. TANF workers have shifted the components of their work they perform online from only determining eligibility to full case management. Welfare recipients' interactions with employees have been found to be a key determinant of overall satisfaction with welfare services, particularly in the employee's use of positive and negative discretion in determining eligibility. The factors that comprise satisfaction with employees (competence, accessibility, and interpersonal relationships) are normally absent from the online application process. As more and more agencies shift to e-services, this is likely to become an issue for some groups, including low-income people, seniors, and non-English speaking immigrants. It is far from clear whether more advanced technology provides a solution or only exacerbates the problem.

Besides cost reduction and other efficiencies, e-services provide other advantages. Benefits of online applications, for example, include the loss of negative discriminatory discretion—online applications are perceived as less judgmental, more convenient, and to cause less anxiety for the applicant. Some people are more likely to trust and respect an online application process, as by definition, it must be impartial to the clients' particulars. "Self-service welfare", however, could be seen as meeting the needs of organizations more than those of the clients. Furthermore, some potential applicants may avoid self-service welfare out of fear of privacy loss, security concerns, and their own technological incompetence. Some persons might think that an online application is unreliable, too difficult, not secure, or unresponsive to their needs, and so they might not even complete an application. Suggestions for improving self-service welfare include: improved technical support, either over the phone or online; more nuanced questions (such as recognizing that a 1-year-old does not have a grade in school), ensuring website security; and integration of online and in-person applications.

6.6   Challenges of Connecting the Unconnected

The ability of e-government to meet the needs of society's most underserved (low-income adults, seniors, and people with disabilities) is also weakened by the fact that these segments of the population tends to be the least connected in terms of technology and the Internet. If inclusiveness is indeed a true priority for e-government and e-democracy, a means must be found to link non-ICT users to the Internet. Not being connected is fast becoming the twenty-first-century equivalent of illiteracy: it effectively excludes one from participating in modern life and enjoying the full benefits of technological innovations. Some of those excluded from the Net choose to be "off the grid." They do not want their personal information being made available for every government agency to see. Additionally, the process is rather cumbersome (despite being online) and many fear a significant loss of privacy.

These fears are far from being unfounded. Government uses of private information that is different from what was originally intended include: authorizing agencies to compare applicant-provided data with federal data to prevent fraud; the PATRIOT Act allowing sharing of information provided to agencies (to ensure no material support is provided to terrorists); prosecuting people who provide false or incorrect information to social service agencies; and requiring applicants to have government-issued identification when applying for social services, allowing for corroboration with federal databases. All are well-intended pieces of legislation, designed to prevent fraud and other criminal activities. Taken all together, however, they result in clients not owning their personal data, which can be freely used by other agencies without their permission. This issue of finding the proper balance between legitimate government concerns and protecting privacy is likely to increase with the growing sophistication of technology to gather and analyze massive amounts of data. It becomes an issue of inclusiveness, moreover, when people are forced to choose between benefits they're eligible for and loss of privacy.

6.7 Technologies that Create Barriers to Access

Another example of the ways technology can hinder efforts to build inclusiveness is the barriers it sometimes creates to access. Although ICT can allow easier, private access to public agencies, the government has used ICT instead to take an approach that favors bloated data collection over serving citizens [32]. Agencies that serve low-income people require similar or identical information, but typically each uses a separate application process. Creating one application that could be used to streamline the process across agencies would solve a problem that has plagued social service agencies for years: the time commitment required by low-income people to access and participate with disparate social service agencies. Using a universal application, while it solves one problem, potentially makes the privacy issue worse since it now becomes easier to corroborate personal data across many agencies using the same application process. Wilson [32] points out that by understanding the impacts on low-income persons of implementing strategies involving ICT, policy makers can develop a deliberately inclusive approach that leverages technology to support access to assistance in a manner that can be implemented at the federal, state, and county levels. According to Wilson, such efforts can further democratize the government-to-citizen relationship and support greater accountability to taxpayers.

The situations described above make it clear that technology-related structural constraints are a critical component in the issue of online communication and political deliberation. These structural aspects are dual in nature; they are either an artifact of technological constraints (e.g., the presence or absence of Wi-Fi in an area) or legal-regulatory constraints. In both cases, they constrain the way users interact in online environments. Often, whether or not the configuration of a virtual space makes it more conducive to the virtual public sphere ideal is a matter of the particular purpose and population addressed. Policies, moderators, and user-friendly applications can ensure that all voices are heard, which allows e-democracy to better able to fulfill its democratic potential. These issues of altering some of the structural constraints of e-government are taken up in the next section.

7 The Way Forward: Reforming Major Structural Aspects of E-Government

Suggestions have been made to improve ICT as a tool for e-democracy that include changing certain aspects of network architecture and training political actors to make more effective use of the technology. To counter the corporate manipulation of online information, for example, Noveck [33] recommends that governments mandate the use of value neutral search filtering tools for the Web. Additionally, applications need to be developed that integrate online discussion forums and information sources to enhance debate and foster more civil online discussions. Another issue is the privacy of citizens needs to be better protected as e-government initiatives continue to grow. Both industry and government should promote the use of basic privacy protection measures (e.g., encryption) as well as collaborate on educating the public on the use of these measures as a means to keep invasions of privacy at a minimum. Through the implementation of some structural reforms and changes, Noveck argues that the Internet's value for society can be maximized.

In light of the structural challenges, Noveck also recommends that several preconditions must be met before e-democracy can flourish. These include: free and easily available Internet access; easy to use applications for all ages and skill levels; easy to find and use e-democracy sites; e-democracy sites that support encryption; sites that facilitate conversation, interaction, deliberation, education, and engagement; and sites that encourage people to slow down, read, deliberate, and then engage in dialogue. Noveck made these recommendations before the advent of social media but most of his recommendations still apply, particularly the last one. If anything, social media has made slowing-down more difficult. One thinks of the rapid volleys of tweets between United States presidential candidates, their supporters and opponents, in 2016 as evidence of this troubling trend.

Finally, e-forums must demand accountability from all participants and provide assurance that every participant can be actively involved. In many respects, these preconditions represent a bare minimum of structural adaptations needed to allow virtual public spheres to thrive and flourish.

7.1   New Role for Political Intermediaries

Another challenge in the transition from e-government to e-democracy is re-envisioning the role played by intermediaries in the political process. Due to the Web's ability to directly connect users, many e-democracy proponents have predicted the demise of interest groups and political parties, the traditional middlemen of politics. In one of the very few studies to examine the critical position of political parties, legislative representatives, traditional interest groups and journalists on the Internet, Edwards [34] finds "the Internet encourages the emergence of various new intermediaries, including voter information websites, moderated online discussion forums and mobilization platforms on specific issues. Increased competition between intermediaries and an ensuing reconfiguration of positions between 'old' and 'new' intermediaries in democracy thus appears a more likely outcome than does the outright disappearance of intermediaries." (p. 163).

Intermediaries need to pursue different online strategies to strengthen relationships or develop new ones with citizens. The quality of e-democracy thus depends on the complex interplay between different types of democratic practices, citizenship roles, and intermediaries. Edwards [34] elaborates on the strategies used by the intermediary groups as they attempt to reconnect with the public by means of technology. Technology exerts its chief influence on both the information and interaction intermediaries; in other words, technology makes inroads into the powerbase of traditional political actors and the corporate media, which threatens their influence over the political system. The preference intermediaries, or political parties, (which have been accorded a privileged place in the political process by virtue of the fact that they have been institutionalized through laws, traditional customs, the economy, etc.) are the central actors in Edwards' explanation. Edwards and others suggest that re-designing current political structures and procedures to empower and encourage citizens to participate constitute a set of conditions necessary to successful e-democracy. The focus on improving e-democracy by designing new governance arrangements that successfully solicit, incorporate, and build public participation is still in its relative infancy. In an examination of the online formats used by the Dutch since 1994 to increase public participation and engagement [35] in the policy formation process, Bekkers found three motives underlie these efforts. First, the desire to bridge the gap between politics and administration on one hand, and citizens and government on the other. Second, valuing the input of citizens and other stakeholders in the policy formation/implementation process. Third, introducing competing policy viewpoints to enrich and stimulate debate on a wide variety of political issues and topics.

7.2 Linux Online Community as a Model for E-Democracy

Overall, governmental efforts have not produced the desired outcomes in these three areas, which [35] leads Bekkers to examine different types of online communities as possible models. One example of cyber-community that has shown significant success in fulfilling each of the three criteria is the Linux community, which has evolved into a worldwide network of open source software developers, as part of an effort to create and disseminate an alternative to Microsoft Windows. This community has been successful because it allows for (1) creative competition that allows participants to discuss, critique, and improve on each other's ideas, (2) accessibility of all relevant information, and (3) embracing trial and error along with feedback on outcomes. Other attributes that increase the viability of online, deliberative communities include ensuring that there is bottom-up policy creation and that issues are narrow and clear, rather than general and vague. In addition, a trial-and-error process that requires participants to be not only diligent, but also critical of themselves as well as others, and to be willing to improve deliberative, online processes is required. Generally, a truly effective e-democracy cannot be wholly the task of government. Ultimately, e-democracy must have firm support and participation from the citizenry.

8 Conclusion: The Future of Virtual Public Spheres and E-Democracy

Political decision-making and policy-making are two areas that are ripe for improvement by means of virtual public spheres. Until recently, information and communication channels have been controlled by a powerful few in society—the political, corporate, and media elite. Meanwhile, ICT provides an alternative source of information and access to government for ordinary citizens, which can, in theory, lead to more bottom-up, participatory decisions. Many problems still exist, however, and some of the most important of these have been discussed in this chapter.

It is unlikely that 10 years from now people will be relying on Facebook to mobilize vast numbers of people. Who can, however, predict with any accuracy what the new platforms will be? Educated guesses, however, can be made taking account of certain broad trends in technology and society. We know, for example, that computing power continues to grow while hardware continues to shrink in size. Today people carry tiny computers in their pockets that are more powerful by many orders of magnitude than the ones NASA used to safely guide astronauts to the moon and back in 1969. There does not appear to be any limit to how powerful or how small computers will become. This stimulates more demand for the Internet to be available everywhere and at all times. From the standpoint of e-government and e-democracy, this translates into the increasing demand by citizens that all government services, including democratic deliberation and voting, be accessible to everyone via ICT.

E-government can point to a number of notable successes, but we are still far from realizing the dream of early activists of the virtual republic. A growing body of research, nevertheless, indicates the conditions and prerequisites that need to be met in order for e-democracy to be implemented. In light of all the structural changes that need to occur, however, it is unlikely that the United States will see successful implementation of e-democracy anytime soon. In the meantime, technology continues to play an essential role in citizens' lives and one can expect to see further improvements in e-government. Although the virtual republic appears to be far off, government helping to make citizens' lives better through technology is very much a current reality.

References

1. Habermas J (1995) The structural transformation of the public sphere: an inquiry into a category of bourgeois society, 7th edn. (T. Burger, Trans.). MIT Press, Cambridge
2. Dawes S (2002) The future of e-government. http://www.ctg.albany.edu/publicaTons/reports/future_of_egov/future_of_egov.pdf
3. Heeks R (2001) Understanding E-governance for development. The i-Government Working Paper Series 11. http://unpan1.un.org/intradoc/groups/public/documents/NISPAcee/UNPAN015484.pdf
4. Misuraca GC (2006) e-Governance in Africa: from theory to action: a practical-oriented research and case studies on ICTs for local governance. In: ACM international conference proceeding series, 151, pp 209–218
5. Swope C (Mar 2004) E-gov's new gear. Governing, 40. http://www.governing.com/topics/politics/E-Govs-New-Gear.html
6. Henman P (2010) Governing electronically: E-government and the reconfiguration of public administration, policy and power. Palgrave Macmillan, Houndmills, Basingstoke, Hampshire
7. Gil-Garcia J, Luna-Reyes L (2006) Integrating conceptual approaches to e-government. In: Encyclopedia of e-commerce, e-government and mobile commerce. Idea Group Reference, Hershey, pp 636–643
8. Rubinstein C (2012) China's government goes digital. The Atlantic, 12 Nov 2012
9. Putnam R (1995) Bowling alone: America's declining social capital. J Democr 6(1):65–78
10. Barber BR (2004) Fear's empire: war, terrorism, and democracy. W.W. Norton & Co., New York
11. Clift S (2003) E-democracy, e-governance, and public net-work. http://www.publicus.net/articles/edempublicnetwork.html
12. Cropf R, Casaregola V (2007) Community networks. In: Anttiroiko AV, Malkia M (eds) Encyclopedia of digital government. IGI Reference, Hershey
13. Dahlberg L (2001) The Internet and democratic discourse: exploring the prospects of online deliberative forums extending the public sphere. Inf Commun Soc 4(4):615–633
14. Papacharissi Z (2002) The virtual sphere: the Internet as a public sphere. New Media Soc 4(1):9–27
15. Keane J (1998) Civil society: old images, new visions. The Polity Press, Cambridge
16. Garrett R, Jensen M (2011) E-democracy writ: the impact of the internet on citizen access to local elected officials. Inf Commun Soc 14(2):177–197
17. Van der Graft P, Svensson J (2006) Explaining eDemocracy development: a quantitative empirical study. Inf Polity 11(2):123–134
18. North D (2005) Understanding the process of economic change. Princeton University Press, Princeton

19. Takao Y (2004) Democratic renewal by "Digital" local government in Japan. Pac Aff 77(2):237–262
20. Wright S (2006) Government-run online discussion fora: moderation, censorship and the shadow of control. Brit J Polit Int Relat 8(4):550–568
21. Wright S (2006) Electrifying democracy? 10 years of policy and practice. Parliam Aff 59(2):236–249
22. Albrecht S (2006) Whose voice is heard in online deliberation?: a study of participation and representation in political debates on the internet. Inf Commun Soc 9(1):63–82
23. Dimaggio P, Hargittai E (2001) From the 'digital divide' to 'digital inequality': studying Internet use as penetration increases. Center for Cultural Arts and Policy Studies working paper. https://www.princeton.edu/~artspol/workpap/WP15%20-%20DiMaggio+Hargittai.pdf
24. Norris P (2001) Digital divide: civic engagement, information poverty, and the Internet worldwide. Cambridge University Press, New York
25. Ismail S, Wu I (2003) Broadband Internet access in OECD countries: a comparative analysis. A Staff Report of the Office of Strategic Planning and Policy Analysis and International Bureau. https://apps.fcc.gov/edocs_public/attachmatch/DOC-239660A2.pdf
26. Kvasny L (2006) Cultural (Re)production of digital inequality in a US community technology initiative. Inf Commun Soc 9(2):160–181
27. Dobransky K, Hargittai E (2006) The disability divide in Internet access and use. Inf Commun Soc 9(3):313–334
28. Kraut R, Patterson M, Lundmark V, Kiesler S, Mukophadhyay T, Scherlis W (1998) Internet paradox: a social technology that reduces social involvement and psychological well-being? Am Psychol 53(9):1017–1031
29. Bimber B (2000) The study of information technology and civic engagement. Polit Commun 17(4):329–333
30. Jaeger P (2004) The social impact of an accessible e-democracy. J Disabil Policy Stud 15(1):16–26
31. Hetling A, Watson S, Horgan M (2014) "We live in a technological era, whether you like it or not": client perspectives and online welfare applications. Adm Soc 46(5):519–547
32. Wilson S (2014) E-government legislation: implementation issues for programs for low-income people. Gov Inf Q 31(1):42–29
33. Noveck BS (2000) Paradoxical partners: electronic communication and electronic democracy. Democratization 7(1):18–35
34. Edwards A (2006) ICT strategies of democratic intermediaries: a view on the political system in the digital age. Inf Polity 11(2):163–176
35. Bekkers V (2004) Virtual policy communities and responsive governance: redesigning on-line debates. Inf Polity 9(3/4):193–203

Chapter 2
Exploring the Emergence of Open Spatial Data Infrastructures: Analysis of Recent Developments and Trends in Europe

Glenn Vancauwenberghe and Bastiaan van Loenen

Abstract In the past 20 years, European public authorities have invested considerable resources in the development of spatial data infrastructures. With the European INSPIRE Directive as an important driver, national spatial data infrastructures were developed throughout Europe to facilitate and coordinate the exchange and sharing of geographic data. While the original focus of these spatial data infrastructure was mainly on data sharing among public authorities, it became more and more evident that these data could also be of great value to users outside the public sector. In recent years, several countries and public administrations started to make a shift towards the establishment of an 'open' spatial data infrastructure, in which also businesses, citizens and non-governmental actors were considered as key stakeholders of the infrastructure. This chapter provides an analysis of the measures and solutions implemented in four European countries (the Netherlands, the United Kingdom, Denmark and Finland) to make their spatial data infrastructures open to businesses, citizens and other stakeholders. The analysis shows that in these four countries the move towards more open spatial data infrastructures can mainly be seen in the increased availability of geographic data and spatially enabled services to citizens, businesses and other stakeholders.

Keywords Open data • Geographic data • Open spatial data infrastructures • Citizens • Businesses • Spatially enabled e-services

1 Introduction

Since the 1990s public administrations in Europe and worldwide have invested considerable resources in the development of infrastructures for promoting, facilitating and coordinating the exchange and sharing of geographic data [1]. These so-called spatial data infrastructures have increased the availability and accessibility

G. Vancauwenberghe (✉) • B. van Loenen
Knowledge Centre Open Data, Delft University of Technology, Delft, The Netherlands
e-mail: g.vancauwenberghe@tudelft.nl

© Springer International Publishing AG 2018
S. Saeed et al. (eds.), *User Centric E-Government*, Integrated Series in Information Systems 39, DOI 10.1007/978-3-319-59442-2_2

of geographic data collected and managed by governments. Geographic data, i.e. data that refer to a location on the earth [2], are increasingly important for governments, as most of the societal, environmental and economic challenges that governments are facing, require spatial understanding and insight. Typical examples of geographic data are topographical maps, address data, road data, and hydro-graphical data [3, 4]. In Europe, an important trigger in the development of spatial data infrastructures was the 2007 INSPIRE Directive establishing an Infrastructure for Spatial Information in the European Community [5]. The Directive had an important impact on the way governments in European countries organized the access to and sharing of their geographic data. Its aim was to develop a European infrastructure based on the creation, operation and maintenance of the national spatial data infrastructures established and operated in the different member states of the European Union.

The original focus of most spatial data infrastructure developments, not only in Europe but also in other parts of the world, was on promoting and stimulating data sharing within the public sector. Also the primary aim of INSPIRE was to create a European Union (EU) spatial data infrastructure for enabling the sharing of environmental geographic information among public sector organizations, within and between member states and especially between member states and the European Commission. In many European countries, data sharing with organizations and individuals outside the public sector for a long time remained limited, as the mechanisms and instruments to support and facilitate this type of sharing were missing [6]. This formed an important barrier to a more effective and efficient use of geographic data throughout society [7]. In recent years, several countries and public administrations in Europe started with the implementation of an open data policy, with the aim of making their government data 'open', i.e. freely available for use and re-use without restrictions. In most countries, also geographic data were under the scope of these open data policies and programmes, and were made available to citizens, businesses and other potential user groups outside the public sector. At the same time also in the development of spatial data infrastructures these private organizations, research institutions and other non-profit institutions were recognized as important stakeholders, and became more actively involved in the governance and implementation of the infrastructures.

The aim of this chapter is to empirically examine the multifaceted and changing role of non-government actors in the development of spatial data infrastructures in Europe. An analysis will be made of how four European countries have been dealing with the challenge of opening their spatial data infrastructures to actors outside the public sector. The chapter will analyse the measures and solutions implemented by European countries in the past 10 years to make their spatial data infrastructures open to businesses, citizens and other stakeholders. In the following section of this chapter, a brief overview is provided of the main concepts, views and research on the role of citizens and businesses in spatial data infrastructures. Next, the EU legal framework on geographic data sharing is described and the four national spatial data infrastructures that will be analysed are introduced. The fourth section presents the main actions and measures taken in these four spatial data infrastructures to make geographic data available to citizens, businesses and other users. In the fifth section, the analysis is focused on the governance and implementation of the infrastructures, and the involvement of non-government actors in both processes. The chapter ends with a discussion of the main findings and some conclusions.

2 Towards Open Spatial Data Infrastructures

Spatial data infrastructures often are defined and described as a complex and dynamic phenomenon [8, 9]. Giff and Crompvoets [10] see several reasons for the complex character of these infrastructures: the many components a spatial data infrastructure consists of, the diversity of involved stakeholders, and the many different objectives and ambitions of these stakeholders. Technological advancements, such as the emergence of web 2.0 technologies, and societal changes, such as the increasing use of geographic information in everyday life, are often mentioned as important drivers behind the dynamic character of spatial data infrastructures. A key characteristic of spatial data infrastructures is the involvement of a large and diverse group of actors [11]. Governments are often considered as the central actors in the development and implementation of spatial data infrastructure, since they are the major producers and users of geographic information [12]. Governments at different administrative levels and in different thematic domains are involved in the creation, management, use and sharing of geographic data [13]. But also private companies, non-profit organisations, research and education institutions and even citizens can participate in the development and implementation of a spatial data infrastructure [14]. Some authors even argued that the involvement and engagement of each of these stakeholders group is essential to the realization of a successful spatial data infrastructure [2, 14–16]. Also the development of spatial data infrastructures for particular users groups, such as scientists or citizens, is proposed as an alternative approach for addressing the needs of these users [17].

For many years several authors have suggested and explored the introduction of a new generation of more user-driven spatial data infrastructures and the need to redefine or expand the SDI concept [18–21]. In reality most spatial data infrastructures in the world were government initiatives to facilitate and coordinate the exchange of geographic data among producers and users in the public sector. In recent years however, several technological, institutional and societal developments suggested a shift towards more open spatial data infrastructures in which also businesses, citizens and other non-governmental actors were considered as key stakeholders of the infrastructure. The concept of open data spatial data infrastructures entails at least four core but interrelated changes in the role and position of actors outside the public sector in the development and implementation of spatial data infrastructures.

First, open spatial data infrastructures primarily deal with opening geographic data, and making these data freely available to citizens, businesses and other users for re-use without restrictions. Since President Obama's Memorandum on Transparency and Open Government announcing the creation of a transparent and collaborative government through public participation, the concepts of open government and open data have attracted considerable attention from researchers, practitioners and decision makers. Open government data became a very popular topic in many parts of the world, including Europe, Australia, New Zealand and Azia [22]. Open spatial data infrastructures in essence are about applying the principles of open data to geographic data. This means all geographic data should be made available for free, unless they are subject to legitimate privacy, security or privilege limitations. The data should be license-free, machine processable, and timely available to the widest range of users in an open format [23].

Second, spatial data infrastructures can be considered as a framework supporting the delivery of e-services to citizens, businesses and other stakeholders [24]. Some authors even argue that spatial data infrastructures will only be successful if they are well connected to e-government [13]. The data and other components of a spatial data infrastructure should be used to improve and enhance all types of online services: information services, contact services, transaction services, and participation services. These spatially enabled services, i.e. services built on top of geographic data and other components of a spatial data infrastructure, will ensure that also businesses, citizens and users could optimally take advantage of the benefits of geographic data. In addition to opening up geographic data sets to businesses, citizens and other users, open spatial data infrastructures also include the provision of different types of spatially enabled e-services to these citizens and businesses.

Third, in order to take into account the needs and requirements of different stakeholder groups, also data users and producers outside the public sector should be involved in the governance of the SDI [25]. The governance of spatial data infrastructures deals with the adoption of structures, procedures and instruments for managing the relationships and dependencies between all involved actors, units and organizations. The key challenge of governance is reconciling collective and individual needs and interests of different stakeholders in order to achieve common goals [26]. Therefore, open spatial data infrastructures is also about refining existing governance instruments and adopting new governance instruments to involve organizations and actors outside government in the governance of spatial data infrastructures.

Fourth, spatial data infrastructures only are open in case all stakeholders can contribute to the development of these infrastructure, which means they can also add their own data and components to the infrastructure. The contribution of non-government actors to the development and implementation should go further than the traditional contribution, i.e. working as contractors for public administrations and providing services to these administrations [6]. Open spatial data infrastructures can only be realized by putting in place processes, methods and tools that stimulate and enable non-government actors to add their own data sets and other components to the infrastructure. A particular challenge is to optimally take advantage of voluntary geographic information (VGI), i.e. geographic data provided voluntarily by individuals [27]. As it was argued by Budhathoki et al. [20], open spatial data infrastructures require a redistribution of data production activities among different types of organizations and users.

3 The European Framework for Geographic Data Sharing

The EU legal framework for the availability and sharing of geographic data is formed by several legal instruments. The two most prominent instruments are the PSI Directive 2003/98/EC on the re-use of public sector information and the INSPIRE Directive 2007/2/EC establishing an Infrastructure for Spatial Information in the European Community (INSPIRE). Both Directives lay down a set of rules on governing the re-use and availability of government data, and geographic data in particular.

3.1 The European PSI Directive

The European Directive on the re-use of public sector information (Directive 2003/98/EC, known as the 'PSI Directive') entered into force on 31 December 2003. After a review of the Directive and a proposal by the European Commission in 2011 to revise the Directive, the new PSI Directive entered into force in July 2013 [28, 29]. The PSI Directive focuses on the economic aspects of public sector information and encourages the Member States to make as much information available for re-use as possible.

The PSI Directive establishes a minimum set of rules governing the re-use and the practical means of facilitating re-use of existing documents held by public sector bodies of the EU Member States. The Directive rules that all documents held by public sector bodies of the EU Member States are re-usable, unless access is restricted or excluded under national rules on access to documents and subject to the other exceptions laid down in this Directive. The PSI Directive does not contain an obligation concerning access to documents. If information is not accessible also the re-use obligations of the PSI Directive do not apply.

The Directive promotes the use of open licenses, although the use of open licenses is not obliged. The Directive also addresses the use of open and machine-readable formats and the provision of metadata on the documents. Another issue addressed in the Directive are possible charges for public sector information. The Directive supports the re-use of this information by setting marginal cost of reproduction as the rule, although certain exceptions still are possible. In addition, the PSI Directive requires transparency of the amount of, and the calculation basis for all charges.

3.2   The INSPIRE Directive

While an important driving force for public organizations to open their data came from the revised PSI Directive, also the INSPIRE Directive establishing an infrastructure for Spatial Information in the European Community of 2007 had an important impact on the way public administrations in Europe organize the access to and sharing of their spatial or geographic data [5]. INSPIRE aims to overcome the major barriers affecting the availability and accessibility of geodata, through the development of a European spatial information infrastructure. This European infrastructure will be based on the creation, operation and maintenance of the national spatial data infrastructures established and operated by the 28 Member States of the European Union, but also Switzerland, Norway and Iceland.

The INSPIRE Directive requires public authorities to publish all spatial data related to the environment according to specific technical and non-technical specifications. For each data set, a description of the data should be provided in the form of metadata and these metadata should be accessible through discovery services making it possible to search for data sets. In addition, view services should be put in place making it possible to view the data sets and download services should be developed enabling to download the data—or parts of it—and access them directly. Data should be conform to the INSPIRE data specifications, while also the metadata and network services should be INSPIRE compliant. Moreover, public authorities should adopt measures for the sharing of spatial data sets and services between its public authorities enabling these public authorities to gain access to and exchange and use these spatial data sets and services.

The INSPIRE Directive aimed to tackle many barriers to the—commercial— re-use of data and services: a central access point is established where users can discover all available data and services of all member states and also view most of these data and services free of charge; download services for getting direct access to spatial dataset need to be put in place, and data providers need to provide information on the conditions applying to access to, and use of, spatial data sets and services and on the corresponding fees. Also the need to make data available harmonized to the INSPIRE specification enables the re-use of this data by other parties. Analysing the different components and requirements of INSPIRE, it can be concluded that the Directive makes an important contribution to promoting the re-use of spatial data, by enhancing the legal and physical attainability of the data but also the usability [30].

3.3   Open Geographic Data in EU Member States

The European INSPIRE Directive and PSI Directive both have an impact on the way governments and public authorities in Europe are dealing with the management and exchange of spatial or geographic data through the establishment of a national spatial data infrastructure. With the entrance into force of the INSPIRE Directive but also the PSI Directive, countries in Europe started or continued with the development of their national spatial data infrastructure according to the principles, rules and guidelines of INSPIRE and PSI.

It is the aim of this chapter to investigate the role and position of non-government actors, such as citizens, businesses, research institutions and other organizations, in the development of these national spatial data infrastructures. The study focuses on four countries that have been very active in promoting and facilitating the participation of non-government actors in their national spatial data infrastructure and thus can be considered to be at the forefront of the development of open spatial data infrastructures in Europe: the United Kingdom, Finland and Denmark and the Netherlands. The study is based on a document analysis of relevant publicly available documents on the development and implementation of the national spatial data infrastructure and the implementation of INSPIRE in each of these four countries. Key documents are the official country reports on the implementation and use of infrastructures for spatial information that have to be submitted by all EU member states every 3 years.[1] In addition to these official country reports, also other policy documents were analysed, including implementation strategies, legislation and other policy reports.

In the United Kingdom, the UK Location Strategy of 2008 was a crucial step in the development of the UK spatial data infrastructure [31]. Because of the synergies between the Strategy and the European INSPIRE Directive, both were implemented jointly as part of the UK Location Programme. Strategic coordination of the implementation originally was provided by the UK Location Council and the UK Location Programme board, in which all the key stakeholders were represented. In 2013, both were replaced by the UK INSPIRE Compliance Board, which now is the main governance body of the UK spatial data infrastructure. The Board is led by the Department for Environment, Food and Rural Affairs (Defra), the national contact point of the UK spatial data infrastructure.

In Denmark, it was the Danish Act on the infrastructure for spatial information, the so-called SI Act, that provided the legal basis for the development of the infrastructure for spatial information, based on the INSPIRE Directive. In Denmark, the development of the national spatial information infrastructure is strongly connected with the national eGovernment strategy, and with the Basic Data Programme in particular. The Coordination Committee on Infrastructure for Spatial Information was established in 2010, with the aim of facilitating and maintaining an effective spatial data infrastructure. The Danish Geodata Agency, which is part of the Ministry of the Environment, is responsible for the infrastructure and for coordinating and supporting the tasks of different involved parties.

In Finland, a first initiative to coordinate the sharing of geographic data was taken in the beginning of the 80s, with the initiation of the national Land Information System (LIS) project. At that time, around 20 public agencies, ministries, local

---

[1] All reports can be found at http://inspire.ec.europa.eu/INSPIRE-in-your-Country

governments, companies and research units participated in the collaboration on the
LIS project. The transposition of the INSPIRE Directive into national legislation in
2009 with a law and a decree on the infrastructure for geographic data provided a
new boost to the development of a spatial data infrastructure in Finland. The national
coordination of the infrastructure is in hands of the Ministry of Agriculture and
Forestry, who is supported by the National Council for Geographic Information.

In the Netherlands the political responsibility for implementing the national
spatial data infrastructure but also INSPIRE lies with the Minister of Infrastructure
and Environment. While it is the Ministry of Infrastructure and Environment that
acts as the principal and budget holder of the SDI, the technical implementation
of the infrastructure is delegated to Geonovum. The Ministry of Infrastructure and
Environment also chairs the national administrative council for geographic data
which incorporates all ministries that are involved in the SDI. INSPIRE is led
by a steering committee, in which the main parties concerned in INSPIRE are
represented, and which is advised by a consultative group. In addition to INSPIRE,
the development of the SDI is strongly related to the key registries of the national
e-government policy and the national data facilities, that are based on national
legal acts.

4   Open Data and E-Services

The aim of this chapter is to empirically investigate to what extent and in which
manner a move was made towards a more open data spatial data infrastructure in
the United Kingdom, Finland, Denmark and the Netherlands. This section analyzes
the actions and measures taken in these four countries to open the main outputs
of these infrastructures, i.e. the data and services on top of these data, to citizens,
businesses and other users.

4.1   Open Data

The United Kingdom, Finland, Denmark and the Netherlands all were among the
first countries in Europe where the central government decided to release its government data as open data and an open data programme was announced. Although
these open data policy programmes and related actions focused on all types of
government data, in all four countries they strongly influenced the availability
of open geographic data. Important elements in the opening of geographic data
were the establishment of single access points and the development of a license
framework with standard licenses.

4.1.1 Policy Initiatives

In the United Kingdom, Prime Minister Gordon Brown announced in the summer of 2009 his 'Making Public Data Public' policy programme to increase the availability of government data for re-use by businesses, citizens and other stakeholders. From July 2010, government departments and agencies should ensure that any information published includes the underlying data in an open standardised format. In the following years, similar policies and initiatives were announced and implemented in other European countries.

In March 2011, the Finnish government published its resolution on sharing of government data and increasing the re-use of government data. As a result of this resolution, many government organizations in Finland started opening their data in 2012. In 2013, the Finnish Ministry of Finance launched a 2-year Open Data Program to accelerate the implementation of open data in Finland. The objective was to open all major government database by the year of 2020. From the very beginning, geographic data and maps were considered as one of the pilot target databases.

With the Danish Basic Data Programme "Good Basic Data for Everyone – a driver for growth and efficiency", the Danish government, local governments and regions agreed to make several key data sets in Denmark freely accessible and re-usable for all public authorities, but also for citizens and companies. As 'open and efficient access to geographic data' was one of the seven key priorities of the Basic Data Programme, also geographic data sets were under the scope of the programme.

In the Netherlands, the Ministry of Internal Affairs is the responsible Ministry for access to public sector information. In 2013, the Ministry presented a vision and associated plan of action for an open government. Partly based on the international Open Government Partnership, the Ministry adopted the general policy 'publicly accessible, unless'. Starting point for publicly accessible data is that these should also be available for re-use. Government needs to make the data publicly accessible either on request of a citizen or pro-actively. In anticipation of this vision, action plan and related legislation, the Dutch Ministry of Infrastructure and Environment already adopted an open data policy for the entire Ministry in the Summer of 2012. All the data of the Ministry should be available as open data, unless there was a good reason not to do so (privacy, national security, confidentiality). All departments of the Ministry were provided a single strict deadline to release their data as open data. All government data coming under the Ministry of Infrastructure and Environment by 2015 at the latest.

4.1.2 Availability of Open Geographic Data

Encouraged by these initiatives, and often mandated by a new legal framework, in all four countries many geodatasets became publicly available. However, some organizations already had an open data policy in place before the introduction and implementation of the government-wide open data programme. In Finland, environmental data had been made available free-of-charge by the Finnish Environment Institute in 2008, several years before the government resolution on open government data. The National Land Survey of Finland opened several small scale data sets in 2011, and all its topographic data, including topographic database and aerial photos, in 2012. Many other data providers opened their data prompted by the resolution on sharing of government data: the Geological Survey of Finland, the Finnish Forest Research Institute, the Statistics of Finland, the National Board of Antiquities and several of the largest municipalities. At the moment, more than half of all data falling under the scope of the INSPIRE Directive are open.

In Denmark, the definition of geographic 'base' data as part of the Basic Data Programme especially focused on data themes recognized by the INSPIRE Directive as reference data. Among the geodata considered as basic data sets, and thus freely available since the beginning of 2013, are the land register, the geographical boundaries (the National Administrative Geographical Classification), Denmark's elevation model, the national geographical names, and the so-called Map Data. Two major geographic data providers are the Danish Geodata Agency and the Ministry of Housing, Urban and Rural Affairs.

In the Netherlands, the Ministry of Infrastructure and Environment, including the different agencies that are part of the Ministry, is the key provider of open geographic data. Almost half of the datasets available on the national open data portal, are geographic data. According to a report of the Dutch Algemene Rekenkamer [32] on the status of open data in the Netherlands, approximately 95% of all map data in the Netherlands are available as open data. Among the open geographic data sets in the Netherlands are several small-scale data sets, but also very detailed data and even 3D data.

In the United Kingdom, the Environment Agency and the Department for Environment, Food & Rural Affairs are among the top providers of open government data, and have also opened several key geographic data sets. Among the most popular and valuable open geographic data are LIDAR data, flood data, geological maps, and land registry data. Also the UK Ordnance Survey has made several geographic data sets openly available, including the road data, river data, terrain data and administrative boundaries.

4.1.3   Single Access Points and Harmonized Licenses

Two key elements in the realization of the open data programmes in the different countries were the establishment of a single access point to data and the development of a license framework. In the UK, the creation of a single online access point for public data, data.gov.uk, was one of the first pillars of the Making Public Data Public programme. Also geographic data sets are made available through data.gov.uk,[2] and form a considerable portion of all government data available on

---

[2]https://data.gov.uk/

this platform. Also in Denmark the creation of a Common Basic Data distribution solution was one of the key priorities of the Basic Data Programme. The common Data Distributor[3] was launched in in 2015, and now is an alternative data distribution channel in addition to Digital Map Supply,[4] the distribution solution of the Danish spatial data infrastructure through which spatial data and services are made available to the public since 2005. In the Netherlands, the National Geo Register[5] is the central access point to spatial data in the Netherlands. Open geodata from the National Geo Register automatically are included in the Dutch Open Data Portal,[6] which was launched as part of the national 'Open Data Programme'. In Finland the national geoportal Paikkatietoikkuna,[7] which was created in 2010, still is the main access point to spatial data.

Also the development and implementation of a licensing framework and standard licenses was an important element in improving the access to and stimulating the re-use of geodata. Since many barriers to sharing and use of geographic data were related to the conditions for use, the Netherlands started with the development of the 'Geo Gedeeld' framework[8] to harmonize conditions for use. The framework was based on the principles of Creative Commons and was built on a set number of standard conditions for use with an individual icon, layperson's wording and a legally binding text [33]. Each data owner had to specify which of the conditions for use (one or more) were applicable to his/her data or services. In 2014, it was decided to bring the Dutch spatial data policy in line with international standards, and to apply where possible the Creative Commons framework. A 'Creative Commons, unless' principle was introduced for INSPIRE data, which means governments now have to apply one of the Creative Commons licenses when making their data available, unless they want to impose specific conditions the Creative Commons framework does not cover. In that case, they have to apply the 'Geo Gedeeld' framework.

In most other European countries, the development of a common license framework from the beginning focused on all government data. In Finland, the Ministry of Finance published an open data license recommendation for public administration in 2014, and the use of the Creative Commons framework now is recommended. In Denmark, several projects dealing with the development of common data licenses across authorities and the private sector were included in the Basic Data Programme. In the United Kingdom, the development of a UK Government Licensing Framework was an important element of the UK Open Data strategy. The UK Government Licensing Framework (UKGLF) provides a policy and legal overview of the arrangements for licensing the use and re-use of

---

[3] http://datafordeler.dk/

[4] http://kortforsyningen.dk/

[5] http://nationaalgeoregister.nl/

[6] https://data.overheid.nl/

[7] http://www.paikkatietoikkuna.fi/

[8] http://geogedeeld.geonovum.nl/

public sector information. The Open Government Licence (OGL) is promoted as the default licence for public sector information. The UKGLF has been endorsed as the licensing framework for the use of spatial datasets covered by the INSPIRE Regulations.

Table 2.1 provides a summary of the main elements of the geographic open data initiatives in the four countries.

4.2 Open E-Services

The realization of an open spatial data policy to make geographic data freely available to citizens, businesses and other stakeholders in many European countries was an important step in the realization of an open spatial data infrastructure. By making geodata accessible and re-usable for actors outside the public sector, also these non-government actors could directly benefit from the large volumes of geographic data collected and managed by public authorities. Opening up geographic data meant the spatial data infrastructure was made more open by making the key output of the infrastructure, i.e. the data, directly available to businesses, citizens and other stakeholders. An alternative way in which European countries opened their spatial data infrastructure was through the provision of spatially enabled services, which were built on top of the geographic data sets. Most European countries strongly focused the implementation of their national spatial data infrastructure on improving the availability and accessibility of geodata, especially in the first years of implementation. An important parallel in the actions and initiatives of the four countries in our analysis is their strong focus on the development of spatially-enabled services to citizens and businesses. These spatially-enabled services have evolved from more simple information services and contact services to more advanced transaction services.

4.2.1 Information Services

The Dutch Atlas Living Environment[9] is a good example of a so-called information service built on top of the national spatial data infrastructure. With the development and provision of these spatially-enabled information services, governments make use of geographic data to make information on their activities, processes and products available to citizens and business, in a user-friendly and accessible manner. The Atlas Living Environment provides citizens and professionals access to up-to-date and correct information on environment and health. The Atlas contains a wide range of digital maps from many different sources, often at a very detailed level, and on several topics: air quality, noise, soil conditions etc. Similar spatially-

---

[9]http://www.atlasleefomgeving.nl/en/

Table 2.1 Key elements of the open geographic data initiatives in the four countries

	United Kingdom	Finland	Denmark	Netherlands
Primary open data policy initiative	Making Public Data Public Programme (2009)	Government resolution to open public data (2011) and Open Data Program (2013)	Danish Basic Data Programme (2013)	Vision and Action Plan on Open Government (2013) and Open Data Policy of the Ministry of Infrastructure and Environment (2012)
Important open geodata providers	Environment Agency; Department for Environment, Food & Rural Affairs	Finnish Environment Institute; National Land Survey of Finland	Danish Geodata Agency; Ministry of Housing, Urban and Rural Affairs	Ministry of Infrastructure and Environment
Access point(s)	data.gov.uk	Paikkatietoikkuna	Data distributor and digital map supply	National Geo Register and the Dutch Open Data Portal
License framework(s)	UK Government Licensing Framework (UKGLF)	Creative Commons	Under the scope of the Danish Basic Data Programme	Creative Commons and Geo Gedeeld

enabled information services can also be found in the United Kingdom, Denmark and Finland, not only in the area of environment, but also in other thematic areas. The Danish MapMyClimate[10] platform informs citizens and other stakeholders about the potential impact of climate change on their life and environment. Also the Finnish Mol.fi[11] website, the national job website where jobseekers can search for vacancies, includes a map interface based on a spatial data service by the national SDI, and can be considered as a spatially enabled information service. The best known example of information services on top of geodata are the multi-modal traffic planners (e.g. Rejseplanen[12] in Denmark or Reittiopas[13] in Finland) providing citizens information on all types of public transport and allowing them to plan their journey.

4.2.2   Contact Services

One of the first spatially enabled contact services was developed and implemented in the United Kingdom. With the online FixMyStreet[14] service citizens could report potholes, broken street lights and other problems with streets and roads. FixMyStreet services now exist in many different European countries and are a good example of spatially enabled contact services, i.e. online services based on geographic data that allow citizens or other stakeholders to contact public administrations and provide them with relevant information. Similar applications exist to allow citizens to report on illegal dumping, other garbage related complaints or cases of pollution. But contact services also include services that can be used by specific stakeholders or professionals to submit an application. One example of this is the Finnish Vipu[15] service, an electronic service farmer can use to submit their application for agricultural subsidies. The service contains a map interface supported by the national spatial data infrastructure, where farmers can submit cultivation plans.

4.2.3   Transaction Services

Also in Denmark farmers can use an online e-service to submit their applications for EU agricultural subsidies. As the entire process has been digitized and also the processing of the application and the final payment of the subsidy is integrated into the system, the service has developed towards a spatially enabled transaction ser-

---

[10]http://mapmyclimate.dk/

[11]http://mol.fi

[12]http://www.rejseplanen.dk/

[13]https://www.reittiopas.fi/

[14]https://www.fixmystreet.com/

[15]https://vipu.mavi.fi/

vice. These transaction services, which refers to the electronic intake and handling of requests and applications of rights, benefits and obligations, can be considered as a third type of spatially enabled e-services. Because these transaction services demand two-way interactions between government and citizens/businesses, they are more complex and more difficult to realise than information services and contact services, which are mostly one-way services. In Denmark, Finland, the Netherlands and the United Kingdom several examples of spatially enabled transaction services can be found. A typical example is the online application and processing of building permits. Under the Finnish Action Programme on eServices and eDemocracry, several services to support the process of building permits were developed based on the national spatial data infrastructure.

5 Open Infrastructure

In the previous section it was shown how several European countries have opened their national spatial data infrastructure to citizens, businesses and other actors outside public administration by making geographic data and e-services on top of these data available to these parties. The provision of data and services to non-government actors can be seen as opening the main outputs of the infrastructure to other parties. Another way of opening the infrastructure is by allowing other stakeholders to contribute to and participate in building up the infrastructure. A distinction can be made between two main types of active participation: participation in the governance of the infrastructure and participation in the implementation of the infrastructure.

5.1 Open Governance

Open governance of spatial data infrastructures implies that also non-government actors and bodies are actively involved in the governance of the infrastructure, and particular effort is done to respect and reconcile the needs and interests of different parties. Two main ways to do this are through the establishment of appropriate governance structures and through the development of a shared vision and strategy on the spatial data infrastructure.

5.1.1 Governance Structures

A common instrument for the governance of national spatial data infrastructures is the creation of a coordination or governance structure through which stakeholders can participate in decision making on the development and implementation of the infrastructure. SDI governance bodies are in place in all European countries, although they come in many different sizes and shapes. Originally, the United Kingdom had a UK Location Council and a UK Location Programme board, which in 2013 were replaced by the UK INSPIRE Compliance Board. The Netherlands still has two main governance bodies for INSPIRE, with the steering committee and the consultative group. The national SDI has an informal governance structure in the top team and strategic platform with representatives of the 'golden helix' (government, business, and academia) in both teams. National government governs the government part in the SDI through the national administrative body for SDI (GI Council). In Finland, the governance structure of the national SDI consists of the National Council for Geographic Information, while in Denmark this role is fulfilled by the Coordination Committee on the Infrastructure for Spatial Information. Although similar structures and bodies are in place in other European countries, the governance of the SDI in the United Kingdom, Finland, Denmark and the Netherlands is characterized by a relatively strong involvement of non-government actors.

In the Netherlands, the involvement of the non-government actors in the decision making process on SDI takes place in the INSPIRE Consultative Group, in which besides INSPIRE data providers also users, universities and the business community are represented. The Consultative group provides advise to the central Steering Committee of INSPIRE, and the chair of the consultative group is also member of the Steering Group. The Consultative Group is considered to be an important factor in the quality assurance procedure of the INSPIRE programme in the Netherlands, as the group examines the main results delivered by the INSPIRE programme and advises the steering committee on the implementation of the programme. For the general geodata policy, a 'top team' and strategic platform have been established in which the private sector is represented to align supply and demand, consisting out of leaders and representatives from the public, private and academic sector. Together they determine the priorities and direction of the geo-sector.

The SDI governance structures of Finland and Denmark formally consist of one single body, i.e. the Coordination Committee in Denmark and the National Council in Finland. In both countries, non-government actors are directly involved in the governance body. The National Council for Geographic Information in Finland consists of representatives of eight central ministries, but also of several members representing several producers and users, the municipalities, collaboration networks and the research community. In Denmark, the Danish universities are directly involved in the Coordination Committee, in which also Geoforum is represented. Geoforum is the Danish forum for spatial information, with members from both public authorities and the private sector. A similar role is fulfilled by the National INSPIRE network of Finland, which is a voluntary network of 350 experts from around 120 organisations, including government institutions, companies and research and education institutions.

In the United Kingdom, representatives from the wider GI sector, including the private, research and non-profit sector, participated in the original UK Location Council, the executive group that provided strategic direction to the UK Location Programme, but also in the UK User Group, an advisory board that monitored the UK Location Programme and ensured that wider end user needs and priorities were met. Experts from private, academic and third sectors are also involved in different working groups of the INSPIRE governance structure. The Association for Geographic Information (AGI), the association representing the UK GI industry, is seen as a key partner in the implementation of the infrastructure. Especially in the starting phase of SDI implementation, many individual experts contributed to the definition of the overall architecture and strategy. However, in the new governance structure the GI industry and wider GI community are not formally part of the new structure, but still remain involved in the implementation.

5.1.2 Strategic Planning and Management

Besides in the governance structure the ambition to develop an Open SDI is also reflected in the strategic planning and management of the implementation of the SDI. All four countries in our analysis have developed an SDI strategic plan in recent years, and each of these plans clearly expressed a move towards an open spatial data infrastructure. In Denmark the development of the strategic document on 'Location – A gateway to eGovernment' mainly was in hands of the Danish National Survey and Cadastre. The document contained a presentation of the National Survey and Cadastre, but also provided a broader view on the national spatial data infrastructure and a detailed discussion of the importance of geographic data.

In the United Kingdom, Finland and Netherlands, the process of developing the strategic plan was a more open process, as actors outside the public sector were involved in the planning process. In Finland, the National INSPIRE network prepared the national spatial data strategy for 2010–2015 entitled 'Location: the Unifying Factor' [34], and actively contributed to the implementation of the strategy. The network was also involved in updating the strategy in 2013 and 2014, which resulted in the Finnish national spatial data strategy 2016 'Position for spatial data'. In the Netherlands, the implementation approach and strategy for the development of national spatial data infrastructure between 2008 and 2011 was described in the GIDEON policy document [35]. Besides several public authorities, also the association for Geo-ICT companies (GeoBusiness Nederland) and several academic institutions contributed to the creation of this strategic document. Also the 2014 policy document, the 'Partners in GEO' vision, is a shared vision of both the private, academic and public sector on the geo-information infrastructure in the Netherlands [36]. The Location Strategy for the United Kingdom was launched by the UK Geographic Information Panel, a high-level advisory board providing advice on location information issues of national importance [31]. Also the members of this panel represent key interest groups in government, business and the wider location information community in the UK.

The idea of an open spatial data infrastructure is not only expressed in the way these strategies were developed, but also in the content of the strategies. All strategies explicitly emphasize the significance of geodata for businesses, citizens and the society in general. The original Dutch GIDEON strategy made a distinction between government-provided products and services for the public and businesses, and products and services that are developed by businesses. Location information provides governments at different levels the opportunities to improve their interactions with citizens and businesses. Moreover, if businesses but also citizens are able to work with location information and create new products and services, economic value is added to governmental location information. The more recent 'Partners in GEO' vision document strongly focuses on the importance of geographic data to address key societal challenges and the need for improved cooperation between government, the private sector and the academic sector.

The UK Location Strategy highlights the significance of location information for realizing innovation, as existing information is used in new and innovative ways, and added value is generated at no additional costs [31]. According to the original Finish 'Location: the Unifying Factor' strategy, geographic data can serve as a basis for new companies to develop their ideas into new products and services for a growing market [34]. The Finish strategy also mentions the role of geo-information in support of participation of citizens. Making available forecasts, plans and decisions as interoperable and easy accessible maps allows citizens to assess them easily and to provide their feedback and proposals. The strategy of Denmark states that geographic data and information will make it easier for citizens and businesses to find information from governments [37]. Presenting administrative information together with location information will make it easier to communicate and understand public sector activities and decisions. Moreover, geodata increase the opportunities of citizens and business to participate in the public debate and secure their individual rights.

Table 2.2 summarizes the key elements of the governance structures and strategic plans of the four national spatial data infrastructures.

5.2   Open Implementation

Besides their involvement in the governance and decision making on the SDI, non-government actors could also actively contribute to the implementation of the spatial data infrastructure through the provision of data, products and services. Businesses but also other institutions such as research institutions often play a significant role in the development of national spatial data infrastructure by collecting data on behalf of public authorities or by handling the data collection and processing at the request of a public authority. Geo-ICT companies also provide tools and services for supporting the distribution of geodata. In many cases, public authorities especially rely on local companies within their own country to support them with the processes of creation metadata, setting up catalogues, setting up view and download services, harmonizing data sets and monitoring the performance of the infrastructure. However, some Geo-ICT companies and SMEs in particular are also active outside their own country and provide support to the implementation of spatial data infrastructures worldwide. Two examples of such internationally

Table 2.2 Key elements of open governance of the national SDI in the four countries

	United Kingdom	Finland	Denmark	Netherlands
Governance structures	UK Location Council, UK User Group and INSPIRE working groups	National Council for Geographic Information	Coordination Committee on the Infrastructure for Spatial Information	INSPIRE Consultative Group
				'Partners in GEO' top team and strategic platform
Key associations and networks	Association for Geographic Information (AGI)	National INSPIRE network of Finland	Geoforum	GeoBusiness Nederland
Strategic documents	Place matters—the Location Strategy for the United Kingdom (2008)	Location: the Unifying Factor (2010) and Position for spatial data (2014)	Location—A gateway to eGovernment (2011)	GIDEON—Key geo-information facility for the Netherlands (2008) and Partners in GEO (2014)

recognized companies can be found in the Netherlands and in Finland. While the Dutch company GeoCat has contributed to the development of many national metadata catalogues based on the opensource software GeoNetwork, many national spatial data infrastructures rely on the products and services of the Finnish company Spatineo for monitoring and evaluating the performance of their spatial web services.

Interesting to notice is also how some of the associations and networks connecting different stakeholders have contributed to the development of the national spatial data infrastructure. In the United Kingdom for instance, the Association for Geographic Information (AGI) played a major role in the development of the UK GEMINI standard for describing metadata. In Denmark, the Geoforum association developed a WMS cookbook that focused on how international standards are linked and how they can be used in practice. Besides these examples of concrete products delivered by associations, the different associations in Denmark, the United Kingdom but also in Finland and the Netherlands contributed to the implementation of the national spatial data infrastructure through the organization of meetings, workshops and conferences for exchanging knowledge and experiences. The organization of competitions and the provision of prices and awards is a way of promoting the development of new and innovative solutions, and raise awareness on the possibilities of using open geodata. For instance, in Finland a Maps4Finland competition was organized and an award was given to the best application using spatial data. In Denmark, the Geodataprisen hands out awards to the best solutions, innovations and ideas dealing with spatial data.

The Netherlands have a strong tradition of joint testing and development activities among public sector parties and other stakeholders in the GI domain. Through the organization of pilot projects and testbeds, different stakeholders are involved in knowledge exchange and experimenting with new technological developments we are considered to be relevant for the future SDI. In 2010, a pilot project was organized on 3D GI to promote and facilitate the development of 3D applications. The pilot led to the development of a 3D toolkit to guide and assists organizations in starting with 3D developments, but also the definition of a 3D standards for the Netherlands. A similar initiative was the pilot project on linked data, which was launched in 2012. Again, the aim of this pilot project was to bring together different actors and organizations to explore the possibilities of linked data for publishing spatial data, define potential use cases and exchange knowledge and expertise related to this topic. In 2015, a testbed on 'Spatial data on the web' was launched in which academic and private organizations were invited to explore the possibilities for publishing spatial data as a usable and integrated component of the web. The testbed consisted of four smaller research projects, focusing on particular research questions. An interesting rather recent evolution is the opportunity given to non-government actors to add their own geographic data to the national SDI and make their geographic data sets available to the central access point. In the Netherlands, for example, several businesses have added their data to the National Geo Register.

6 Discussion and Conclusion

The goal of this chapter was to analyse the role and position of non-government actors in the development of national spatial data infrastructures in Europe and investigate to what extent the current spatial data infrastructures can be considered as open spatial data infrastructures. The analysis focused on four European countries that have taken several measures to facilitate and stimulate the involvement of non-government actors in the development of their spatial data infrastructure: the Netherlands, the United Kingdom, Finland and Denmark, all have taken. The analysis showed that in these four countries the move towards more open spatial data infrastructures can mainly be observed in the increased availability of spatial data and spatially enabled services to citizens, businesses and other stakeholders. Despite their efforts to also increase the involvement of these non-government actors in the governance and implementation of the infrastructure, government still remains the major player in the development and implementation of spatial data infrastructures in Europe.

In other words, it can be argued that the development of spatial data infrastructures in Europe so far has been successful in opening the data but less in opening the infrastructure. Driven by recent open data initiatives and EU legislation, the four countries in the analysis have opened most of their geographic data sets to the public, and allowed the re-use of these data sets for many purposes. Access to these data is provided through the national geoportals and more recently established open data portals, and the conditions for access to and use of the data have been simplified and harmonized through the use of common licenses. In addition to making the data available and accessible, the four countries also have been very active in the development of spatially enabled e-services to citizens and businesses. The development and online provision of different types of services on top of geographic data is about making the data valuable for different stakeholder groups. Citizens but also businesses and professionals outside the geographic data domain will especially benefit from the development of services on top of the data and customized to their needs, rather than from the data themselves. Making data available will be an important enabler for the development of such services and applications, as it allows businesses and other organizations to take control of the development of these services and products. The key challenge for public authorities will be to decide on which services should be provided by the government and which services should be left to the market. In some cases, even the co-design of location enabled services should be considered.

While European countries have been successful in opening their spatial data to citizens, businesses and other stakeholders in society, still a lot of progress can be made in also opening the infrastructure. The analysis of the four national spatial data infrastructures revealed some interesting approaches and practices of involving businesses, research institutions and other organizations in the governance of these infrastructures, especially through the design of an appropriate governance structure and the development of strategic plans. However, even in the most advanced spatial data infrastructures in Europe, public sector bodies still remain dominant in the decision making process and in the implementation of the infrastructure. Based on this observation it can be argued that spatial data infrastructures in Europe still are far away from being truly open infrastructures. A truly open spatial data infrastructure would not only contain and make available government data, but would provide an access point to all geographic data in society, including government data, private sector data and citizen data. The fundamental challenge in realizing such an open spatial data infrastructure will be to consider and treat all involved parties, i.e. public sector organizations, businesses, research institutions but also citizens, as equals and to look for the most effective approaches, methods and technologies for embedding non-government actors in the development and implementation of the spatial data infrastructure. Only then the SDI will be able to arrive at its full potential.

References

1. Dessers E, Crompvoets J, Janssen K, Vancauwenberghe G, Vandenbroucke D, Vanhaverbeke L (2011) SDI at work—the spatial zoning plans case. Spatialist, Leuven
2. Van Loenen B (2006) Developing geographic information infrastructures: the role of information policies. DUP Science, Delft
3. Groot R, McLaughlin J (2000) Introduction. In: Groot R, McLaughlin J (eds) Geospatial data infrastructure: concepts, cases, and good practice. Oxford University Press, New York, pp 1–12
4. Nedović-Budić Z, Crompvoets J, Georgiadou Y (eds) (2011) Spatial data infrastructures in context: North and South. CRC-Press—Taylor & Francis Group, Boca Raton
5. European Commission (2007) Directive 2007/2/EC of the European Parliament and of the Council of 14 March 2007 establishing an infrastructure for spatial information in the European Community (INSPIRE), OJ L 108/1
6. Vancauwenberghe G, Dessers E, Crompvoets J, Vandenbroucke D (2014) Realizing data sharing: the role of spatial data infrastructures. In: Gascó-Hernández M (ed) Open government. Opportunities and challenges for public governance. Springer, New York, pp 155–169
7. McDougall K (2009) The potential of citizen volunteered spatial information for building SDI. In: GSDI 11 world conference: spatial data infrastructure convergence: building SDI bridges to address global challenges, Rotterdam
8. Groot R (1997) Spatial data infrastructure (SDI) for sustainable land management. ITC J 3(4):287–294
9. Grus L, Crompvoets J, Bregt A (2010) Spatial data infrastructures as complex adaptive systems. Int J Geogr Inf Sci 24(3):439–463
10. Giff G, Crompvoets J (2008) Performance indicators a tool to support spatial data infrastructures assessment. Comput Environ Urban Syst 32(5):365–376
11. Rhind D (2000) Funding an NGDI. In: Groot R, McLaughlin J (eds) Geospatial data infrastructure: concepts, cases and good practice. Oxford University Press, New York, pp 39–55
12. Janssen K (2010) The availability of spatial and environmental data in the EU at the crossroads between public and economic interests. Kluwer, Dordrecht
13. Warnest M (2005) A collaboration model for national spatial data infrastructure in federated countries. University of Melbourne, Department of Geomatics, Melbourne
14. Craglia M (2006) Introduction to the international journal of spatial data infrastructures research. Int J Spat Data Infrastruct Res 1(1):1–13

15. Wehn de Montalvo U (2001) Strategies for SDI implementation: a survey of national experiences. In: 5th global spatial data infrastructure conference, Cartagena de Indias, 21–25 May 2001
16. McLaughlin J, Nichols S (1994) Developing a national spatial data infrastructure. J Surv Eng 120(2):62–76
17. Bernard L, Mäs S, Müller M, Henzen C, Brauner J (2013) Scientific geodata infrastructures: challenges, approaches and directions. Int J Digital Earth 7(7):613–633
18. Hendriks P, Dessers E, Van Hootegem G (2012) Reconsidering the definition of a spatial data infrastructure. Int J Geogr Inf Sci 26(8):1479–1494
19. Masser I (2009) Changing notions of a spatial data infrastructure. In: Loenen B, Besemer JWJ, Zevenbergen JA (eds) SDI convergence. Netherlands Geodetic Commission, Delft, pp 219–228
20. Budhathoki NR, Bruce BC, Nedovic-Budic Z (2008) Reconceptualizing the role of the user of spatial data infrastructure. GeoJournal 72(3):149–160
21. Coleman DJ, Rajabifard A, Kolodziej KW (2016) Expanding the SDI environment: comparing current spatial data infrastructure with emerging indoor location-based services. Int J Digital Earth 9(6):1–19
22. Wirtz BW, Birkmeyer S (2015) Open government: origin, development, and conceptual perspectives. Int J Public Adm 38(5):381–396
23. OpenGovData (2016) Eight principles of open government data. http://www.opengovdata.org
24. Latre MA, Lopez-Pellicer FJ, Nogueras-Iso J, Bejar R, Zarazaga-Soria FJ, Muro-Medrano PR (2013) Spatial Data Infrastructures for environmental e-government services: the case of water abstractions authorisations. Environ Model Softw 48:81–92
25. De Kleijn M, van Manen N, Kolen JCA, Scholten HJ (2014) Towards a user-centric SDI framework for historical and heritage European landscape research. Int J Spat Data Infrastruct Res 9:1–35
26. Box P (2013) The governance of spatial data infrastructure: a registry based model. University of Melbourne, Department of Infrastructure Engineering, Melbourne
27. Goodchild M (2007) Citizens as voluntary sensors: spatial data infrastructure in the world of Web 2.0. Int J Spat Data Infrastruct Res 2:24–32
28. European Commission (2003) Directive 2003/98/EC of the European Parliament and of the council of 17 November 2003 on the re-use of public sector information, OJ L 345/90
29. European Commission (2013) Directive 2013/37/EU of the European Parliament and of the council of 26 June 2013 amending Directive 2003/98/EC on the reuse of public sector information, OJ L 175/1
30. Van Loenen B, Grothe M (2014) INSPIRE empowers re-use of public sector information. Int J Spat Data Infrastruct Res 9:86–106
31. UK Geographic Information Panel (2008) Place matters: the location strategy for the United Kingdom. Communities and Local Government, London
32. Rekenkamer A (2014) Trendrapport open data. Algemene Rekenkamer, Den Haag
33. Van Loenen B, van Barneveld DW (2010) Implementing INSPIRE: the process towards the harmonization of licenses for public sector geographic information in the Netherlands. In: The 4th INSPIRE conference, Krakow, 22–25 June 2010
34. Finnish Ministry of Agriculture and Forestry (2010) Location: the unifying factor. Finnish national spatial data strategy 2010–2015. Ministry of Agriculture and Forestry, Helsinki
35. Netherlands Ministry of Housing, Spatial Planning and the Environment (2008) GIDEON—key geo-information facility for the Netherlands. Approach and implementation strategy (2008–2011). Ministry of Housing, Spatial Planning and the Environment, The Hague
36. Bregt A, Nijpels E, Tijl H (2014) Partners in GEO: shared vision of government, private sector and scientific community on the future of the geo-information sector. http://geosamen.nl
37. Danish National Survey and Cadastre (2011) Location—a gateway to eGovernment. Strategic basis for the National survey and cadaster 2011–2015. Danish Ministry of the Environment, Copenhagen

Chapter 3
Improving Domestic Revenue Mobilisation in African Countries Using ICT: A Literature Review Analysis

Emmanuel Eilu

Abstract Many countries in Africa do not have adequate capacity to mobilize domestic fiscal resources for economic growth and development. This has led to an extremely low tax-to-GDP ratio in many African countries. Countries in the Sub-Sahara Africa region continue to fall below 7% growth rate. For economic development and growth to happen, a country should have an effective and efficient tax system to mobilize domestic fiscal resources to finance the provision of essential public goods and services. For domestic taxation is a panacea for development. Currently, there are extensive calls for reforms in the tax systems. One of the reforms that can greatly change the face of many tax bodies in Africa and has a great potential to improve domestic revenue collection is the integration of ICT into the tax systems. A number of African countries have started an array of initiatives to exploit ICT with a view of improving domestic tax revenues. Indeed, in this modern age, it is quite difficult to conceive of a tax administration system that can perform to its expectation without making considerable use of ICT. However, high expectations on the use of multi-million dollar ICT resources to improve the tax systems in Africa has either not materialized or has proven to be a much more time-consuming and costly than originally envisaged. There is a need to investigate the current use of ICT in Tax Administrations and the extent to which ICT addresses significant challenges in Tax Administration. The lessons outlined in this chapter may be important in informing governments in Africa on how to successfully improve Tax Administration using ICTs.

Keywords E-Tax Systems • African Countries • Economic Growth • Economic Development

E. Eilu (✉)
School of Computing and Informatics Technology, Makerere University Kampala, Kampala, Uganda
e-mail: eiluemma@yahoo.co.uk

© Springer International Publishing AG 2018
S. Saeed et al. (eds.), *User Centric E-Government*, Integrated Series in Information Systems 39, DOI 10.1007/978-3-319-59442-2_3

1 Introduction

Taxation is one of the most important ways in which developing countries can mobilize their own resources for sustainable development. It supports the basic functions of an effective state, enabling it to raise the resources needed to deliver essential services, and creates the context for economic growth [1, 2]. For economic development and growth to happen, a country should have adequate capacity to mobilize fiscal resources to finance the provision of essential public goods, a capacity that many developing countries lack [3–5]. Governments with a bare minimum of tax administration infrastructure, as is typically the case in developing countries, find it costly to monitor earnings and enforce tax compliance [6]. Many developing country have for long been grappling with huge challenges in tax administration and taxation. For example, in 2006, the average GDP share of government revenue in low-income countries was 12.1%. However, for high-income OECD countries, the figure stood at 25.2%, twice as high for low-income countries [6]. A report from the African Development Bank Group [7] indicates that domestic revenue collection through taxation is still below its potential in many African Countries. For example, between 2006 and 2008, tax-to-GDP ratios in the East African Community sub-region ranged between 12.3 to 22.1%, compared to an average of 35.6% and 25.4% for the Organisation for Economic Cooperation and Development (OECD) countries and South Africa respectively. The bank also reports that other measures such as revenue productivity and Value Added Tax (VAT) efficiency are also still low. Bird [8] explains that, for developing countries to benefit from the opportunities presented by this contemporary era such as globalization—or even to recover from the global negative economic waves, they must be able to mobilize adequate fiscal revenues. The most reliable way to effectively mobilize fiscal revenue is to revamp the tax administration systems.

Although there have been various tax administration reforms in the many African countries such as, establishment of autonomous revenue authorities, simplifying tax systems and reducing tax evasion/avoidance, much of the significant reforms have generally been centered on the use of Information and Communication Technology (ICT) as a tool to improve the efficiency and effectiveness of the tax bodies [7, 9]. ICT has broadly been utilized to accumulate and handle tax payer's data, undertake specific checking in view of risk analysis, automatically exchange data between government agencies, provide convenient data to bolster decision making by leaders and inform tax policy formulation [10]. Indeed, in this modern age, it is quite difficult to conceive of a tax administration that can perform its tasks effectively and efficiently without making substantial use of ICT. However, much of the expectation of greater effectiveness as a result of adopting ICT has either not materialized, or has proven to be a much more time-consuming and a very costly process than originally envisaged [9]. Bird [8] observes that the success of an ICT aided tax system requires not just "automating" existing structures and methods, but instead reconsidering, updating and streamlining tax systems, frameworks and strategies. This chapter sets out to establish how to increase the tax-to-GDP ratio in many African countries by improving tax administration using ICT.

2 The Purpose of This Chapter

This chapter, therefore, examines the state of Tax administration in Africa. It also establishes current reforms being implemented in Tax administration particularly using ICT, and the extent to which ICT addresses significant challenges in Tax administration. This chapter further identifies challenges of Implementing ICTs in tax administration, and remedies to those challenges. The lessons outlined in this chapter may be important in informing governments in developing countries, especially in Africa, on how to successfully improve tax administration using ICTs, for an effective tax administration may thus play a critical role not only in shaping economic development but in developing an effective state.

Three major research questions are asked in this chapter

1. What is the state of tax administration in Africa?
2. To what extent do ICTs address major challenges in week tax administration systems in Africa?
3. What are the likely challenges of Implementing ICTs in tax administration, and remedies to those challenges?

3 Methodology

A systematic review was the main method used in this chapter. In the last 30 years or so, narrative-style literature reviews have been criticized for being biased and inadequate in terms of the rigor of research performed [11]. This has led to the emergence and widespread use of systematic review method of research. A systematic review is a 'rigorous method used to map the evidence base on an unbiased way as possible and to assess the quality of the evidence and synthesize it' [12]. Systematic review method follows a formal process for appraising literature and minimizing bias [13]. According to Zanker and Mallett [14], a systematic review is considered by some to offer 'the most reliable and comprehensive statement about what works and how it worked. It has been generally utilized for a long time as a part of various field studies, for example, in medical research, and in natural sciences. A systematic review has many times been employed in evidence-informed policymaking within the arena of international development. It is much preferred by international agencies as such the UK's Department for International Development (DFID) and the Australian Agency for International Development (AusAID). These agencies have funded a series of systematic reviews over the past few years, with the express aim of finding out 'what works and how it worked' in generating development outcomes [14]. In 1984 Cooper [15] proposed a five stage systematic review process that was followed in this chapter'

- Problem formulation—statement of objective.
- Data collection—an unbiased literature search.

- Data evaluation—assessing the studies for inclusion in the review.
- Analysis and interpretation—qualitative or quantitative aggregation of individual research studies.
- Public presentation—discussion and context of findings.

According to Kowalczyk and Truluck [13], a systematic review is considered original research as it follows a standard scientific protocol.

4   The State of Tax Administration in Africa

Despite the recent economic gains made in the last decade by a number of African countries in terms of export revenue, it is important to note that the growth rate in Sub-Sahara Africa as a region continues to fall short of the 7–8% necessary to achieve the Millennium Development Goals (MDGs) target of halving poverty [16]. To raise the development rate and manage it at the level that will permit African nations to halve poverty requires a critical increment in the volume of foreign and local resources earmarked for economic development of the country, and particularly improve the standard of living of the citizens. Accomplishing the Millennium Development Goals, for example, may require some low-wage countries to raise their duty Gross Domestic Product (GDP) proportions by around 4 percentage points [17]. However, increasing the GDP by 4 percentage points has proven to be a daunting task for many African countries. This is because the domestic revenue collection in many African countries is still low. For example, the Mozambique Revenue Authority has registered about 2,600,000 taxpayers, both citizens and companies. However, only less than 10% of these tax payers really document or pay tax charges [18]. As already said before, the mean tax-to-GDP proportions in Uganda, Kenya, Tanzania, Burundi, and Rwanda from 2006 and 2008 was between 12.3 and 22.1%, far much underneath their OECD partners whose normal tax to-GDP proportion was 35.6 and 25.4% [6]. About 32 African countries collect less than USD 1 of tax per person per day. Those with the lowest tax-to-GDP ratios also tend to be those with the lowest effort [19].

Although Foreign Direct Investment (FDI) flows to Africa have increased over years from USD 27.4 Bn in 2003 to USD 47.8 Bn in 2010, contributing to over 37% of net aid disbursements to all developing countries, it is important to note that this funding is still too limited in geographical coverage, and it is mainly directed towards extractive industries [20]. Because of this deficit, effectively harnessing domestic financial resources could help raise additional financing to narrow Africa's resource gap. Increased domestic revenue would also help to accelerate the process of economic development and poverty reduction in many of these countries [16]. Adequate domestic revenue would further reduce dependence on donor funds and its associated conditions. Fjeldstad [1] observes that the importance of strengthening domestic revenue mobilization was emphasized by the G20-leaders at their summit in November 2010. Both the European Commission [21] and the

OECD Development Assistance Committee [2] have firmly underscored domestic tax collection as a panacea for development. A successful tax system is viewed as key to sustainable development because it can stimulate the household income base as a key driver for economic development in many African countries. This would enable these countries to escape from international aid dependency, or single natural resource reliance [1]. Therefore, there is a need to build adequate capacity to mobilize fiscal resources to finance the provision of essential public goods [3, 4, 22]. From the beginning of the twenty-first century, there has been an overwhelming desire to fill Africa's development resource gap and various continuous efforts have been made to attain this [23]. In today's world, advances in Information and Communication Technology (ICT) offers a great potential to improve revenue collection by automating taxation processes, better servicing taxpayers, increasing compliance and a cheaper possibility for gathering and analysing a large amount of data on taxpayers [6, 18, 24–26]. The use of ICT in an attempt to improve fiscal capacity and to better taxation processes has caught the attention of tax authorities throughout developing countries [6]. In the next section, this paper discusses attempts by African countries to improve the efficiency and effectiveness of their tax administrations through the use of ICT.

5 Electronic Tax Systems in Africa

Over the last 40 years, Bird and Zolt [9] observe that reform efforts in tax administration in developing countries has been generally centered on ICT. Allover Africa, there are a number of on going efforts to exploit the benefits of ICT in enhancing efficiency and effectiveness in tax administration [1]. For instance, the use of e-Filing systems for domestic revenue, computerized registration systems for motor vehicles and drivers registration, electronic cash registers for VAT, the use of electronic communication systems for information dissemination and much more [1, 27]. Historically, the most prevalent use of ICT systems in tax administrations is in core tax activities such as, processing returns and payments, and collecting relevant information [27]. IT systems generally enable tax administrations to move away from the overwhelming manual handling to direct its resources to facilitate monitoring and enforcing compliance. ICT also facilitates voluntary compliance by opening multiple interactive and electronic channels with taxpayers [27].

The figure below illustrated a basic electronic tax system used in a typical Revenue Authority (Fig. 3.1).

There are majorly two types of electronic tax systems deployed in African countries today, namely; the custom-built or sometimes called "build it in-house" and "Commercial Off-The-Shelf" (COTS) electronic tax systems [18, 27]. Making a decision to purchase either custom built or COTS is normally referred to as the Make-or-Buy decision [18]. According to Jimenez et al. [27] and Blume and Bott [18], custom built electronic tax systems take a longer time than purchasing a COTS solution, as it has to be built from scratch by the in-house team. The custom built

• TIN/VAT Registrations
• Integration with Automated System for Customs Data (ASYCUDA) • VAT Returns Processing • VAT Payment • VAT Taxpayer Accounting • VAT Revenue Accounting • VAT Refunds
• VAT Refunds • RMS Common Cashiering • Taxpayer Accounting • Revenue Accounting • Taxpayer Enquiries
• Taxpayer Enquiries • VAT Audit/Investigation Tools • VAT E-Tax • Income Tax Pay As You Earn (PAYE) processing/Provisional Taxes
• Income Tax/PAYE returning processing • Advanced Auditing • Income Tax/PAYE returning processing
• Debt Management • Objections • Withholding Taxes • TIN

Fig. 3.1 IT support to tax administration functions with the core tax system [18]

system accommodates specific and usually current business processes of the tax authority. They tend to have lower initial costs, leverage internal experience, and systems. Custom-built solutions, however, depend on internal expertise, which can be difficult to acquire or retain. With custom-built solutions, it inherently involves a higher risk, as it may be difficult for tax administrations to keep pace with technological innovations. Countries that have custom built electronic tax system include among others, Swaziland but later changed to COTS, and Senegal which maintains both custom built and COTS. On the other hand, COTS systems are ready, vendor-made, and transferrable solutions designed to accommodate leading practice in business processes. COTS systems are normally tested and proven to align with best practices. COTS is used by a number of Revenue Authorities across the African continent, such as, the US$ 5 million Integrated Revenue Administration System (IRAS) used by Swaziland Revenue Authority, approximately US$8 million Integrated Tax Administration System used by the Tanzania Revenue Authority was a COTS system-though it was later modified in-house, much of the US$15 million electronic tax system used at the Uganda Revenue Authority is COTS, the US$1.5 million electronic tax system used by the Zambia Revenue Authority is a COTS system-to mention but a few. Blume and Bott (2015) strongly advice that, whenever possible, software should be bought off the shelf rather than developed internally, both for cost reasons, and to accommodate subsequent technological developments.

The table below illustrates the recent electronic tax systems implemented in different African countries.

The Table 3.1 shows a number of ICT-based revenue collection initiatives implemented, or are being implemented in a number of African countries. Other ICT tax systems that have not been reflected in the above table include; The FreeBalance Accountability Suite used by Rwanda Revenue Authority. iTAX used by Tanzanian Revenue Authority (TRA) in 2001, then later the Tanzania Local Government Authorities (LGA). Tax and Revenue Management (TRM) used by Maldives and Zimbabwe [18]. It worth noting that these countries are implementing different types of electronic tax systems, and each implementation is at a different stage. So far, enormous benefits have been realized from the implementation of the above initiatives. Some of the visible benefits of electronic tax systems in Africa are discussed in next section.

6 Importance of Electronic Tax Systems in Africa

A couple of years back, more than 24 developing countries instituted changes that made it less demanding, or less exorbitant for firms to document tax returns and pay charges. The most widely recognized component of tax returns changes was in the upgrading of the manual filing system in to an electronic filing system. Such changes were executed in 18 countries in the Sub-Saharan region including, Mozambique, Zambia, Uganda, Kenya among others [28]. Tax payers in these countries now record tax returns electronically, in this manner investing less energy and time on compliance. These electronic tax systems also increase transparency and limit the opportunity for corruption and bribery [18, 28]. In Uganda, for example, since the introduction of the tax online interface in 2012/13, there were 2.3 million visits to the Uganda Revenue Authority web-based tax filing interface, up from 1.3 m the previous year. There were 4,417,245 tax related electronic exchanges recorded and UgShs 6 trillion (about US$1.8 billion) was collected. This represented 75% of the tax collected by Uganda Revenue Authority [29]. In Tanzania, the electronic tax collection through banks has enabled the Tanzania Revenue Authority reduce operational costs by a high margin, and at the same time improve efficiency in the payment system [22]. The system has minimized settlement risks and eliminated floats between Commercial Banks and the Central Bank. Since the introduction of the system of payment through banks, 97% of total revenue collection is settled under interbank arrangements [22]. Wamathu [30] examined the impact of electronic taxation on the financial performance of audit firms in Kenya and found that, there was an improvement in timely filing of returns since the introduction of I-Tax, and there has been a reduction in audit period due to the introduction of I-Tax, and that the I-Tax system was cost effective. In Zambia, with the launch of Tax Online, it is no longer necessary to physically go to the Zambia Revenue Authority offices to register for taxes, file tax returns or make tax payments. Following the introduction of the web based tax filing and payment system, the time taken to

Table 3.1 Electronic tax systems projects in Africa [18]

Country	Project	Description
Ethiopia	2007–2012 Support Facility for the Public Sector Capacity Building	Support to the Public Sector Capacity Building Programme. Technical assistance included supporting the purchase, installation and configuration of a COTS solution for the tax administration
Uganda	2000–2011 Support to the Uganda Revenue Authority (URA)	Support to the implementation of the eTax system from TATA consulting
Sierra Leone and Liberia	2005–2012 Support for National Revenue Authority	Support to the National Revenue Authority (NRA) Procurement of a VAT processing systems (this is actually provided by Crown Agents and is an older version of the TRIPs system)
Uganda	2012–2015 Oil Taxation Capacity Building Programme	Support to the implementation of a new eTax module for oil and gas
Mozambique	Since 2009 Co-financing of tax administration reform basket fund	Among others Automation/ICT-based tax administration reform
Kenya	2008–2012 Public Financial Management Reform	Working with the Kenyan government to develop a budget framework consistent with government priorities and policies; improving the quality of government records and procurement practices; strengthening revenue and tax systems and Improving the effectiveness of audits
Liberia	Since 2011 Economic Governance & Institutional Reform-Additional Financing	The project assists with strengthening public financial management through improving revenue administration by covering the cost overrun of the installation of an integrated tax administration system. Support to the installation of an integrated tax administration system (ITAS) in the BIR by providing equipment hardware, software, technical assistance and training

comply with tax obligations dropped by 3% in 2013, and by a further 11% in 2014, and reduced the payments sub-indicator by 11 payments between 2013 and 2014. This is because the majority of taxpayers now file and pay their VAT online. Taxpayers can also now file their tax returns within 2 hours instead of the previous 15 working days needed to manually capture all tax payers' data into the system. As by 2014, 57% of all registered taxpayers filed their tax returns online [31, 32]. In Sierra Leone, with support from international donors, there has been a massive drive to modernise the National Revenue Authority (NRA) using locally developed ICT solutions. According to the World Bank report of 2012, Sierra Leone jumped from 159th to 76th country in paying tax elements, and NRA exceeded its 2012 target by 28% to an impressive US$417m.

Undeniably, as stated earlier in this chapter, it is difficult to imagine of a modern tax administration that can perform its tasks efficiently and efficiently without making considerable use of ICT [33]. However, just like any other computerized system, deploying and utilising an ICT aided tax system also includes some tough challenges in conceiving, deployment and sustenance [18]. In the next section, this paper discusses some of the challenges always encountered during the implementation of ICT aided Tax systems in many African countries, and their probable solutions.

7   Challenges and Remedies of Electronic Tax Systems in Africa

In this section, this chapter highlights the main challenges along with recommendations for electronic tax systems in Africa.

7.1   ICT Infrastructure

One of the major problems faced by African countries in the implementation of electronic tax systems is the inadequate ICT support infrastructure. In many developing countries, taxpayers have limited internet resources that can facilitate the use of electronic tax filing system. There is limited internet access, low network speeds, power shortages and system failures, and the electronic system can be quite slow and unreliable. In Kenya, for example, the online filing system introduced in 2009 took 3 years for the system to gain acceptance with taxpayers, this was as a result of the slow processing speed of the filing website [28]. In Zambia, there are 200,000 registered taxpayers in the Zambian Revenue Authority (ZRA) database, and three-quarters of these are Small and Medium scale Enterprises (SMEs). Ordinarily, an SME tax payer in Zambia needs at least a minimum of a computer with internet connection in order to do e-business with ZRA. However, studies show that a high number of SMEs have no PCs and those who own PCs have no connection to internet facilities. Others are not well versed in PC and web use. Due to these difficulties, it is exceptionally troublesome for SMEs to do business with ZRA [34]. In Senegal, sporadic power supply has in some cases hampered the effective rollout of the electronic tax systems throughout the country. In certain cases, the buildings in which the tax offices are accommodated need to be renovated, as serious issues like leaking roofs are hampering IT deployment [18]. Ezomike [28] observes that, although ensuring that taxpayers and tax officials are properly educated on the use of the system can be a herculean task, an adequate sensitisation plan should be drafted, and the system must be designed to be user-friendly for ease of acquaintance by the users. Government and donor agencies need to provide the necessary infrastructure needed for a successful deployment and usage of electronic tax systems.

7.2 Administrative Capacity

Many conclusions have been made that the tax administration systems in developing countries are simply insufficient and lacks "administrative capacity", usually defined in terms of skilled human capital for the tax administration to function properly [33]. Blume and Bott [18] observe that, each stage of the modernisation procedure, including ICT integration into the tax system, will require sufficient capacity and capabilities within the tax administration. Depending on the stage of the project, these shortages will become visible in the area of IT, business analysts, tax officers and managers alike in the respective areas of expertise. One of the biggest technical challenges encountered in Mozambique Revenue Authority (MRA) reform projects was the Oracle System which ran on Java. It required IT personnel to undergo extensive training before they are able to undertake any changes in the system. As a consequence of the tight schedules and a difficult relation with Oracle vendor, the MRA was forced to employ a team of approximately four Oracle consultants to carry out the required alterations on the ground [18]. With donor support, Ghana computerized its tax processes, however, the human resource was not adequately trained and the recruitment of staff was not to the recommended numbers, therefore leading to the ineffective implementation of the ICT reforms [38]. IMF et al. [35] observe that many tax bodies continue to be staffed by poorly trained and low paid officials, have structures which do not encourage an integrated approach to different taxes, and are marked by imbalanced service and enforcement functions. There is a need to build capacity before, during and after the implementation of ICT in the tax systems. One of the tax Authorities that managed to address the issue of unskilled personnel is Zambia Revenue Authority (ZRA). In conjunction with training programs for tax officers, ZRA has been successful in improving the collection and processing of taxpayer data through consistent training, and the project has built up technical expertise within the ZRA to effectively use ICT [20]. There is also a need to build a competitive salary structure throughout the Authority. Competitive salaries are needed to attract and retain suitably qualified staff, such as skilled professional managers, and to reduce incentives for corruption [36]. In Uganda, for example, salaries for staff working at the Uganda Revenue Authority was increased by an average of 250%, which aided in the recruitment and maintenance of highly skilled staff [20].

7.3   Conflicting Interest (Donor-Government)

As expressed before, despite the fact that the general pattern of aid towards the different tax bodies in developing countries has essentially increased from USD 21.3 Bn in 2002 to USD 47.8 Bn in 2010, donors continue to have mixed reactions and approaches towards supporting the improvement of tax administration capability on a sustainable basis [20]. Clashing interests and uncoordinated activities have been registered between the donor agencies and the tax bodies or governments. When several donors are involved in a given modernisation program at the same time, and they are pursuing parallel tax projects, it has maximum potential to fragment, foster inconsistency and elevated transactions costs of the project [18]. There were situations where a number of donors were undermining coherent reform effort in Tanzania Revenue Authority (TRA), where the introduction of information technology project and Taxpayer Identification Number (TIN) project were not coordinated. There were also incidents where the reforms processes were managed offshore in the donor country, leaving the recipient country (Tanzania) inexperienced [20]. Furthermore, for a long time, the donor community sent mixed signals and inhibited strengthening the TRA as a single integrated authority. Therefore, from the onset, donors should pursue a proactive systematic approach of coordinated technical support to tax administration reform in African countries. The basket funding approach has been successful in Uganda's modernization of tax processes. Basket funding arrangement plays a major role in the successful coordination of donor supported reform. With support from various donor agencies like Netherlands, the UK, DFID, World Bank, IMF, Japan, China, CIDA and Denmark, the government of Uganda successfully implemented the modernization of the tax processes supported through an integrated technical co-operation and basket funding framework for an approximated amount of USD 15 million [20].

7.4   Inadequate Planning

Blume and Bott [18] observe that some countries do not put in enough energy and time to fully examine and understand the business processes of the Authority before planning and tendering for a new system. Without this prior examination, unnecessary delays and unwanted budget overruns will likely be the consequence. The impact of this action will be realized when funding for remedial measures over shoots, and the total cost of the project inflates. For example, in Mozambique, the tax body began to venture into e-taxation without simplifying and redesigning its processes in a proper way, and this led to numerous setbacks during implementation, which led to unnecessary delays. Likewise, the interaction between the authority and Oracle which was contracted to supply the e-tax system was far from optimal, so the desired results could not be achieved. Consequently, the tax authority was pushed to hired external consultants on the business side, to mediate with the supplier (Oracle) and to introduce best practices on a business process level [18]. Blume and Bott [18] make an observation that, carefully planning the structure and procedures during the full implementation process is no guarantees for success, however, without it, the chance of success will be reduced to almost zero. Blume and Bott [18] recommend best practices in the area of project management, like Prince2 or PMI, will help to structure the project and the internal processes and procedures. A carefully thought-out detailed plan must be in place prior to system implementation, and more importantly, lessons should be drawn and learned from other countries.

7.5 *Corruption*

Bird and Zolt [9] acknowledge that, since silver linings seldom arrive without clouds, there is a possibility that technology itself may equally increase corruption. Technology its self, may foster corruption by increasing the opportunities for more sophisticated collaboration between taxpayers and corrupt officials. One of the biggest impediments to reforms in tax administration in the African Revenue Authorities has been the resurgence of considerable corruption. The South African Revenue Service (SARS) at one time reported a plot between corrupt officers employed by tax paying companies, and the intellectual property registration office of SARS to swindle SARS off VAT income. In response to this kind of corrupt tendencies, some revenue entities such as the Uganda Revenue Authority through donor advice, sought after a more radical (but effective) approach. When the tax body was changed into an Authority, all previous tax officers were laid off and were advised to re-apply for positions in the new Authority following an extremely strict vetting process. In South Africa, when the new Authority was instituted, more than 33% of the previous staff were rejected due to prior misconducts [20]. Kagina [20] recommends donors to provide expertise on how to detect corruption within tax administrations, internal investigative units should be explicitly supported, and hiring expatriate personnel for these units, potentially from other African countries should be looked into.

7.6 *In Adequate Legislation*

Throughout the literature, local government revenue systems in many African countries lack strong and consistent domestic tax legislation [37]. This has affected the implementation of electronic tax systems. Kagina [20] observes that administrative positive reforms can work best if they are empowered by enabling legislative enactments. For instance, a tax reform that mandates taxpayers to file returns using the web platform, requires an enactment permitting electronic returns in the tax laws. There is a need to either tailor the electronic tax system to comply with the country's tax legislation or the legislation can be tailored to empower the electronic tax system. For example in Zambia, there were a few situations where Legislation had to be amended to accommodate recognition of e-reports in official courtroom in case there was a dispute. While in Burundi, new and improved legislation was drafted prior to the creation of the Burundais des Recettes (OBR), a semi-independent revenue authority to professionalize tax administration in Burundi, and also as part of a wider strategy addressing the needs for Burundi to harmonize its laws and procedures with all other state members of the East Africa Community (EAC) [18].

8 Conclusion

Indeed, it is true that for economic growth and development to be achieved, a country should have and effective and efficient capacity to mobilize fiscal resources to finance the provision of essential public goods. However, many countries in Africa do not have an efficient and effective capacity to mobilize domestic resource in form of taxes, and hence low levels of economic growth and development have been registered in many countries. There is a need to reform the tax sector in many of the African countries. One of the reforms that can greatly change the face of many tax bodies in Africa, and has a great potential to improve domestic revenue collection is the integration of ICT into the tax systems. However, successful reforms in the tax systems in Africa require not simply 'computerising' existing forms and procedures, but rather rethinking, redesigning and streamlining processes and procedures in the entire tax system. The successful introduction and use of ICT thus requires fundamental reorganization in both processes and procedures, ICT strategic planning, legislation changes, recruitment, training, incentives and use of COTS.

References

1. Fjeldstad OH (2013) Taxation and development: a review of donor support to strengthen tax systems in developing countries. ISBN 978-92-9230-587-1 WIDER working paper no. 2013/010
2. OECD (2011) Revenue statistics, 1965–2010: 2011 edition [Online]
3. Bird RM (1980) The administrative dimension of tax reform in developing countries. In: Gillis M (ed) Lessons from tax reform in developing countries. Duke University Press, Durham, pp 315–346

4. Braütigam D, Fjeldstad OH, Moore M (2008) Taxation and state-building in developing countries: capacity and consent. Cambridge University Press, Cambridge
5. Vito T, Zee HH (2000) Tax policy for emerging markets: developing countries. Natl Tax J 53(2):299–322
6. Ali M, Shifa A, Shimeles A, Woldeyes FB (2015) Information technology and fiscal capacity in a developing country: evidence from Ethiopia. ICTD working paper 31. Available at SSRN: https://ssrn.com/abstract=2587857. Accessed 12 May 2016
7. African Development Bank Group (2011) Domestic resource mobilisation for poverty reduction in East Africa: lessons for tax policy and administration
8. Bird RM (2015) Improving tax administration in developing countries. J Tax Adm 1(1)
9. Bird RM, Zolt EM (2008) Technology and taxation in developing countries: from hand to mouse. http://www2.law.columbia.edu/taxcolloquium. Accessed 12 May 2016
10. Nakabayashi S (2016) Capacity building for tax administration to mobilize domestic resources for development. In: 12th tax administration conference, Sydney, 31 Mar 2016
11. Hemingway P, Brereton N (2009) What is a systematic review? Hayward Group Web site. http://www.whatisseries.co.uk/whatis/pdfs/What_is_syst_rev.pdf. Accessed 8 Jan 2016. Published April 2009
12. DFID (Department for International Development) (2013) Systematic reviews in international development. https://www.gov.uk/government/publications/systematic-reviews-in-international-development/systematic-reviews-in-international-development. Accessed 10 Mar 2016
13. Kowalczyk N, Truluck C (2013) Literature reviews and systematic reviews: what is the difference? Radiol Technol 85(2):219–222
14. Zanker JH, Mallett R (2013) How to do a rigorous, evidence focused literature review in international development. A guidance note. https://www.odi.org/sites/odi.org.uk/files/odiassets/publications-opinion-files/8572.pdf. Accessed 10 Mar 2016
15. Cooper HM (1984) The integrative research review: a systematic approach. Applied social research methods series, vol 2. Sage, Beverly Hills. In: Randolph JJ (2009) A guide to writing the dissertation literature review. Pract Assess Res Eval 14(13):1–13. http://pareonline.net/pdf/v14n13.pdf. Accessed 12 May 2016
16. UN (2007) Economic development in Africa: reclaiming policy space: domestic resource mobilization and developmental states. In: United Nations conference on trade and development
17. United Nations (2005) Investing in development. United Nations, New York
18. Blume J, Bott M (2015) Information technology in tax administration in developing countries. KfW Development Bank Report
19. De Paepe G, Dickinson B (2014) Tax revenues as a motor for sustainable development. http://www.oecdilibrary.org/docserver/download/4314031ec011.pdf?expires=1463478676&id=id&accname=guest&checksum=5F7BF9FF3D4FF08D927A35EE84D6494F. Accessed 15 June 2016
20. Kagina A (2012) Aid as a catalyst to increase domestic revenue mobilisation in Sub-Saharan Africa. Office for ECOSOC Support and Coordination
21. European Commission (EC) (2010) Tax and development: cooperating with developing countries on promoting good governance in tax matters. Communication from the Commission to the European Parliament, COM(2010)163 final (21 April). The Council and the European Economic and Social Committee, European Commission, Brussels
22. Kitillya HM (2016) We're boosting revenue collection. http://derlimited.com/index.php?option=com_content&view=article&id=234&%E2%88%93Itemid=236. Accessed 10 Mar 2016
23. United Nations (UN) (2009) Enhancing the role of domestic financial resources in Africa's development. A policy handbook. A report written for the United Nations conference on trade and development in Geneva
24. Saeed S, Reddick C (2013) Human-centered system design for electronic governance. IGI Global, Hershey

25. Saeed S, Bamarouf YA, Ramayah T, Iqbal SZ (2017) Design solutions for user-centric information systems. IGI Global, Hershey
26. Saeed S, Bajwa IS, Mahmood Z (2015) Human factors in software development and design. IGI Global, Hershey
27. Jimenez G, Sionnaigh NM, Kamenov A (2013) USAID'S leadership in public financial management: information technology for tax administration
28. Ezomike C (2016) The case of an integrated tax administration system. http://www.thisdaylive.com/index.php/2016/04/27/the-case-of-an-integrated-tax-administration-system/. Accessed 8 Jan 2016
29. Banage SB (2013) URA's E-tax system has contributed to increased revenue. http://www.monitor.co.ug/OpEd/Letters/URA-s-E-tax-system-has-contributed-to-increasedrevenue/-/806314/1925336/-/eagv8oz/-/index.html. Accessed 12 May 2016
30. Wamathu WE (2014) Effects of electronic taxation on financial performance of audit firms in Kenya. Masters Dissertation. http://chss.uonbi.ac.ke/sites/default/files/chss/MSC-Finace%20Esbon%20wandugo%20D63-61264-2013.pdf. Accessed 10 Mar 2016
31. ICF—Investment Climate Facility for Africa (2014) Zambians now can pay their taxes online. http://www.icfafrica.org/news/zambians-now-can-pay-their-taxes-online. Accessed 8 Jan 2016
32. PricewaterhouseCoupers (PwC) (2016) Paying taxes 2016 Zambia. http://www.pwc.com/zm/en/assets/pdf/zambia-article.pdf. Accessed 10 Mar 2016
33. Bird RM, Zolt EM (2008) National Tax Journal Vol. LXI (4), Part 2 Dec 2008
34. Konge W (2014) Tax online's running effects. http://www.times.co.zm/?p=14971
35. IMF, OECD, UN, World Bank (2011) Supporting the development of more effective tax systems. A report to the G-20 development working group by the IMF, OECD, UN and World Bank; Department of Economic and Social Affairs United Nations
36. Besley T, Persson T (2013) Taxation and development. Final Drat JEL: H11, H20, O17, O43. http://econ.lse.ac.uk/staff/tbesley/papers/TaxationAndDevelopment.pdf. Accessed 12 May 2016
37. Fjeldstad OH, Chambas G, Brun J (2014) Local government taxation in Sub-Saharan Africa: a review and an agenda for research (CMI Working Paper WP 2014:2). Chr. Michelsen Institute (CMI), Bergen. http://www.cmi.no/publications/file/5098-local-government-taxation-in-sub-saharan-africa.pdf. Accessed 12 May 2016
38. Tettey WJ (1997) Transforming tax administration in Ghana: the tension between computers and human agency. Dev Policy Rev 15:339–356

Part II
Effectiveness of E-Government Infrastructures

Chapter 4
A Method to Evaluate E-Government Service Quality Attributes

Mohammad Anwar Rahman

Abstract Many government organizations attempted to leverage Internet-based technologies to improve public service through electronic means, termed as e-service. Besides the tangible services, government increasingly encounter and adopt intangible services to meet user needs. Government invests significant financial amounts alongside the non-financial resources to keep e-services up-to-date. E-government service assessment ensures the quality of their services, resource allocation priorities and potential service factors to identify what services may work together to engage users to the government policies. Although a limited studies have been done, researchers proposed several multicriteria decision methods to index e-service quality based on user survey profiles. This study presents a multicriteria decision model combining Analytic Hierarchy Process and entropy weight technique to demonstrate e-government service priority selection. The model synthesize a local and global index priorities among 18 different categories of e-services, classified into three quality dimensions. The presented analysis do not offer the complete roadmap of e-government evaluation. Further research needed to set priorities to specific e-services. The empirical result indicates that improving *e-Efficiency* is the top priority, followed by *e-Support* commitment and *e-Reliability* information in tracing e-government service and engagement.

Keywords E-government • Service quality attributes • Entropy method • Resource allocation

1 Introduction

The evolution of e-government engagement and e-service access in the public domain in both developing and developed nations have changed the way government and policy makers communicate with their citizens. Government services using the web technologies and electronic communication to provide efficient, transparent

M.A. Rahman (✉)
Central Connecticut State University, 1615 Stanley Street, New Britain, CT 06053, USA
e-mail: Rahman@ccsu.edu

© Springer International Publishing AG 2018   65
S. Saeed et al. (eds.), *User Centric E-Government*, Integrated Series in Information Systems 39, DOI 10.1007/978-3-319-59442-2_4

and reliable information are essential for effective governance. The government e-services include developing user-friendly websites with information, guidelines, electronic forms and Frequently Asked Questions etc. In recent years, nearly all transactions with government tend to use electronic communications. Service members use multiple communication channels such as telephone, e-mail, message boards to interact with users for personal advice, track the progresses and update status report of a pending transaction. However, e-government suffers from many fiscal limitations often experienced by general users, and private and public sectors. Users can be significantly affected by the public policies due to unfamiliarity and uncertainty about the future of the policy. The users can significantly contribute to the improvement and the success of e-government development and policies by offering their individual experience, unique insight and knowledge. The e-government success depends on the ability to interact with users and collect interrelated information and communication from the user feedback. The multicriteria method has the potential for e-government personnel to identify the key attributes to focus and allocate resources to keep the e-services on track.

E-service increasingly encounter many intangible service attributes alongside the tangible services. Intangible service attributes include innovative technology ideas, new service attributes, learning principles, and self-service assistance have great impacts on policy success and user satisfaction. These attributes are associated with service personnel actions, interoperability, understanding, preparedness on service tools and technologies, service awareness, and information sharing with users. Improving e-service quality is vital to any government in order to engage users for more effective participation and contribution. The evaluation of e-government service quality attributes can be critically appraised using Multi-Criteria Decision Models (MCDM). A major contribution of MCDM is to identify the high priority weight factors to increase service efforts and resource allocation for improved performance. The study of a multi-dimensional decision making approach helps to understand social signals and recognize users intention to the high priority government services offered in the public sectors. This definitely helps to realign the focus the quality and performance of underlying system, processes and incorporate resource to enhance e-service support.

Previous studies have shown that there are direct connections between e-service quality and specific goals and performance of traditional service channels. E-service quality largely depends on user perception of the service quality, resources and satisfaction. As soon as the user needs are identified, government organizations initiate the arrangement to provide e-services such as creating electronic document, e-forms, up-to-date reports and up-to-date financial statement to meet the expectations. The prerequisite to achieve a high level service quality is mainly the ability to categorize desirable e-services offered, analyze future demand, and effectively manage the needs by anticipating interests and properly allocating resources to respond the evolving needs. E-service attributes are directly associated with design, personalization, interaction between users, private and public sectors, vendors, and professional partners and inter departments between the government organizations.

However, user perception about e-service quality and responses are often not incorporated as a tool to evaluate e-learning and service quality.

The majority of service quality models emphasize e-service reliability, web support by the government personnel, and efficiency of the government website. The factoring analysis of the proposed e-service priority attributes is absence in the model. In this global economy, the understanding of user expectation, service needs, perception of quality, weight factors and technical ability to provide quality feedback are crucial in order to achieve satisfaction. This study measures three dimensions of the e-service factors: 'efficiency of the e-service', 'e-support by the service personnel', and 'e-reliability on information' to develop a coordination between the government and users. This method embraces e-service quality factors existed in the literature and a multidimensional hierarchical model for e-service quality priority analysis. Following are the attributes:

1. E-reliability is the expected response quality of what a customer actually experiences as a result of user interaction with the government agencies. It is important to review the users' perception of quality to develop and enhance e-government facilities.
2. E-support is the perceived service that a user actually receives from the service firm in relation to waiting time to service, service time, and deviation request. This is important to review the users' views of e-service technical performance evaluation.
3. E-efficiency is the ability of a service or product to meet the needs and expectations of the users. This can be achieved by benefit service package, commitment to service, and other factors inclusive (effective e-government site's search engine, organized site map, completeness of information, and updated information).

A better performance in e-service quality in e-government domain gains a competitive advantage and cost effective services. The OECD defined e-government as the use of information and communication technologies, particularly the internet, as a tool to achieve better governance [1]. There are four pillars of e-Government, people, process, technology and resources. Decision making in relation to e-government service priorities is essential for delivering the highest quality services, increased participation, higher retention, and fewer mistakes requiring the e-service performance improvement. E-government engagement should be managed by teams with decades of service quality experience. The World Bank Group noted that e-government initiatives serve a variety of different ends including better delivery of government services to citizens, improved interactions with business and industry, citizen empowerment through access to information, or more efficient government management [2]. Decision-making to identify the best practicing service quality attributes critical to public is not an easy task due to the varying opinions of individuals, groups, and divisions of a public sector. However, a service oriented evaluation to improve the e-service quality performed on a regular basis. World Bank Group noted that the resulting benefits can be less corruption, increased transparency, greater convenience, revenue growth, and/or cost reductions [2].

Following the quality management ideas from W.E. Deming, Joseph Juran and Kaoru Ishikawa to improve organizational effectiveness. There is an emphasis in the use of statistical quality control applications to manage quality assurance and quality control [3]. They also noted that quality as a preventive approach which was integral to everyone's job, rather than the traditional inspection-led reactive approach. The e-service can be attributed to check-do-act (CDA) quality plan and a continuous-improvement-process (CIP) approach to measure the effectiveness of service performance. Other authors explored e-government quality improvement in Australia by the application of information and communications technologies (ICT) to the organization and operation of government [4]. They conclude that there is major difficulties and a careful reworking of the concepts and tools is needed to be applied to the public sector. Developing a service quality index is a major strategy which employs a set of principles and practices to achieve a sustainable competitive advantage in the service industry.

The selection of e-service attributes with respect to improving the service quality is widely varied depending on the implicit expectations of the users. The perception of service quality varies from person to person. People perceive quality differently for the same services and e-learning features. In diverse decision-making groups, members have different experiences, values, attitudes, and cognitive approaches; consequently, they bring divergent perspectives to the group's problem [5]. It is also difficult to measure the quality of a service that is performing well today, but can go wrong tomorrow due to changes in customer needs or behavior, changes in competitive markets, innovations facilitating competitor advantages, and new self-serving technologies. Although the quality of a service means professionalism in all aspects, the expectation is even greater for user satisfaction. Thus, defining a service quality index is unique for a particular service and requires a dynamic, multi-dimensional approach for evaluation.

An ongoing set of studies refer that potential e-government benefits include reduced waiting time, increased level of accessibility, 24/7 access to services, greater transparency of information, and increased levels of citizen participation and satis-faction [4, 6]. Many e-government facilities have limited amounts of resources and capital to invest. The evaluation of e-service attributes is to prioritize service efforts and resource allocation for improved service performance, believed to be a Multi Criteria Decision Making (MCDM) problem which has grown significantly in past decades. In the area of MCDM, fuzzy set theory has given a significant contribution by accepting uncertainty and inconsistent judgment as a nature of human decision making [7]. The purpose of this study is to develop an e-service quality index (e-SQI) essential in the e-government service measures for quality management. The AHP technique prioritizes attributes in a hierarchical decision-making structure, which can be easily modified to incorporate specific attributes [8]. In this study, the hierarchical model technique is adopted to synthesize a systematic decision-making process to prioritize the e-service quality attributes. The ability to determine and analyze users' priority and measure the impact on e-service attribute are likely the procedures to determine the success or failure of e-government. Identification of the desired service quality attributes is essential for government entities to endure effectiveness to its users in an increasingly complex, technological environment. A comprehensive, multidimensional assessment of e-service quality characteristics provides the scope to allocate limited resources, revitalize efforts towards e-services that have the greater impacts on successful e-government implementation. The resource allocation also improve user engagement, enhance the execution of public policies, and increase the provision of government services to benefit its users [9]. Undertaking the e-service priority selection, this study examines the role of quality dimension using multicriteria decision theories integrating entropy technique. The proposed model helps to determine the attributes desired to the users, likely to contribute e-government success. Attribute categories have collected from existing literatures. The pairwise orders based on their relative importance among the e-service factors in the AHP method will identify the factor priorities in a specific e-government domain.

The rest of the chapter is organized as follows: The next section illustrates the background of e-government service, review of popular models and role of government to improve e-service quality. The research methodology adopting the hierarchical model philosophy and entropy technique to prioritize e-service attributes is presented in the next section. An empirical illustration, results, and discussion adopted in this study are presented in the following section. Research findings, limitations, and outlining recommendation for future research is in the conclusion.

2 Literature Review

Over the past decade, many government sectors have established e-services that increasingly affects the lives of people in ever-increasing numbers. There is a considerable amount of literature review on e-government models used in the online environment regarding the effectiveness of e-service quality factors, outcomes and deliverables. Most popular models presented in the earlier literature always receive positive assessment of e-government development. The depth of information technology, easiness of internet service, wave of innovation technology revolutionize users' involvement and interaction with government policy and decision making process. Use of Internet reduces the service costs than traditional government service. The tremendous growth in e-government has created awareness among the users. However, e-government engagement have slowed in growth significantly in recent years, but lack the infrastructure, staffing, and expertise to provide meaningful and relevant services to its users [10]. Re-alignment of service focus and resource allocation is very important to ensure quality services.

Response quality to customer needs has consistently been at the core of research into service organization because it is recognized as a critical determinant of service performance and used as a strategic tool for firms wishing to gain long-term viability [11]. Customer interaction is an important service quality attribute for the successful implementation of service. Reputable customer interaction motivates, avoids misunderstanding, and reduces the cost of quality by avoiding mistakes [12]. Researches showed the interaction with customers helps to provide a better control of processes, which ultimately improves quality [13]. The level of customer knowledge is an important attribute to measure. Response quality may be positively impacted if industries effectively relay information to enhance the knowledge of their customers. Knowledge becomes more important if industries offer tangible and intangible services that become increasingly complex in nature. Thus, an industry's ability to relay accessible information clearly and accurately will be highly valued. Customers will feel more confident and empowered in their decision making and will be less likely to experience feelings of regret or dissatisfaction with services offered. Transparency of information will enable customers and lead to increased levels of trust and perceived service quality [14, 15]. Processing time management is critical for improving service quality that emphasizes waiting time to service, service time (50th percentile), product shortages upon demand, technician evaluation performance, and deviation request. Process management emphasizes conformance to customer requirements by means of error-free services in an efficient manner [16]. A systemic decision-making process enables businesses to achieve an effective approach and process.

E-government can engage its users more effectively by utilizing web technologies, electronic communication and social media. Social media has both the capability to reach out to a large volume of individuals while at the same time interact with citizens personally and allow their collective voice to be heard. Utilizing these technologies can open up opportunities for its citizens to become engaged and allow governments to learn from the collective knowledgebase of its citizens [17]. To benefit appropriately from the government e-services, users can integrate themselves in the open source e-learning platform to accustom with a wide range of information and communication technology (ICT) system. Amongst a variety of e-Learning systems, researchers evaluated the usability issues of open source e-Learning platform such as WebGoat, so that its future versions can improve on usability aspects [18]. The e-service improvement upon yielding the greatest return on investment while maintaining the linear trajectory proposed by earlier models to ensure continued success and growth of e-government facilities depends on the users' participation in the services [19].

The dimension of e-service quality measurement on e-government domain has received attention in recent years. The models of service quality in literature contributed unique perspectives of how service quality can be measured and improved upon. There are a range of factors that may influence how service quality is perceived, measured, and quantified [9, 20]. The purpose of categorizing each model is to examine and observe the similarities and differences between the e-services. It also provides insight into how quality attributes can be further implemented, identified and prioritized. Three main attribute categories: E-Government website reliability (e-Reliability), employees' support (e-support) and website efficiency (e-Efficiency) are determined after assessing the core conceptual attributes of most e-government facility service. The study implements the e-government service evaluation to provide the understanding of e-service factors that are important to users and potential for development of e-government as a good government practice.

A growing number of researches referred e-government services as the degree to which an E-government website facilitates that competent to deliver efficient e-services to help users, businesses and agencies in achieving their governmental transactions [21]. There are several critical factors that have contributed to a decline in e-government adoption and effectiveness. A lack the basic skills, access to the Internet, lack of assistance, low return on investment and unsatisfied demand from users and businesses contributes greatly to the failed initiatives of e-government. Past research indicated in 2001 that 60% of white households in the U.S. had Internet access, while only 34% of African American and 38% of Latino households did. Likewise, roughly 78% of households with income between $50,000 and $75,000 had Internet access compared to only 40% of those with household incomes between $20,000 and $25,000 [22]. Analyzing the basic abilities and services researchers recognized many people lack the basic skills needed to interact with computer hardware and software [23]. Researchers have established that the old, less educated, poor and minority individuals are more likely to need computer assistance, such as help using the keyboard or e-mail [24].

There are other challenges in e-government services such as difficulty in verifying the identity (e-identity), e-security, difficulty in finding reliable models. Public management outcomes are more difficult to discern and measure due to the varying nature of political agendas, strict adherence to the law, negative government reputation, and uncertain methods to measure the success of service deliverables [25]. E-government facilities is well-known to reach out to a diverse population and engage them to the service policies in an effective way. As an alternative, private providers are typically focused on targeting their customers in a way that will maximize profits [4]. The authors also noted that if a service quality problem is accurately defined and disseminated, e-government personnel have a greater likelihood to improve the way in which services are delivered and made transparent to the users. The studies are best described by three generic steps common in all models' construction and verification that include (1) conceptualization, (2) design, and (3) normalization [26]. Steps are the following.

(a) The first step of a model relates to conceptualization of the need of the e-services critical to public after an extensive literature survey.
(b) The second step focuses on validity and reliability analysis given the sample of items on operational issues and users' response.
(c) The third step concerns the effort to normalize the scale to rationalize the model, and e-service verification and validation.

Social media is another mean to connect e-government services via a set of online tools that are designed to provide social interaction and electronic communication. Further, the descriptions of government policy on social media can found in [12]. A collection of web-based technologies and services include blogs, Twitter, social sharing services (e.g., YouTube, Flickr, Stumble Upon, Last.fm), text messaging, discussion forums, collaborative editing tools (e.g., wikis), virtual worlds (e.g., Second Life), and social networking services (e.g. Facebook, MySpace) [27]. Managing perceived service quality means that the user has to match the expected service and perceived service to each other so that consumer satisfaction is achieved [20]. However, e-government provides productivity and efficiency of public services, as well as, provide better and more easy to use services. Three categorical quality attributes are chosen, which further organized with a number of sub-attributes to develop pairwise comparisons. The weights determination of quality factor is crucial in order to facilitate the ranking decision of quality criteria and sub-criteria. This study implements user feedback to determine the e-service priority using the AHP model integrated with entropy weight technique. The motivation to develop the priorities among the e-services factors and sub-factors given the chosen quality dimensions is to demonstrate the quality evaluation of e-service systems and electronic communication.

3   Quality Factor Analysis

A plethora of government agencies offer services through web portals and other Internet based technologies to improve users' relations and services. At the global level, the United Nations (2003) observed that "Governments are increasingly becoming aware of the importance of employing e-government to improve the delivery of public services to the people" [28]. The e-government development index and e-participation index of 10 ten countries is collected from UN e-government survey 2016 [29]; presented in Appendix 1. Key policy and research questions on privacy, security, accuracy, governance policy objectives are in Appendix 2.1 [30].

This study uses a decision-making process model to establish the priorities of government e-service quality attributes by building a service quality index. The study considers global weight factor and local weight factor to identify explicit and implicit e-service attributes at the group service quality and sub-factor levels. Hierarchical model helps to obtain priorities among service quality factors relevant to e-government services that are critical to public. In the pairwise comparison and the attribute selection process, one of the weakness in the AHP model is to find the proper standardized weight vectors. Application of one method often receives criticism for its inability to adequately handle the inherent uncertainty of priority and unknown attribute weights. Merging steps from multiple models and aggregating preferences of different decision makers in the selection process can avoid the biasness in the selection attribute weights and scales. In association with AHP, the entropy based method can improve decision-maker's perception on priority and attribute weights. Using the strength of hierarchical model and entropy method, one can set priorities among different quality factors in systems to underlie different service phenomenon. The integration of AHP with entropy weigh technique strategy is aimed at reducing the uncertainty and inconsistency in human judgment during decision making processes by the policy makers. Based on the interaction with quality management officials and from literature review, three main categorical quality factors and 18 sub-criteria have been identified. Once the e-service priorities are established resources can be allocated according to priority index in order to achieve the maximum benefits from the e-service. The following ten steps demonstrate the AHP approach to identify priorities of the 18 criteria under three quality factors. The priorities are identified according to the global and local quality factor analysis.

The attributes were selected from the opinions of experts, service personnel, and a brief field survey where the respondents stated their expectations about e-service experiences and perceived quality. At the first level, three categorical quality factors are selected to meet the goal and objectives of e-service quality. In the next level, a total of 18 sub-criteria are identified to support the quality attributes. In this hierarchy, the evaluation process measures the priorities among these sub-criteria within a quality factor and the global priority ranking between the factors. These attributes are then used to build a mathematical model to analyze the e-service quality opinion. The model objective is to identify users' perceptions of e-service quality effective to government service via web sites or portals. Prioritization of e-service quality not only provide potential applications and limitations of e-government service, but also involves users in the process through customer feedback in the online environment to improve link and satisfaction.

3.1 Step I: Identify Major Quality Factors

The first step is to identify major e-service quality factors in government service systems. Three major citizen support dimension of service quality factors are identified: (1) government facility website reliability (*e-Reliability*), (2) service support through government employees (*e-Support*), and (3) usability and e-service efficiency (*e-Efficiency*). A number of sub factors under each e-service quality factors have been identified in most literature. Service response measures the quality of the service and customer interaction. Waiting time is the response time to deliver a service, processing time and other service related experiences. Warranty service delineates the contractual service rights and obligations of the purchases. Some of these factors, such as warranties, are not always mandatory for a service industry. However, these factors foster the responsibility of better service quality performance. Figure 4.1 shows the hierarchy framework of service quality factors and the corresponding criteria to each factor.

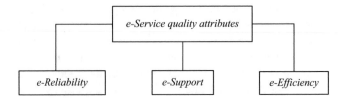

Fig. 4.1 E-service quality factors used in hierarchical decision model

3.2 Step II: Decompose Quality Factors into Criteria or Sub-criteria

This step involves the decomposition each quality factor into several relevant criteria and sub-criteria. Identifying quality factors that affect these attributes may be used to better understand the needs and perceptions of its citizens [26]. Developing a comprehensive model for discerning citizen engagement and satisfaction is an important process necessary to improve a government practice and electronic communication. Following are the quality factors adopted from e-government service quality research [25].

E-government Website Reliability (*e-Reliability*)

1. Fast downloadable e-government forms available at the website.
2. Website is always available and accessible.
3. Website performs the service successfully upon first request.
4. Website provides services in time.
5. Website pages are downloaded quickly enough.
6. Website works properly with users default browser.

E-government Employee's Support (*e-Support*)

1. Employees showed a sincere interest in solving users' problem.
2. Employees give prompt replies to users' inquiries.
3. Employees have the knowledge to answer users' questions.
4. Employees have the ability to convey trust and confidence.
5. Acquisition of username and password in this e-government site is secure.

E-government Website Efficiency (*e-Efficiency*)

1. This e-government site's structure is clear and easy to follow.
2. This e-government site's search engine is effective.
3. This e-government site's site map is well organized.
4. This e-government site is well customized to individual users' needs.
5. The information displayed in e-government site is appropriate detailed.
6. The information displayed in this e-government site is fresh.
7. Information about field's completion in this e-government site is enough.

3.3   Step III: Evaluate Weight Factor Using Entropy Technique

Entropy weight coefficient method determines weight $\tilde{w}_j$ for each criteria, C_j ($j = 1$, $2, \ldots, n$). Using the general normalized decision matrix, P_{ij}, entropy weight coefficient E_j is calculated as follows:

$$E_j = -k \sum_{j=1}^{n} p_{ij} \ln p_{ij} \tag{4.1}$$

where $p_{ij} = x_{ij} / \sum_{i=1}^{m} x_{ij}$, k (constant) $= 1/(\ln (m))$.

The proposed AHP methodology can be integrated with entropy technique to determine the quality factor weights and uncertainty using the subjective reasoning. The principle of entropy method refers that a criterion tends to be more important, if a greater dispersion is observed in the evaluations of the alternatives. The higher D_j value indicates the importance of the criterion in the decision matrix. The measurement of dispersion D_j for a criterion is calculated as the following:

$$D_j = 1 - E_j. \tag{4.2}$$

Weight W_j for each attribute is calculated by using the following:

$$w_j = \frac{D_j}{\sum_{k=1}^{n} D_k} \tag{4.3}$$

$w_j = \tilde{w}_1, \tilde{w}_2, \ldots, \tilde{w}_n$, where $\tilde{w}_j$ is the weight of jth criterion C_j.

3.4   Step IV: Pair-Wise Comparison for Each Quality Factor and Criteria

After identifying weights of quality factors and the corresponding criteria, the next step is to determine how important a quality factor is relative to other factors. The relative priority of a rating is assigned a weight factor between 1 (equal importance) and 9 (extreme importance) to the more important criterion. The study espoused scale of relative preference for pair-wise comparison.

In the AHP approach, the relative importance of a factor is measured by pair-wise comparisons and the results are placed into a matrix form. After identifying the relative importance among the quality factors, relevant empirical information is placed in a matrix form. Comparing the service response and waiting time in Table 4.2, evaluators favor service response as being three times more important over the waiting time. Thus it takes value 1/3 in row 1 and column 2 of the matrix. It is convenient to fill out the upper triangular matrix first. If a_{ij} is the element of row i and column j of the matrix, then the lower diagonal is filled using the reciprocal

Table 4.1 Pair-wise comparison of service quality factor

E-Gov. service quality factors	e-Reliability	e-Support	e-Efficiency
Website reliability (e-reliability)	1	1/3	1/5
Employee's support (e-support)	3	1	1/3
Website efficiency (e-efficiency)	5	3	1

Table 4.2 The weight is determined as the following weight $m = 3$

Entropy weight method	e-Reliability	e-Support	e-Efficiency
$E_j = -k \sum_{j=1}^{n} p_{ij} \ln (p_{ij})$	0.7963	0.7181	0.8528
$D_j = 1 - E_j$	0.2037	0.2819	0.1472
$w_j = D_j / \sum_{j=1}^{n} D_j$	**0.3219**	**0.4455**	**0.2326**

values of the upper diagonal using the formula, $a_{ji} = 1/a_{ij}$. Table 4.1 demonstrates the pair-wise comparison of e-service quality factors.

In this step, the focus is to create the weight factors for the three main e-service quality factor using a normalized matrix and entropy values. The procedure to get normalized weight is summing each column, and then, dividing each element of the matrix by the summed value of the corresponding column. The priority of weight factors is obtained by computing values obtain in normalized matrix and entropy principles. Table 4.2 presented the weight coefficient of e-service quality, calculated using the entropy method, discussed in Step II.

From Table 4.2, it is clear that the priority is given to perceived e-Support (0.445) by the government employees, followed by e-reliability (0.322) of government website, and efficiency (0.233). Next step computes Eigenvector multiplying the matrix in Table 4.1 with weight factors vector in Table 4.2 to obtain the eigenvector.

$$\delta = \begin{bmatrix} 1 & 1/3 & 1/5 \\ 3 & 1 & 1/3 \\ 5 & 3 & 1 \end{bmatrix} \begin{bmatrix} 0.322 \\ 0.446 \\ 0.232 \end{bmatrix} = \begin{bmatrix} 0.516 \\ 1.244 \\ 1.646 \end{bmatrix}$$

3.5 Step V: Pair-Wise Criteria Comparison Under Each Quality Factor

Tables 4.3, 4.4 and 4.5 present the pair-wise comparisons of the sub-criteria under each quality factor. Maturing e-service quality lead to increase in e-government participation.

In pair-wise comparisons, six sub-criteria have been selected for *e-Reliability*, five criteria for *e-Support*, and seven criteria for *e-Efficiency*. Focus here is to find individual quality level influence on e-government participation.

Table 4.3 Pair-wise comparison of government website reliability (*e-Reliability*)

Website reliability (*e-reliability*)	Download forms	Available accessible	Service at first request	In-time service	Fast download	Default browse
Forms downloadable	1.00	3.00	0.50	5.00	4.00	6.00
Available and accessible	0.33	1.00	0.33	4.00	3.00	5.00
Service at first request	2.00	3.00	1.00	6.00	7.00	9.00
In time Services in time	0.20	0.25	0.17	1.00	0.50	2.00
Quick downloadable	0.25	0.33	0.14	2.00	1.00	3.00
Works with default browser	0.17	0.20	0.11	0.50	0.33	1.00

Table 4.4 Pair-wise comparisons of government employee support (*e-Support*)

Employee's support (*e-support*)	Sincere interest	Prompt replies	Knowledge to answer	Trust and confidence	Secure logon
Showed a sincere interest	1.00	0.50	5.00	6.00	3.00
Give prompt replies	2.00	1.00	7.00	9.00	5.00
Have knowledge to answer	0.20	0.14	1.00	3.00	2.00
Convey trust and confidence	0.17	0.11	0.33	1.00	0.50
Secure username and password	0.33	0.20	0.50	2.00	1.00

Table 4.5 Pair-wise comparison of government website efficiency (*e-Efficiency*)

Website efficiency (*e-Efficiency*)	Clear and easy	Search effective	Well organize	Customize to users	Correct fact	Fresh data	Sufficient informa-tion
Structure is clear and easy	1.00	5.00	3.00	4.00	3.00	2.00	7.00
Search engine is effective	0.20	1.00	0.50	0.50	0.33	0.20	3.00
Site map is well organized	0.33	2.00	1.00	2.00	2.00	1.00	2.00
Site is customized to users	0.25	2.00	0.33	1.00	0.50	0.33	4.00
Correct Facts displayed	0.33	3.03	0.50	2.00	1.00	0.17	5.00
Fresh data information	0.50	5.00	1.00	3.00	6.00	1.00	9.00
Sufficient Information	0.14	0.33	0.50	0.25	0.20	0.11	1.00

3.6   Step VI: Investigating Consistency in Pair-Wise Comparison

The perceived value of the e-service quality includes reliability, trust, electronic interaction, access to application forms and e-forms, efficiency critical towards establishing effective e-government facilities. Governments thus need to measure the e-service attributes both in financial and non-financial terms and deploy appropriate resources to ensure the quality of the e-services to be upheld and up-to-date. In the pair-wise comparisons, the assigned weights of the e-service quality factors reflect the evaluator's opinion. The weights of e-service quality are critical in the decision making. The inconsistence and differences in weights may affects the efficiency and effectives of the service priority selection process. Therefore, it is important to observe whether the assigned weight factors are consistent. The equation to compute the eigenvector (λ) is the following

$$\lambda = \frac{i_{th} \text{ entry in } \delta}{i_{th} \text{ entry in priority weight}} \tag{4.4}$$

The consistency ratio (CR) technique provides a measure of the inconsistencies in the AHP model [31]. The consistency ratio (CR) is calculated according to the following equation: $CR = CI/RI$. Consistency index (CI) is obtained by the following equation.

$$CI = (\lambda_{max} - n) / (n - 1) \tag{4.5}$$

The consistency ratio random number index (RI) is computed as.

$$RI = 1.98 \ (n - 2) / n \tag{4.6}$$

Using $CI = 1.38$, and the corresponding random index (RI) = 0.58 (for n = 3), the consistency ratio (CR) = 0.0643. If CR is sufficiently small, the evaluators' comparisons are perceived to be consistent and reliable to provide useful estimates of the priority of the quality factors. If $CR < 0.10$, the degree of consistency is acceptable [29], but if $CR > 0.10$, serious inconsistencies may exist, and the AHP may not yield meaningful results. In such cases, the assessment should be revised. In this example, the maximum value of CR is '0.0643' (in Table 4.6) indicates that the degree of consistency in the model is satisfactory ($CR < 0.10$). The measures of e-service index need to be based on a proper understanding of the factors.

3.7   Step VII: Calculate the Global Weights of Each Criteria and Sub-criteria

In this step, overall ranking for quality factor and criteria under each factor have been identified. The hierarchical model establishes the priority of weights for each quality factor at the individual level as well as the quality factors in group levels.

Results of the pair-wise comparisons of sub-criteria under each quality factor is presented in Table 4.6. The study used the same scale presented in [32]. The nine-point relative preference for pair-wise comparison is presented in Appendix 2.2.

Two types of ranking is provided, (1) rank by 'local weight factors'—the priority weight with respect to the quality factor located under the preceding hierarchical level, and (2) rank by 'global weight factors'—the priority weight with respect to the highest hierarchical level to meet the goal. Tables 4.7 and 4.8 illustrates the local and global weights of quality factor and sub-criteria, respectively.

The rank by 'global weights' is performed by the following equation.

Table 4.6 Pair-wise comparisons of E-Government service criteria

		Weight (w)	Factor (δ)	Eigen vector (λ)	CI	RI	CR
Website reliability (e-Reliability)	Forms downloadable	0.269	1.726	6.417	0.083	1.24	0.067
	Available and accessible	0.160	0.996	6.234	0.047	1.24	0.038
	Service at first request	0.408	2.583	6.330	0.066	1.24	0.053
	In time services in time	0.053	0.321	6.031	0.006	1.24	0.005
	Quick downloadable	0.076	0.463	6.092	0.018	1.24	0.015
	Works with default browser	0.034	0.208	6.127	0.025	1.24	0.020
Employee's support (e-Support)	Showed a sincere interest	0.287	1.552	5.412	0.103	1.12	0.092
	Give prompt replies	0.484	2.582	5.332	0.083	1.12	0.074
	Have knowledge to answer	0.103	0.524	5.079	0.020	1.12	0.018
	Convey trust and confidence	0.043	0.221	5.079	0.020	1.12	0.018
	Secure logon	0.082	0.413	5.028	0.007	1.12	0.006
Website efficiency (e-Efficiency)	Structure is clear and easy	0.316	2.409	7.620	0.103	1.32	0.078
	Search engine is effective	0.055	0.409	7.422	0.070	1.32	0.053
	Site map is well organized	0.140	1.065	7.623	0.104	1.32	0.079
	Site is customized to users	0.079	0.581	7.371	0.062	1.32	0.047
	Correct Facts displayed	0.111	0.807	7.253	0.042	1.32	0.032
	Fresh data information	0.269	2.019	7.510	0.085	1.32	0.064
	Sufficient information	0.030	0.235	7.778	0.130	1.32	0.098

Table 4.7 Rank quality factor by local and global weights

Factors	E-government service quality	Local weights		Global weights	
		Weights	Rank	Weights	Rank
Main factors	Website reliability (*e-Reliability*)	0.106	3	0.106	3
	Employee's support (*e-Support*)	0.261	2	0.261	2
	Website efficiency (*e-Efficiency*)	0.633	1	0.633	1

Table 4.8 Rank quality sub-criteria by local and global weights

Website reliability (*e-Reliability*)	Forms downloadable	0.269	2	0.028	10
	Available and accessible	0.160	3	0.017	14
	Service at first request	0.408	1	0.043	8
	Provide in time e-services	0.053	5	0.006	17
	Quick downloadable	0.076	4	0.008	16
	Works with default browser	0.034	6	0.004	18
Employee's support (*e-Support*)	Showed a sincere interest	0.287	2	0.075	5
	Provide prompt replies	0.484	1	0.126	3
	Have knowledge to answer	0.103	3	0.027	11
	Convey trust and confidence	0.043	5	0.011	15
	Secure logon	0.082	4	0.021	12
Website efficiency (*e-Efficiency*)	Structure is clear and easy	0.316	1	0.200	1
	Search engine is effective	0.055	6	0.035	9
	Site map is well organized	0.140	3	0.089	4
	Site is customized to users	0.079	5	0.050	7
	Correct Facts displayed	0.111	4	0.070	6
	Fresh data information	0.269	2	0.170	2
	Sufficient information	0.030	7	0.019	13

$$\text{Global weights} = \Sigma \, (\text{Weight factor } i \times \text{weight criterion } j \text{ under factor } i) \qquad (4.7)$$

There are immense benefit of e-government in the developing counting since Internet uses reduce the service cost, as well as increase the e-contact between regular users and government employees. Table 4.8 summarizes the priority and rank of e-government service quality factors. In order to make these ranks more effective, the factors weight below 0.01, concerning ranks from 16 to 18 may be viewed as less significant attributes. The rest 1–15 factors can be viewed as representative e-government service criteria. The resource allocation according to suggested priority would provide the maximum benefit in evolving e-government service quality.

4   Results

This study examines the most significant quality factor through decision-making procedures in support to improve e-government service quality. Quality standard improvement happens when the government service providers set the strategic direction to identify public interests and service provider responsibilities with a relentless pursuit to the best of their ability. The prioritization of quality criteria and sub-criterion direct towards the attention of e-government to utilize resources more efficiently and positively to the best of public interests. The weights of the e-service factors was attributed following the entropy weight technique. The model is used to evaluate user feedback and develop quality index for e-government service improvement. The e-services are classified into 18 quality attributes under three main quality dimensions: *e-Reliability*, *e-support* and *e-Efficiency*. The perceived e-service feedback and data was collected from a pilot survey among a number of working professionals focusing on a western country local and federal government web service facilities. In the proposed hierarchical model, three main categorical quality factors in the first level were selected. In the light of the reviewed literature, these quality factors were then divided into sub-attributes. The *e-Efficiency* service factor has seven sub-criteria, while *e-Support* has five sub-criteria, and *e-Reliability* has six sub-criteria. Table 4.7 demonstrates the priority weights and consistency ratios of all quality factors and sub-criteria. The AHP analysis integrated with entropy weight factors used in the comparison matrix provided the rank of the high priority quality determinants.

After creating the conceptual model integrating entropy with AHP approach, the e-government quality attribute have been ranked constructing both the local and global weights factors. The rational of the e-service factor rankings are shown in Table 4.8. When dealing with priorities of the service quality factors, e-government website efficiency (*e-Efficiency*) ranked as the most important criteria, followed by the employee's support (*e-Support*), and the website reliability (*e-Reliability*) with weights of 63.3%, 26.1% and 10.6%, respectively. In the subsequent analysis, the sub-criteria at the second stage are ranked based on the local and global weights. The critical e-service factor priority results are reported separately with respect to local and global weights.

4.1   Local Weight Factor Ranking

The concept of e-service quality has been examined in several studies. In local weight factor analysis, this study reveals the service quality related to e-government website efficiency (*e-Efficiency*) is the most important factor. The corresponding criteria under 'e-Efficiency' prioritize as the following; *structure is clear and easy* (0.316) followed by *fresh data information* (0.269), *site map is well organized* (0.14), *correct facts displayed* (0.111), *site is customized to users* (0.079), *search engine is effective* (0.055), and *sufficient Information* (0.03). The next important quality factor is the Employee's Support (*e-Support*). The order of the five criteria under '*e-Support*' is *employees provide prompt replies* (50th percentile) (0.484), *employees showed a sincere interest* (0.287), *employees have knowledge to answer* (0.103), *support secure logon* (0.082), and *employees convey trust and confidence* (0.043).

The remainder quality factor is website reliability (*e-Reliability*). The order of the six sub-criteria is *service at first request* (0.408), *forms downloadable* (0.269), *website available and accessible* (0.16), forms q*uick downloadable* (0.076), *provide in time Services* (0.053), and *website works with default browser* (0.034). Collectively, the result suggests that e-service quality is a multidimensional construct although the content of what constitutes e-service quality varies across studies. The e-service quality factors affecting e-government include convenience of using the web portal, faster processing time, ease of use, new technologies. Information security, transparency, and trust level are the dominant factor that inspire users to engage or disengage in the e-government involvement.

4.2   Global Weight Factor Ranking

The difficulty of dealing with e-service and website quality in public sector environment is the identification of the service priorities in meaningful ways. The responses of the global weights indicate that website information s*tructure is clear and easy* (0.2) is the most important factor among the 18 quality criteria. This is followed by *fresh data information* (0.170) and *employees provide prompt replies* (50th percentile) (0.126). These are the three most important quality criteria. The fourth factor is e-government provided *site-map is well organized* (0.089), followed by *employees showed a sincere interes*t (0.075), *correct facts displayed* (0.070), *site is customized to users* (0.050), provide service at first request (0.043), search engine is effective (0.035), and downloadable forms (0.028). The rest of the global order rankings are e-government employees *have knowledge to answer* (0.027), *support secure logon* (0.021), *sufficient Information* (0.019), *available and accessible* (0.017) employees convey trust and confidence (0.011), *quick downloadable forms* (0.008), *provide in time Services* (0.006), and employees works with default browser (0.004). Users will be more likely to engage in e-government service if information is presented clearly and found quickly.

The feasibility of ranking the priority and improving the quality standard depend on a specific e-government service domain. The type of service delivery, influences of policies and accountability and the technological means are the important determinants to the feasibility of such endeavors. There are other critical factors which are not included in this study include in the visual appeal, sensitivity to users' involvement, intuitive use across various devices, maintainability, and intractability of the e-government web portal. The results demonstrate the importance of electronic communication enhancing the decision making with creative and innovative approaches supported by individual, group, and industry learning. In this finding, the e-service quality attributes are not necessarily integrated by the opinions of all participants in the final decision. Since the quality of the decisions are made vital to e-government service performance, both divergent and convergent thinking are needed for this decision-making process. The decision-making process by the AHP approach requires both a systemic and creative thinking approach: both of which are vital to rank quality factors for effective decision making.

5 Conclusion

E-governments are increasingly becoming aware of the importance of e-services that need frequent communication with general users as well as public sectors and private businesses. The quality of e-government services has become the subject of great interest as it affects the public engagement in government-run activities, satisfaction and government policy success. E-government services involves financial and non-financial investments. Government cannot allocate equal amounts of effort or resources to each area of e-services due to the limitations of human and monetary resources. The methodology to identify e-service priorities plays a key role to improve government services by allocating resources to the important service areas. The model evaluated and indexed 18 e-services attributes, distributed into three quality dimensions: *e-Reliability*, *e-Support* and *e-Efficiency*. The data of the perceived e-government benefit used in the AHP model was collected from a pilot survey focusing on e-system reliability, service support and website efficiency of local and federal government e-service facilities in a western country. The findings of this study indicate that the e-service efficiency '*e-Efficiency*' generated the highest impact (which is about 63.3%). The next important e-service criteria to public engagement ranked the following. The employee's support to the users (*e-Support*) is the next highest priority, followed by e-government website information reliability (*e-Reliability*) with weights of 26.1% and 10.6%, respectively. The ranking of the sub-criteria based on the local and global weights provides a good understanding of how different factors work together to influence adoption of e-government services for public engagement. This study has reviewed literature to identify e-service factors associated with public interests, easy to understand and use, user friendly systems, technological skills, motivation for community engagement, as well as facilitating different conditions for adoption. The result obtained from this study is specific to the selected e-service factors, and may not be generalized to all other applications.

The multicriteria methods generally require subjective judgment to make decision on activities and direction which e-services to be offered. The experts who have substantial experience in the field of e-service quality should engage in decision planning. The entropy weight method is an easy to use model, avoids the shortcoming of the subjective judgement. There is an absence of a single model factoring both multicriteria decision making and weight factors of e-service to evaluate whether a factor to adopt or not adopt. The study proposed the application of AHP method integrated with entropy weight technique to identify the e-service priorities, lead towards the effectiveness of e-service identification. The strategic analysis of the public response benefits government to improve e-service performance, critical to public engagement and satisfaction.

However, the study holds few limitations that it did not include few service quality dimensions which may be an interest for future research. For example, demographic variables such as race, education level, and ethnicity have an effect on e-service quality dimensions in both developed and developing countries. Further research may be directed to examine the interaction between larger decision-making processes and the relationships among different demographic variables to create an environment that fosters both a systemic approach and creative thinking. Since e-government expansion has now reached a point of critical form with services provide at cities, states, federal and government agencies, the study may be extended to adopt quantitative information and unanimous consent on operations and services to develop innovative prioritization of service index and advance theoretical models for the future services and quality implications.

Appendix 1: E-Government Development Index

E-government development index top 12 countries		E-participation index 12 countries	
Country	Index	Country	Index
United Kingdom	0.9193	United Kingdom	1
Australia	0.9143	Japan	0.9831
Republic of Korea	0.8915	Australia	0.9831
Singapore	0.8828	Republic of Korea	0.9661
Finland	0.8817	Netherlands	0.9492
Sweden	0.8704	New Zealand	0.9492
Netherlands	0.8659	Spain	0.9322
New Zealand	0.8653	Singapore	0.9153
Denmark	0.851	Canada	0.9153
France	0.8456	Italy	0.9153
Japan	0.8440	Finland	0.9153
United States	0.8420	United States	0.8983

Source: UN E-Government Survey 2016 [29]

Appendix 2

Appendix 2.1: Key Policy and Research Questions Related to Privacy, Security, Accuracy, and Governance Policy Adopted from [30]

Privacy, security, accuracy, and archiving

- How will agencies ensure the privacy of individuals, particularly when data may not be owned by government agencies?
- What data and information search tools are necessary to facilitate access to and location of government data?
- What review processes are required prior to government data dissemination through open government initiatives such as data.gov to ensure privacy, security, and accuracy?
- What data validity, reliability, and quality check processes could be adopted in order to ensure appropriate uses, combinations, and extrapolations of combined government (and other) datasets?
- What cybersecurity measures, tools, and approaches are necessary to ensure national, agency, and individual security?
- What tools and applications do agencies need to archive and preserve their social media-based activities?
- What is the "document" that agencies preserve based on their social media activities?
- What policies and procedures are necessary to govern the scheduling and archiving of government social media activities?
- What is the role of GPO and the FDLP, if any, in the social media technology environment of the federal government?

Governing and governance

- How do we build social and political trust and who/what makes decisions on what authority?
- What collaborative governance processes and structures do social media technologies enable?
- What policy structures and frameworks are necessary to government use and interaction with social media technologies?
- In what ways can the federal government harmonize across a range of policy instruments to comprehensively account for the evolving policy context of social media technologies?
- Will social media technology privilege certain types of policy substance over others?
- Will social media technology result in new policies that rely on the existence of viable social media?

- What policy barriers to using social media technologies exist, and how to resolve the impediments?
- How do we create policies to encourage social media technologies?
- How can agencies and governments incorporate the results of social media technology use into agency strategies, goals, objectives, services, and resources?
- What review and analysis processes should agencies develop to assess social media-based participatory feedback and solicitations into agency workflows?

Access and social inclusion

- What tools and approaches best promote universal access to social media technologies?
- How do we ensure that social media technologies are inclusive, rather than exclusive?
- Are there social media technologies that can facilitate access to persons with disabilities?
- What mechanisms (e.g., partnerships, collaborations) can promote access to and participation in social media technologies to all members of society?
- How can agencies leverage partnerships to extend social media applications and use within communities across the country?
- What types of partnerships best promote use of and interaction with government through social media technologies?
- How can agencies and organizations develop mutually beneficial partnerships?
- What organizational, management, and operational structures are necessary to create successful partnerships?

Appendix 2.2: Saaty's Nine Point Scale [32]

Intensity of importance	Definition	Explanation
1	Equal importance	Two factors are equally contributing to objective
3	Moderate strong	One factor is marginally superior over other
5	Strong importance	One factor is strongly superior over other
7	Very strong or demonstrated importance	Experience and judgment strongly favor one activity over another
9	Absolute strong	The highest level of superiority of one factor over other
2, 4, 6, 8	Intermediate values	Scale between two factor, negotiation required

References

1. OECD (2003) The e-government imperative. OECD Publ., Paris
2. World Bank (2010). Introduction to e-government: what is e-government? http://www.worldbank.org/en/topic/ict/brief/e-government. Accessed 5 Dec 2016
3. Wilkinson A, Redman T, Snape E, Marchington M (1998) Managing with total quality management: theory and practice. Macmillan Business, Basingstoke
4. Teicher J, Hughes O, Dow N (2002) E-government: a new route to public sector quality. Manag Serv Qual 12(6):384–393
5. Elsass PM, Laura MG (1997) Demographic diversity in decision-making groups: the experiences of women and people of color. Acad Manag Rev 22(4):946–973
6. Sharma SK (2015) Adoption of e-government services. Transf Gov People Process Policy 9(2):207–222
7. Chiou H, Tzeng G, Cheng D (2005) Evaluating sustainable fishing development strategies using fuzzy MCDM approach. Omega 33:223–234
8. Banuelas R, Anthony J (2003) Going from six sigma to design for six sigma using AHP. TQM Mag 15:34–44
9. Alanezi MA, Kamil A, Basri S (2010) A proposed instrument dimensions for measuring e-government service quality. Int J u-and e-Serv Sci Technol 3(4):1–17
10. Coursey D, Norris D (2008) Models of e-government: are they correct? An empirical assessment. Public Adm Rev 68(3):523–536
11. Gale BT, Robert CW (1994) Managing customer value: creating quality and service that customers. Free Press, New York
12. Cohen S, Brand R (1993) Total quality management in government: a practical guide for the real world. Jossey-Bass, San Francisco
13. Bunse C, Verlage M, Giese P (1998) Improved software quality through improved development process descriptions. Automatica 34:23–32
14. Eisingerich AB, Simon JB (2008) Perceived service quality and customer trust. J Serv Res 10(3):256
15. Harrison-Walker L (2012) The role of cause and effect in service failure. J Serv Market 26(2):115–123
16. Duggirala M, Chandrasekharan R, Anantharaman RN (2008) Patient-perceived dimensions of total quality service in healthcare. Benchmarking 15(5):560–583
17. Bertot JC, Jaeger PT, Hansen D (2012) The impact of polices on government social media usage: issues, challenges, and recommendations. Gov Inf Q 29:30–40
18. Amin MA, Saeed S (2015) Role of usability in e-learning system: an empirical study of OWASP WebGoat. In: Saeed S, Bajwa IS, Mahmood Z (eds) Human factors in software development and design. IGI Global Press, Hershey
19. Syamsuddin I, Hwang J-S (2010) A new Fuzzy MCDM framework to evaluate e-government security strategy. In: Proceedings of the IEEE 4th international conference on application of information and communication technologies, IEEE
20. Seth N, Deshmukh SG, Vrat P (2005) Service quality models: a review. Int J Qual Reliab Manag 22(8):913–949
21. Tan C-W, Benbasat I, Cenfetelli RT (2008) Building citizen trust towards e-government services: do high quality web sites matter? Paper presented at the 41st Hawaii international conference on system sciences, pp 1530–1605
22. Wright N (2002) The economics of privacy in the information age. Annual meeting for the Academy of Marketing Studies
23. Massenburg K, Tolbert C, Stansbury M (2003) Virtual inequality: beyond the digital divide. George Washington University Press, Washington
24. Jackson L, Von Eye A, Harbalsis G, Hincca F, Fitzgerald H, Yong Z (2004) The impact of internet use on the other side of the digital divide. Commun ACM 47(7):43 47

25. Papadomichelaki X, Mentzas G (2012) E-GovQual: a multiple-item scale for assessing e-government service quality. Gov Inf Q 29:98–109
26. Aladwani AM, Palvia PC (2002) Developing and validating an instrument for measuring user-perceived web quality. Inf Manag 39:467–476
27. Hansen DL, Shneiderman B, Smith MA (2011) Analyzing social media networks with NodeXL: insights from a connected world. Morgan Kaufmann, Burlington
28. United Nations (2003) Comparative worldwide analysis of city e-government performance and services. Division for Public Administration and Development Management. United Nations, New York
29. UN E-Government Survey (2016) E-government in support of sustainable development. https://publicadministration.un.org/egovkb/en-us/Reports/UN-E-Government-Survey-2016. Accessed 26 Feb 2017
30. Dyer RF, Forman EH (1992) Group decision support with the analytic hierarchy process. Decis Support Syst 8:99–124
31. Crowe TJ, Noble SJ, Machimada SJ (1998) Multi-attribute analysis of ISO9001 registration analysis using AHP. Int J Qual Reliab Manag 15(2):205–222
32. Saaty T (2008) Decision making with the analytic hierarchy process. Int J Serv Sci 1(1):83–98

Chapter 5
Trust in the System: The Mediating Effect of Perceived Usefulness of the E-Filing System

T. Santhanamery and T. Ramayah

Abstract This study examines the mediating effect of perceived usefulness on the relationship between trust in the system (correctness, response time, system support, availability and security) and continuance usage intention of e-filing system in Malaysia. Data was collected from two urban cities in Malaysia; Selangor and Kuala Lumpur. A total of 355 data was collected and analyzed using Partial Least Squared Method (PLS). The result showed that Perceived Usefulness has a mediating effect on the relationship between trust in the system variables (correctness, response time and security) with the continuance usage intention and trust in the system variables (correctness and response time) has significant positive relationship with continuance usage intention. Perceived usefulness was found to be the most important predictor of continuance usage intention meanwhile response time was found to be the most important predictor of perceived usefulness. However the variables of system support and availability does not have any significant impact on perceived usefulness and also on continuance usage intention.

Keywords Trust in the system • Perceived usefulness • Continuance usage intention • E-filing system

1 Introduction

E-government can be termed as the utilization of ICT, mobile computing, web based networks and the Internet to deliver citizens with necessary services, improve government agencies performance, to assist successful public participation and to transform relations with citizens, business and other arms of government,. The

---

T. Santhanamery
Faculty of Business Management, University Teknologi MARA, Penang, Malaysia

T. Ramayah (✉)
School of Management, Universiti Sains Malaysia, Penang, Malaysia

UTM International Business School (UTM-IBS), Universiti Teknologi Malaysia, Kuala Lumpur, Malaysia
e-mail: ramayah@usm.my

© Springer International Publishing AG 2018
S. Saeed et al. (eds.), *User Centric E-Government*, Integrated Series in Information Systems 39, DOI 10.1007/978-3-319-59442-2_5

success of e-government projects will depend on the best utilization of such investment in these projects [1, 2]. The influence of e-government has witness a dramatic increase particularly by governments in developing countries. More and more developing countries are using ICT to modernize and increase internal efficiency as well as improve service delivery [3, 4]. Today, similar to e-Commerce, citizens' adoption of e-Government services has moved to the post-adoption stage [5]. The use of these services after the initial adoption are subject to changes based on usage experiences [6], which may potentially increase or decrease [7]. Therefore, an understanding of what factors affect citizen's continuous usage intention plays a vital role in e-Government development.

The use of information technology has given a new perspective to the development and integration of Malaysia's tax administration system. Tax administrators understanding of the e-filing system will improve the level of service provided and encourage the users of the system to continuously use it which will lead to the increase in revenue generation [8, 9]. E-filing system as a whole integrates tax preparation, tax filing and tax payment, which serves as a major advantage over traditional manual procedure [10]. Since its introduction in 2006, e-filing has evolved each year in order to provide better service to the taxpayers. The online tax system makes an effective impact on the economic towards improving the level of income generation and tax compliance by the tax payers. This could be due to benefits provided by e-filing system such as convenience, time saving, cost effectiveness for both the tax administrator and tax payers [8]. Therefore, this study will examine the impact of perceived usefulness in mediating the relationship between trust in the system and e-filing continuance usage intention.

The research questions of this study are (1) Do perceived usefulness significantly influences the continuance usage of the e-filing system; (2) Is there a mediating effect of perceived usefulness on the relationship between trust in the system and continuance usage of e-filing system; (3) What is the influence of trust in the system on the continuance usage intention? These questions were answered with the objectives of this study which are (1) to examine the significant relationship between perceived usefulness and continuance usage intention of e-filing system, (2) to examine the mediating effect of perceived usefulness on the relationship between trust in the system and continuance usage intention of e-filing system, (3) to examine the relationship between trust in the system and continuance usage intention of e-filing system. Figure 5.1 below represents the theoretical model.

2 Literature Review

2.1 Trust in the System

Papadopoulou et al. [11] defined trust in the system as the interpretation of the system's functions which will display availability, fault tolerance and its security

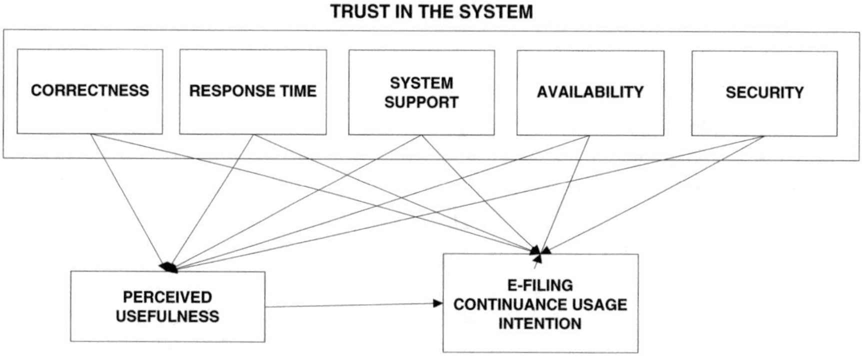

TRUST IN THE SYSTEM

Fig. 5.1 The theoretical model

and correctness is guaranteed together with stability in system response time. Azmi and Aziz [12] have studied the effect of trust on continued use of e-filing by tax practitioners in Malaysia and they found that trust is one of the important factors that determined continued use of e-filing system. Similarly Gao et al. [13] has investigated the impact of perceived usefulness and trust on users intention to return and use e-government services and revealed that both the variable have significant impact on the intention. The study also found that trust has a significant relationship on perceived usefulness towards intention to return and use. In the current study, however, is not investigating the general trust towards e-filing continuance usage intention but more specifically the effect based on the dimensions of availability, correctness, security, response time and system support. As such, in this study, the trust in the system component factors such as responsiveness (response time), reliability (correctness), system support, availability and security will be evaluated to determine their impact on the continuance usage intention of the e-filing system. *Response Time* means the system reacts to requests within minimal time. It is also defined as the duration between the time the users initiated request and the reply to the request [14], *System Support* is defined as the automated and personalized support to access the needed information without problems. It includes help desks, online support services, tailored support and other facilities [15] and *Correctness* is defined as the assurance that the system works properly and produces correct output. Bailey and Pearson [14] defined accuracy as the correctness of the output information. **Availability** is defined as the assurance that the system is up and running, is fully functional whenever needed and is protected from denial of service. It is also classified as the dimensions or items that measures system quality [16]. **Security** is the guarantee that the system is protected against intimidations interference's. Bailey and Pearson (1983) defined security as the protection of data from embezzlement or unlawful alteration or loss.

2.2   Continuance Usage Intention

Continuance intention is defined as ones intention to reuse or repurchase decision after their initial usage of services or products [17]. The research on e-government nowadays are focusing to evaluate the continued usage intention by citizens rather than initial intention. Wangpipatwong et al. [18] examined the role of perceived usefulness, perceived ease of use and computer self-efficacy in determining the citizens continuance intention to use e-government websites. The study found that perceived usefulness is the strongest predictor of continuance intention. Similarly, Ambali [10] also found that perceived usefulness has a strong relationship towards continuance usage intention of e-filing system in Malaysia. Further Gao et al. [13] has concluded that both trust and perceived usefulness has a significant relationship towards continuance usage intention e-government services.

2.3   Perceived Usefulness

Perceived usefulness (PU) was defined as the prospective user's subjective probability that using a specific application system will increase his or her job performance within an organizational context [19]. Research by Min Jiang and Heng Xu [20] found that satisfaction and perceived usefulness have direct impact on continuance intention of e-government in China. Compatibly, Hu et al. [21] found that perceived usefulness as one of the key predictor of continued use of e-tax services in Hong Kong. Similarly, McCloskey [22] found a significant relationship between trust and perceived usefulness which indicates that the higher the trust that consumer has the higher their belief on the usefulness of the system. Similarly, Pavlou [23] also found that trust has a substantial consequence on intention to use electronic commerce through perceived usefulness; which means that there exist mediating effect of perceived usefulness on the relationship between trust and intention to use. Study by Horst et al. [24] revealed perceived usefulness as the main determinant in intention to use e-government services, however the study also found that trust is the main determinant of perceived usefulness. As such, this present study adapts perceived usefulness to mediate the relationships that exist between continuance usage intention of an e-filing system and trust in the system. The hypotheses developed are based on the study model.

H1a: There is a direct positive relationship between correctness and continuance usage.

H1b: There is a direct positive relationship between response time and continuance usage.

H1c: There is a direct positive relationship between system support and continuance usage.

H1d: There is a direct positive relationship between availability and continuance usage.

H1e: There is a direct positive relationship between security and continuance usage.

H2a: There is a direct positive relationship between correctness and PU.

H2b: There is a direct positive relationship between response time and PU.

H2c: There is a direct positive relationship between system support and PU.

H2d: There is a direct positive relationship between availability and PU.

H2e: There is a direct positive relationship between security and PU.

H3: There is a direct positive relationship between PU and continuance usage.

H4a: PU mediates the relationship between correctness and continuance usage intention.

H4b: PU mediates the relationship between response time and continuance usage intention.

H4c: PU mediates the relationship between system support and continuance usage intention.

H4d: PU mediates the relationship between availability and continuance usage intention.

H4e: PU mediates the relationship between security and continuance usage intention.

3 Methodology

3.1 Data Collection Method

A total of 900 questionnaires were distributed among the taxpayers in Selangor and Kuala Lumpur, Malaysia using self-administered questionnaire. A total of 401 questionnaires were received back and out of it, 355 were usable while the other 46 were unusable. As such, the response rate was 44.5%. The questionnaire consists of five sections. The first section elicited the screening question, the second section collected the demographic data, the third section extracted information on trust in the system dimensions, section four measured the perceived usefulness, and last section measured continuance intention. The sample selected were taxpayers who had used the e-filing system before at least once as the measures required them to express the trust in the system, perceived usefulness and continuance intention.

3.2 Measures

The measures were all adapted from the published literature. The measures for continuance intention were from Bhattacherjee [17]. Perceived Usefulness were from Davis [25] whereas measures for correctness were adapted from Nicolaou and McKnight [26], system support were adapted from Wangpipatwong et al. [27], response time from Liu and Ma [28], availability from Ojha et al. [29] and security from Carlos Roca et al. [30].

3.3   Sample Profile

The demographic of the respondents tabulated in Table 5.1 were derived from descriptive analysis. The majority of the age group were in the category of 30–34 years old (23.3%). Male (63.8%) outnumbered the females (36.2%). In terms of ethnicity, the result somewhat reflects the ethnic group distribution in Malaysia whereby the majority of the respondents were Malays (55.2%), followed by Chinese (25.0%) and Indians (19.8%). About 60.3% of the total respondents are highly educated with Bachelor degree and followed by Master's degree. In terms of earnings, greater part of the respondents (31.9%) are earning within RM3000–RM3999 per month with majority (81.0%) are married respondents. Lastly, about 84.5% and 57.8% of the respondents claimed to have experience in computer usage and internet usage approximately 10 years and above, respectively.

4   Data Analysis

Smart PLS version 3.0, a variance based Structural Equation Modelling (SEM) was used to analyze the hypotheses generated. The two step analytical procedure suggested by Anderson and Gerbing [31] was adopted to analyze data whereby the measurement model was evaluated first and then followed by the structural model. Also following the suggestion of Chin [32], the bootstrapping method (500 resample) was done to determine the significant level of loadings, weights and path coefficients. The research model of this study is as below (Fig. 5.2).

4.1   Measurement Model

Convergent validity is the degree to which the items that are indicators of a specific construct should converge or share a high proportion of variance in common [33]. According to Hair et al. [33], factor loadings and Average Variance Extracted (AVE) of more than 0.5 and Composite Reliability (CR) of 0.7 or above is deemed to be acceptable. As can be seen from Table 5.2, all loadings and AVE are above 0.5 and the composite reliability values are more than 0.7. Therefore, we can conclude that convergent validity has been established.

Next, we assessed the Discriminant Validity which is the extent to which a construct is truly distinct from other constructs [33]. This can be established by the low correlations between all the measure of the interest and the measure of other constructs. To address discriminant validity, the square root of the AVE is compared against the correlations of the other constructs, when the AVE extracted is greater than its correlations with all the other constructs then discriminant validity has been established [34] (refer Table 5.3).

Table 5.1 Demographic of
the respondents

Age	Frequency	Percent
20–24 years	3	0.80
25–29 years	41	11.50
30–34 years	68	19.20
35–39 years	70	19.70
40–44 years	30	8.50
45–49 years	62	17.50
50–54 years	57	16.10
55 years and above	24	6.80
Gender		
Male	116	32.70
Female	239	67.30
Ethnicity		
Malay	276	77.70
Chinese	42	11.80
Indian	33	9.30
Others	4	1.10
Education		
Diploma/College	34	9.60
Bachelor Degree	87	24.50
Master's Degree	146	41.10
Doctoral Degree	63	17.70
Others	24	6.80
Income		
RM2000–RM2999	36	10.1
RM3000–RM3999	83	23.4
RM4000–RM4999	68	19.2
RM5000–RM5999	30	8.5
RM6000–RM6999	33	9.3
RM7000–RM7999	41	11.5
RM8000–RM8999	15	4.2
RM9000–RM9999	22	6.2
RM10,000 and above	19	5.4
Marital status		
Single	69	19.4
Married	281	79.2
Others	5	1.4
Computer usage		
1–3 years	1	0.30
4–6 years	9	2.50
7–9 years	18	5.10
10 years and above	327	92.1
Internet usage		
1–3 years	7	2.0
4–6 years	24	6.80
7–9 years	55	15.5
10 years and above	269	75.8

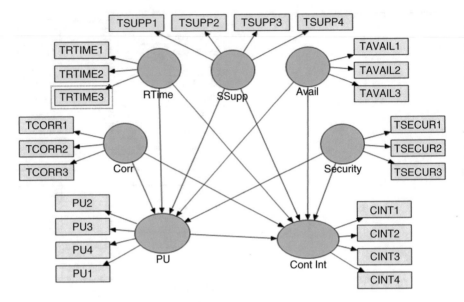

Fig. 5.2 The research model

4.2 Structural Model

The structural model represents the relationship between constructs or latent variables that were hypothesized in the research model. The goodness of the theoretical model is established by the variance explained (R^2) of the endogenous constructs and the significance of all path estimates [35]. Together the R^2 and the path coefficients indicate how well the data support the hypothesized model [32]. Figure 5.3 and Table 5.4, shows the results of the structural model from the PLS output. Correctness was significantly related towards Continuance Intention ($\beta = 0.211$, $p < 0.05$) and Perceived Usefulness ($\beta = 0.293$, $p < 0.01$) thus supporting H1a and H2a of this study. Response Time was found in this study to be significantly related to Continuance Intention ($\beta = 0.181$, $p < 0.1$) and Perceived Usefulness ($\beta = 0.463$, $p < 0.01$), thus supporting H1b and H2b. Perceived Usefulness was found to be statistically significant to Continuance Intention ($\beta = 0.536$, $p < 0.05$), thus supporting H3. However, System Support, Availability and Security was found to be insignificantly related to both Continuance Intention ($\beta = -0.021$; $\beta = -0.018$; $\beta = -0.011$) and Perceived Usefulness ($\beta = 0.027$; $\beta = 0.002$; $\beta = -0.071$), thus rejecting H1c, H1d, H1e, H2c, H2d and H3e.

In verifying the mediating effect of perceived usefulness, Chin [35] testing method for mediation was followed. To establish the mediation effect, the indirect effect between (a) (independent variable and dependent variable) × (b) (moderator

Table 5.2 Result of the measurement model

Model construct	Items	Loadings	AVE	CR
	PU1	0.905	0.838	0.954
	PU2	0.909		
	PU3	0.922		
	PU4	0.925		
Continuance intention	CINT1	0.936	0.895	0.971
	CINT2	0.947		
	CINT3	0.945		
	CINT4	0.954		
Correctness	TCORR1	0.936	0.830	0.936
	TCORR2	0.914		
	TCORR3	0.883		
Response time	TRTIME1	0.879	0.744	0.897
	TRTIME2	0.909		
	TRTIME3	0.796		
System support	TSUPP1	0.864	0.766	0.929
	TSUPP2	0.850		
	TSUPP3	0.882		
	TSUPP4	0.903		
Availability	TAVAIL1	0.899	0.835	0.938
	TAVAIL2	0.929		
	TAVAIL3	0.913		
Security	TSECUR1	0.957	0.905	0.966
	TSECUR2	0.966		
	TSECUR3	0.930		

Table 5.3 Discriminant validity of constructs

	1	2	3	4	5	6	7
1. Availability	**0.914**						
2. Continuance	0.492	**0.946**					
3. Correctness	0.678	0.585	**0.911**				
4. PU	0.491	0.743	0.551	**0.915**			
5. Response time	0.679	0.613	0.608	0.625	**0.862**		
6. System support	0.660	0.487	0.640	0.495	0.693	**0.875**	
7. Security	0.602	0.384	0.599	0.367	0.527	0.597	**0.951**

Note: Diagonal represents the square root of Average Variance Extracted (AVE) while the other entries represent squared correlations

and dependent variable) has to be significant [36]. To test for significance, the t-value based on bootstrapping result is calculated [35]. If the t-value exceeds 1.28 at $p < 0.1$ (1 tail) the hypotheses can be accepted. The t-value is formally defined as follows:

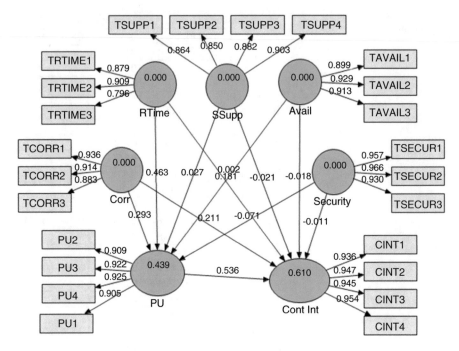

Fig. 5.3 The structural model

Table 5.4 Summary of the structural model

	Path coefficient	Standard error	t-value
Availability → Continuance	−0.018	0.116	0.151
Availability → PU	0.002	0.120	0.019
Correctness → Continuance	0.211	0.113	1.867**
Correctness → PU	0.293	0.122	2.409***
PU → Continuance	0.536	0.118	4.554***
Response time → Continuance	0.181	0.134	1.351*
Response time → PU	0.463	0.143	3.252***
System support → Continuance	−0.021	0.106	0.195
System support → PU	0.027	0.124	0.217
Security → Continuance	−0.011	0.085	0.135
Security → PU	−0.071	0.096	0.736

***p < 0.01, **p < 0.05, *p < 0.1

$$t = \frac{a^{*}b}{StandardDeviation\ (a^{*}b)}$$

The result supports the mediating effect of perceived usefulness between correctness and continuance usage intention ($t = 5.125$), response time and continuance intention ($t = 5.691$) and security and continuance intention ($t = 1.628$), which

Table 5.5 Blindfolding results

	CV Red	CV Comm
Continuance intention	0.535	0.796
Perceived usefulness	0.368	0.838

implies that there is a mediation effect of correctness, response time and security on continuance usage intention via perceived usefulness, thus supporting hypotheses H4a, H4b and H4e. However System Support and Availability are not significant ($t = 0.467$ and $t = 0.034$ respectively), hence H4c and H4d are not supported.

Apart from that, "blindfolding" procedure was also performed to measure the predictive relevance (Q^2) of the model fit. The Q^2 "represents a measure of how well observed values are reconstructed by the model and its parameter estimates" [32]. Models with Q^2 greater than zero imply that the model has predictive relevance. Table 5.5 shows the result of the blindfolding results. Omission distance of 7 was utilized as Chin [32] indicates that values between 5 and 10 are feasible (refer to Table 5.5).

5 Discussion

The purpose of this study was to test the role of mediating effect of perceived usefulness towards trust in the system variables; correctness, response time, system support, availability and security towards continuance usage intention of e-government services in Malaysia. The study also examines the relationship between the five elements of trust in the system; correctness, response time, system support, availability, security and perceived usefulness towards continuance usage intention.

The result revealed that trust in the system variables; correctness and response time was found to be positively related to perceived usefulness. This result is similar to the previous studies by Yang and Fang [37], Floropoulos et al. [38], Carlson and O'Cass [39]. Result of this study also consistence with findings by Al-maghrabi and Dennis [40], Shiau et al. [41], Wheelen and Hunger [42], and Brahmasrene and Lee [43] whereby perceived usefulness was found to be positively influence continuance usage intention. Similarly a significant mediating effect of perceived usefulness was found towards trust in the system variables; correctness, response time and security towards continuance usage intention. This is consistent with the previous studies that also found a significant mediating effect of perceived usefulness, such as Ratna and Mehra [44], Belkhamza and Wafa [45] and Money and Turner [46]. On the other hand, the insignificant effect of system support towards perceived usefulness and continuance usage intention could be due to the fact that the support received by the taxpayers will highly influence the satisfaction of the taxpayers and not on the perception of the usefulness and continuance usage intention. This has been confirmed in the study by Delone and McLean [47] claimed that

that effective system support improves user satisfaction of the system. Availability on the other hand is considered as relative advantage of the e-government website by previous researchers [48] and as a system quality [49] which is more likely to provide convenience and operational efficiency to the users [49], as such the direct effect of availability on these variables may deem to be irrelevant. Likewise, the insignificant effect of security towards continuance usage intention could be due to the fact that e-filing system is provided by the government and such the security of the system is believed to be upheld. Previous researches also has claimed that security is more concerned towards the behavior of the taxpayers which has a strong influence towards the attitude of the taxpayers [50] (and not on the usefulness of the system).

The model adopted in this study shows that the perceived usefulness, correctness and response time can explain about 61% of the variance in continuance usage intention. These results showed that the model has relatively good predictive power on continuance usage intention. Further, the blindfolding result in Table 5.5 shows that the CV Comm and CV Red are all above 0 which indicates the model has predictive relevance [51].

As for the implication of the findings, theoretically, this study adds to the growing body of literature of continuance usage intention by supporting the evidence towards the determinant of the usage particularly in Malaysian context. On the other hand, practically, it is important information to the Inland Revenue Board of Malaysia (IRBM) to pay more attention and continuously improve the correctness and response time of the system from time to time to boost optimistic attitude towards the system. In the case of e-filing system in Malaysia, since it is a voluntary based, trust is deemed to be very important.

5.1   Limitation and Suggestion for Future Research

Despite the useful findings of this study, there are several limitations that need to be acknowledged. Firstly, the sample size of the study is only limited to 355 respondents due to the limited time. Secondly, the scope are limited to two states in Malaysia only, as such caution need to be taken when generalizing to the whole country. Lastly, this study only focus on testing the effect of trust in the system variables; correctness, response time, system support, availability, security, perceived usefulness and continuance usage intention and does not incorporate the actual usage behaviour in the proposed model.

Therefore, this research can be done further in future by (1) expanding the study to other states in Malaysia, (2) extend the model by incorporating the actual usage behaviour or any other relevant variables such as availability or security of the system, (3) replicate the study to any other e-government services.

6   Conclusion

In this study, it was found that perceived usefulness is an important determinant of continuance usage intention. This is supported by previous researchers such as Li and Shi [52] and Islam [53]. This result implies that a web portal has to provide all necessary and fundamental capabilities to avoid turning away users after their initial usage [54]. Study by Ambali [10] has indicated that any technological devices that are provided to enhance the service provided by the government must be found to be useful by the citizens. Thus, in the case of e-filing system to be accepted and continued use, it must be perceived as a better alternative, failure on this will lead to citizens discontinue the usage of the system in long run. Furthermore, the findings of this study reveal that perceived usefulness mediates the relationship between the dimensions of correctness, response time and security towards e-filing continuance usage intention. This indicates that correctness and response time had a primary and secondary influence on taxpayers' continuance usage intention of the e-filing system while security has a secondary impact on continuance usage intention. It appears that the system that works properly and produces correct output and a short and reasonable response time is not only able to determine the usefulness of the e-filing system but also affect their intention to continuously use the system.

References

1. Abu-Shanab EA (2017) E-government familiarity influence on Jordanians' perceptions. Telematics Inform 34:103–113. Elsevier
2. Saeed S, Reddick CG (2013) Human-centered system design for electronic governance. IGI Global, Hershey
3. Bhatnagar S (2009) Unlocking e-government potential: concepts, cases and practical insights. SAGE, New Delhi
4. Saeed S, Bajwa IS, Mahmood Z (2014) Human factors in software development and design. IGI Global, Hershey
5. Tran HP, Tan FB, Mills AM, Wang WYC (2014) Information transparency and citizen's continuous use intention of e-Government services. In: The International Conference on Information Resources Management (Conf-IRM), an affiliated conference of the Association for Information Systems (AIS)
6. Venkatesh V, Thong JYL, Chan FKY, Hu PJ-H, Brown SA (2011) Extending the two-stage information systems continuance model: incorporating UTAUT predictors and the role of context. Inf Syst J 21:527–555. Wiley Online Library
7. Reddick CG (2004) A two-stage model of e-government growth: theories and empirical evidence for US cities. Gov Inf Q 21:51–64. Elsevier
8. Mustapha B, Obid SNBS (2015) Tax service quality: the mediating effect of perceived ease of use of the online tax system. Procedia Soc Behav Sci 172:2–9. Elsevier
9. Saeed S, Alsmadi I (2013) Knowledge-based processes in software development. IGI Global, Hershey
10. Ambali AR (2009) E-government policy: ground issues in e-filing system. Eur J Soc Sci 11:249–266

11. Papadopoulou P, Nikolaidou M, Martakos D (2010) What is trust in e-government? A proposed typology. In: 2010 43rd Hawaii international conference on system sciences (HICSS), IEEE, pp 1–10
12. Azmi AC, Aziz NF (2015) Trust, justice and the continued use of e-filing. Electron Gov Int J 11:207–222. Inderscience Publishers (IEL)
13. Gao X, Zhong W, Mei S (2013) Security investment and information sharing under an alternative security breach probability function. Inf Syst Front 17:423–438. doi:10.1007/s10796-013-9411-3
14. Bailey JE, Pearson SW (1983) Development of a tool for measuring and analyzing computer user satisfaction. Manag Sci 29:530–545. INFORMS
15. Cho V, Edwin Cheng TC, Jennifer Lai WM (2009) The role of perceived user-interface design in continued usage intention of self-paced e-learning tools. Comput Educ 53:216–227. Elsevier
16. Liu C, Arnett KP (2000) Exploring the factors associated with Web site success in the context of electronic commerce. Inf Manag 38:23–33. Elsevier
17. Bhattacherjee A (2001) Understanding information systems continuance: an expectation-confirmation model. MIS Q 25:351–370. JSTOR
18. Wangpipatwong S, Chutimaskul W, Papasratorn B (2007) The role of technology acceptance model's beliefs and computer self-efficacy in predicting e-government website continuance intention. WSEAS Trans Inf Sci Appl 4:1212–1218
19. Davis FD, Bagozzi RP, Warshaw PR (1989) User acceptance of computer technology: a comparison of two theoretical models. Manag Sci 35:982–1003. INFORMS
20. Jiang M, Xu H (2009) Exploring online structures on chinese government portals: citizen political participation and government legitimation. Soc Sci Comput Rev 27:174–195. doi:10.1177/0894439308327313. SAGE Publications: Los Angeles
21. Hu PJ-H, Brown SA, Thong JYL, Chan FKY, Tam KY (2009) Determinants of service quality and continuance intention of online services: the case of eTax. J Am Soc Inf Sci Technol 60:292–306. Wiley Online Library
22. McCloskey DW (2006) The importance of ease of use, usefulness, and trust to online consumers: an examination of the technology acceptance model with older consumers. J Organ End User Comput 18:47. IGI Global
23. Pavlou PA (2003) Consumer acceptance of electronic commerce: integrating trust and risk with the technology acceptance model. Int J Electron Commer 7:101–134. Taylor & Francis
24. Horst M, Kuttschreuter M, Gutteling JM (2007) Perceived usefulness, personal experiences, risk perception and trust as determinants of adoption of e-government services in The Netherlands. Comput Hum Behav 23:1838–1852. Elsevier
25. Davis FD (1989) Perceived usefulness, perceived ease of use, and user acceptance of information technology. MIS Q 13:319–340. JSTOR
26. Nicolaou AI, Harrison McKnight D (2006) Perceived information quality in data exchanges: effects on risk, trust, and intention to use. Inf Syst Res 17:332–351. INFORMS
27. Wangpipatwong S, Chutimaskul W, Papasratorn B (2010) Quality enhancing the continued use of e-government web sites: evidence from e-citizens of Thailand. Applied Technology Integration in Governmental Organizations: New E-Government Research: New E-Government Research. IGI Global, p 20
28. Liu L, Ma Q (2006) Perceived system performance: a test of an extended technology acceptance model. ACM SIGMIS Database 37:51–59. ACM
29. Ojha A, Sahu GP, Gupta MP (2009) Antecedents of paperless income tax filing by young professionals in India: an exploratory study. Transform Gov People Process Policy 3:65–90. Emerald Group Publishing Limited
30. Carlos Roca J, García JJ, Vega JJ d l (2009) The importance of perceived trust, security and privacy in online trading systems. Inf Manag Comput Secur 17:96–113. Emerald Group Publishing Limited
31. Anderson JC, Gerbing DW (1988) Structural equation modeling in practice: a review and recommended two-step approach. Psychol Bull 103:411–423. doi:10.1037/0033-2909.103.3.411. American Psychological Association

32. Chin WW (1998) Commentary: issues and opinion on structural equation modeling. MIS Q 22:7–16. JSTOR
33. Hair JF, Black WC, Babin BJ, Anderson RE (2010) Multivariate data analysis: a global perspective. Pearson, Upper Saddle River
34. Fornell C, Larcker DF (1981) Evaluating structural equation models with unobservable variables and measurement error. J Market Res 18:39–50. JSTOR
35. Chin WW (2010) How to write up and report PLS analyses. In: Handbook of partial least squares. Springer, pp 655–690
36. Helm S, Eggert A, Garnefeld I (2010) Modeling the impact of corporate reputation on customer satisfaction and loyalty using partial least squares. In: Handbook of partial least squares. Springer, pp 515–534
37. Yang Z, Fang X (2004) Online service quality dimensions and their relationships with satisfaction: a content analysis of customer reviews of securities brokerage services. Int J Serv Ind Manag 15:302–326. Emerald Group Publishing Limited
38. Floropoulos J, Spathis C, Halvatzis D, Tsipouridou M (2010) Measuring the success of the Greek taxation information system. Int J Inf Manag 30:47–56. Elsevier
39. Carlson J, O'Cass A (2010) Exploring the relationships between e-service quality, satisfaction, attitudes and behaviours in content-driven e-service web sites. J Serv Market 24:112–127. Emerald Group Publishing Limited
40. Al-maghrabi T, Dennis C (2009) Understanding the factors that derive continuance intention of e-shopping in Saudi Arabia: age group differences in behaviour. Available: http:// bura.brunel.ac.uk/handle/2438/3826
41. Shiau W-L, Huang L-C, Shih C-H (2011) Understanding continuance intention of blog users: a perspective of flow and expectation confirmation theory. J Converg Inf Technol 6:306–317. Advanced Institute of Convergence IT
42. Wheelen T, Hunger D (2011) Strategic management and business policy: toward global sustainability, 13th edn. Prentice Hall, Upper Saddle River
43. Brahmasrene T, Lee J-W (2012) Determinants of intent to continue using online learning: a tale of two universities. Interdiscip J Inf Knowl Manag 7:1–20
44. Ratna PA, Mehra S (2015) Exploring the acceptance for e-learning using technology acceptance model among university students in India. Int J Process Manag Benchmark 5:194–210. Inderscience Publishers
45. Belkhamza Z, Wafa SA (2009) The effect of perceived risk on the intention to use e-commerce: the case of Algeria. J Internet Bank Comm 14(1):1–10
46. Money W, Turner A (2004) Application of the technology acceptance model to a knowledge management system. In: Proceedings of the 37th annual Hawaii international conference on system sciences, 2004. IEEE, 9 p
47. Delone WH, McLean ER (2003) The DeLone and McLean model of information systems success: a ten-year update. J Manag Inf Syst 19:9–30. Taylor & Francis
48. Akkaya C, Wolf P, Krcmar H (2012) Factors influencing citizen adoption of e-government services: a cross-cultural comparison (Research in progress). In: 2012 45th Hawaii international conference on system science (HICSS). IEEE, pp 2531–2540
49. Lin H-F (2010) An application of fuzzy AHP for evaluating course website quality. Comput Educ 54:877–888. Elsevier
50. Jahangir N, Begum N (2008) The role of perceived usefulness, perceived ease of use, security and privacy, and customer attitude to engender customer adaptation in the context of electronic banking. Afr J Bus Manag 2:32. Academic Journals
51. Fornell C, Cha J (1994) Partial least squares. Adv Methods Market Res 407:52–78
52. Li G, Shi X (2012) The determinants of consumers' purchase intention to online group-buying. Adv Mater Res 459:372–376. Trans Tech Publ.
53. Islam AKM (2012) The role of perceived system quality as educators' motivation to continue e-learning system use. AIS Trans Hum Comput Interact 4:25–43
54. Lin CS, Sheng W, Tsai RJ (2005) Integrating perceived playfulness into expectation-confirmation model for web portal context. Inf Manag 42:683–693. Elsevier

Chapter 6
Administrative Efficiency and Effectiveness with the Application of E-Government: A Study on Bangladesh Public Administration

Md. Abir Hasan Khan

Abstract Administrative efficiency and effectiveness is the key to positive administrative changes. Notably, most government in developing world have lack in efficient and effective administrative mechanisms to meet the citizen demands. The governments have a promise to gain administrative efficiency and effectiveness with substantial administrative changes. Information and Communication Technologies (ICTs) are considered as one of the most important tools behind these changes. ICTs can leverage the concept of online or e-government where citizen can be a part of government and actively participate to its functions to make the administration effective and efficient. However, the administrative systems in the developing world are more often reluctant in communicating with its customers and getting feedback from them for positive administrative changes. The application of e-government has failed to achieve its goals due to rigid administrative approach in these countries. Bangladesh is not an exception where government has introduced e-government with a bunch of positive visions without supportive administrative systems. This paper finds some loopholes and crucial reasons of failing to achieve the efficiency and effectiveness in the administration of Bangladesh.

Keywords E-government • ICTs • Efficiency • Effectiveness • Bangladesh public administration

1 Introduction

The efficiency and effectiveness of an administration depends on multifarious variables that should be carefully monitored by the administrators. With the demand of time and the necessity of administrative modernization, these variables have been replaced by the new one. An example of the administrative modernization process is the New Public Management (NPM). In the early 1980s of last century,

Md. A.H. Khan, Ph.D. (✉)
School of Management, University of Tampere, Tampere, Finland
e-mail: abir.uta.fi@gmail.com

© Springer International Publishing AG 2018
S. Saeed et al. (eds.), *User Centric E-Government*, Integrated Series in Information Systems 39, DOI 10.1007/978-3-319-59442-2_6

NPM has been considered as the most innovative appliance to replace the old administrative system. However, it has been noticed that except some developed countries, most of the countries in the world have become unable to install NPM into their administrative mechanisms [1]. In principle, most of the innovations have been initiated in order to improve administrative efficiency and effectiveness. However, in most cases changes in the efficiency and effectiveness remain unseen and the innovations have been remarked as failure [1, 2].

The process of administrative modernization cannot remain stagnant for failure in innovations, rather the development process is to be continued with alternate technique. A new tool with new hope using the most vibrant ICTs application called e-government has been introduced into the process of administration. E-government has been incorporated into public administration in the later part of 1990s [3–5]. Analysts [6, 7] believe that the benefits of e-government are enormous and administrative modernization process is very much possible with the application of e-government. If we focus on the specific benefits of e-government, we would notice that the efficiency and effectiveness of administration is the logical sequence from the application of ICTs into the administration where citizens and other parties can interact for mutual benefits. However, this has been considered as a failed initiative for most of the administration in the world [8]. The reason of this failure, could be assumed as because of rigid administrative approach in citizen participation, and the overall vision of e-government being obscure to the administrative staffs.

Since e-government is initiated by the government, so, the government should be aware of the vision that e-government has been incepted for. Moreover, the administration should have to be well trained for the achievement of e-government targeted goals through changing rigid administrative systems and establishing multi-sectoral communication methods.

2   Objectives and Methodologies

The OECD E-Leaders conference [7] formulated four directives for the future e-government agenda:

- Increasing coherency and integration of the public sector through IT,
- Citizen-centricity of the public sector,
- Local service delivery,
- Globalization of public services.

Here, emphasis has been given on the citizen-centric public services for the national and global users using ICTs into the administration. However, ICTs itself cannot gain the expected e-government benefits. The administration needs to be efficient and effective in communicating and promoting available citizen participation into their services. In this regard, the government should focus upon the coherent administrative approach to gain administration effectiveness and efficiency. The administration in developing countries, particularly Bangladesh public administration, are expecting to offer their services online since they have initiated e-government into the mainstream of government administration. However, their success is minimal due to bureaucratic and strategic reasons.

Considering the above scenario of e-government, the main aim is to see how the government has planned for the implementation of e-government to gain administrative efficiency and effectiveness in the long run. In order to have an insight into the subject, the objectives are to see how government has set the strategies for different e-government modules, such as the application of ICTs, human resource development, change of management to ensure citizen participation and make the administration open for all with available services.

This is a qualitative research where data has been gathered from the secondary sources, i.e., from books, journals, reports, web-sources, etc.

3   Theoretical Background

Administrative process, all over the world, has been greatly impacted by the evolution of ICTs. Although unknown in the 1970s, ICTs have been incepted into the mainstream government operations in early 1980s [9], however, e-government has been coined into government and its management since the 1980 [10]. Eventually, the momentum of e-government has been spread worldwide basically in the field of public administration since the late 1990 [11] Therefore, since late 1990s of the last century, governments all over the world have paid their proper attention on the application of ICTs in the mainstream of their administrative process.

3.1   ICTs into Government

ICTs have been considered as the fundamental tools for the success of e-government. However, use of ICTs along is not a solution for gaining efficiency and effectiveness among the administration. The administration should develop, in one hand, human resources through available training facilities, on the other hand, management should have proper spaces to work as a responsible body for the delivery of public services. The most important factors behind the success of e-government might be the creation process: plans and strategies must be proper for the context i.e. the readiness, to get the expected outcomes from e-government [12–14]. In this section these issues has been elaborated and explained with other related factors of e-government.

Before we go into the deep of how e-government plans and strategies facilitate ICTs and other readiness for achieving targeted outcomes, here, it is important to focus upon the incremental benefits from the application of e-government. The e-government is supposedly considered to bring forth the following benefits [2, 6],

- Improving services to citizens;
- Improving the productivity and efficiency of government agencies;
- Strengthening the legal system and law enforcement;
- Promoting priority economic sector;
- Improving the quality of life for disadvantaged communities; and
- Strengthening good governance and broadening public participation.

If we go through the benefits targeted to be obtained from the application of ICTs into the government it would be noticed that all these benefits are impossible without efficient and effective administrative process. That means proper plans are very necessary for meaningful implementations and successful outcomes. Put together it appears that a successful e-government initiative needs some background work called creation process, context, and the content. Therefore, before starting e-government application a government should focus upon this issues.

Context is considered the general condition, for example, organizational culture, electronic knowledge of employees, technological requirements, and administrative maturity of the realization of e-government. The creation process, on the other hand, indicates the method of determining the progression of content where content is the general indicator of e-government assessment, such as efficiency, citizen relationship management, electronic trust, and e-justice. The creation process relates to policy-making, developing strategy, identifying expected functions, identifying critical success factors and barriers to developing architectural structure, selecting methods of implementation, and evaluating results [15].

Government mainly starts e-government application following different implementation phases of digital efforts. The necessary digital efforts could be focused in different ways [3]. The ways could be in the 'back end' of the administrative organization and processes associated with e-government initiatives. This mainly relates to the reform effort of the public sector with 'digital divides' to decrease the gap between those who are able to access, create and use information through ICTs and those who are not. Digital divides are basically to support the front end through the open government data via portal where portal is considered as the most popular one stop service point that facilitates primary website for e-participation. In order to make portal as a means of connecting government with its customers through the online structure with integration of both horizontally and vertically service delivery, the portal should be regularly monitored and researched thoroughly.

Meanwhile, digital efforts should have proper plans and strategies to turn the system of governance from ineffective to an effective and efficient type [16, 17]. The notion of digital effort through the term e-government is to make the government not only transparent and accountable but also to produce competent administrative institution through their effective and efficient institutional practice [11, 18]. Recent study shows that almost every part of the developing world has been administered by an old system of administrative procedures [19]. However, the importance of substantial administrative changes have been raised by people of their own, by the community, and of course by the academics all over the world.

3.2 E-Government Trend Towards Administrative Change

In early age, bureaucratic organizations have different kind of orientations and scales of measuring the effectiveness and efficiency. Theoretically, these orientations have changed with the change of time and demand from the society. In early bureaucratic age the context of bureaucratic organizations had some basic features as explained by Jain [20]:

1. Bureaucracies had a formal and clear-cut hierarchical structure of power and authority;
2. Bureaucracies had an elaborate, rationally derived and organized division of labor;
3. The governed process of bureaucracies were set by a general, formal, explicit, exhaustive and largely stable rules that were impersonally applied in decision making. Furthermore, all decisions and communications have been recorded in permanent files and such records were used to refine existing rules and derive new ones.

Based on the above features it could be seen that bureaucracy (basically in old administrative system) was to maximize administrative efficiency only within their given structures. They were not accountable to the citizen, whereas, they used to serve their superiors. With the change of time the scenario changed with the availability of computers and other advanced electronic gadgets. Governments felt the necessity of using these tools into their system to cope with the new era. As a result, governments started reforms and incepted ICTs into the administrative process to change the old administrative system and make the administration efficient and effective. Primarily, the outset of ICTs into government was for the electronic commerce to deliver services to the citizen 'on-line' [10]. At present, ICTs have been considered as the media to shift the ownership of government to external users with the digital entities by an efficient and effective administrative system [3].

An effective and efficient administrative system can never be possible only with incorporation of digital entities. Prior to putting attention on digital entities an important task is to make the administration ready so that they can proficiently handle ICTs and achieve the respective goals. Moreover, an elaboration on the digital entities are required with mentions of plans, strategies and how to explore maximum benefits. As the plans and strategies of ICTs are for the success of e-government, hence the success of e-government is dependent on the different approaches of administration and governance.

Before the evolution of ICTs into the government and its administration the functions of administration were governed with four types of governance models: hierarchical model, rational goal model, open systems model, and self-governance model [21]. In the hierarchical model, the total control of policy development and implementation is restrained following the strict bureaucratic hierarchies. The rational model, on the other hand, disperses the power across the wide range of agencies rather focusing on the hierarchical model. The open system model is more dynamic and can constantly be reshaped to respond to new challenges and demands. The self-governance model focuses on the relationship between state and government rather limiting notion of governance of action of the state only.

In order to shift from traditional governance system to e-government, four typologies in e-government approaches are available in practice [2]: such as reform oriented e-government, authoritarian e-government, managerial e-government, and open e-government.

Reform oriented e-government generally promotes the involvement of all social actors, e.g., citizens, business, etc. It is worth mentioning that the traditional system of administration follows vertical system of communication and considered as rigid and one-way service providing system. Moreover, in this system actors of different social sectors have been avoided or somehow neglected. Some countries have followed the traditional administrative system in a reverse way where citizen could be focused to initiate policies in case of public service through introducing bottom-up approach replacing the old top-down approach of communication system.

On the other hand, authoritarian e-government is mainly the application of e-government but not to shift power to the citizens or practice the process of democracy. Here, government mainly tries to establish strong communication system with the local government, so that, the central government could easily monitor their work and impose the decision taken by them. Moreover, this seems a top-down approach of controlling the whole government system. The system also controls the web from national and international access and favors the administrative systems for the economic and social growth of the country.

The managerial form of e-government utilizes the management system of private organizations to increase the economy, efficiency, and effectiveness. The main approach of introducing 'e' into the form of managerial type of government is to reduce the cost of staff by introducing the application of e-government.

Finally, the open type of e-government mainly focuses on the transparency, accountability, equity, and inclusion. The belief is that e-democracy is possible if the opportunity for equal right of participation could be ensured. After ensuring the participation of social actors government mechanisms will be transparent and accountable automatically. Ghosh et al. [22] suggested using 'open-source software' within the public administration with the slogan of everyone can get insight, everyone can give his or her contribution and everyone can change the result of decision. Moreover, open e-government combine institutional practice with cultural ethos in a contemporary democracy in order to safeguard the fundamental entitlement of individuals. It encourage the e-participation through the e-vote, and finally contribute to the process of drafting and implementing policies.

It is an obvious fact that e-government effort cannot be accomplished without the digital entities. Moreover, digital entities have benchmark to understand the highest level of e-government maturity. Scholars [23–26] have emphasized that in order to achieve the highest e-government levels a specific technological set-up should be beset. In principle, five e-government matured levels have been outlined by the scholars. The starting level (level one) has been termed where only web-link is presented whereas in the highest matured level many other technological set-up, i.e., web, e-mail, digital signature, public key infrastructure, portals, secure sockets layer and other available technologies should be available to cross the departments and layers of government.

4 E-Government to Make the Administration an Efficient and Effective in Bangladesh

Before going through the details of e-government setup in the administration of Bangladesh it is necessary to outline the reform movement that has been started since its independence. Bangladesh has got its independence in 1971 from Pakistan. Since its independence different reform efforts have been pertained to generate an effective and efficient administrative system. At present, the country could be seen as a unitary administrative form of government. Prime Minister is the executive head of the country who along with his/her cabinet is solely responsible for overall policies and strategies. Subsequently, cabinet member are basically responsible for specific Ministry and has been assisted by a senior permanent civil servant known as secretary. The policies of the national administration is formulated by the Minister in cooperation of the secretary in the secretariat and implemented by the field administration [27].

Presently, the government of Bangladesh has four tiers of field administrations [28]. These tiers are named as the division, district, upazila/thana, and the union parishad. In Bangladesh there are seven administrative divisions and 64 district with several upazilas/thanas, and the union parishads. The administration is unitary in form and follow the instructions from the highest administrative authority i.e. secretariat; the field administration only implement polices without comments or any further recommendations.

If we go back bit upper-part of our discourse it would be noticed that after independence, Bangladesh initiated reforms to speed-up administrative effectiveness and efficiency. Therefore, e-government has been welcomed as a most vibrant reform effort to the administration of Bangladesh. Moreover, after the commencement of e-government in the later part of 1990s the government of Bangladesh has initiated and implemented various projects in cooperation with the donors (i.e. UNDP, World Bank, etc.) to promote administrative efficiency, effectiveness and to make the administration more transparent and accountable to the citizens [29]. Eventually, the present government took over power in 2009 and re-elected in 2014 with a slogan of 'Digital Bangladesh' to ensure the state services closer to the citizens. Accordingly, the government has been emphasizing on e-government in all of its administrative sectors.

The ICTs application in the administration of Bangladesh started in 1986 with a vision of transforming public services to the citizens and business, to promote democracy with achieving the highest level of transparency, accountability among the government and its administration, to become a mid-income country enhancing the social equity. However, the first ICTs policy was formulated by the government of Bangladesh in 2002 with an aim of becoming an ICTs driven nation by the year of 2006 [30]. In order to succeed the ICTs policy 2002, government allocated 890 million Bangladeshi currencies (approximately US$12 million) in 2003 [4]. However, it has been noticed that after 6 years the outcomes were very minimal compare to its expectations. Some reasons of the poor outcomes was pointed out by the Ministry of Science and ICT, [30] as:

1. Underdeveloped internet facilities: the government of Bangladesh has very limited internet facilities to operate their functions online,
2. Inability of responsible authority: The authority responsible for ICTs and the related issues has inability to achieve the goals of the ICT policy 2002,
3. Inadequate capacity: Due to the lack of infrastructure to harness the benefits of ICTs for improving the management and the processes of public sector ultimate goal still in question,
4. Limited usability: Due to the small access of internet and e-mails of civil servants the vast e-government application in administration is limited,
5. Improper planning: The ICTs planning and its strategic actions are not properly maintained for the overall success of ICT policy 2002.

To overcome the identified problems, the government of Bangladesh took two new partners Spinnovation and DNet to develop a short, medium, and long term National ICT Action Plan or Roadmap for Bangladesh on the basis of the National ICT Policy 2002 [30]. A detail action plan was drafted by these two partners and in 2009 the government adopted a revised plan emphasizing the following issues [31]:

• Expand and diversify the use of ICTs to establish a transparent, responsive and accountable government;
• Develop skilled human resources;
• Enhance social equity;
• Ensure cost-effective delivery of citizen-services through public-private partnerships;
• Support the national goal of becoming a middle-income country within 10 years and join the ranks of the developed countries of the world within 30 years.

The adopted revised plan basically required to make the government more open and create an atmosphere to promote e-government [32]. In principle, this revised plan was undertaken in two movements in cooperation with the UNDP (United Nations Development Program). These two movements are: Firstly, Assistance to SICT project (taken in the 2002 policy as SICT), and secondly, Access to Information (A2I). In short, A2I is for the administrative efficiency generation through the facilitation of online-services to the citizen and other stakeholders of government. The vision of the ultimate success of e-government application and its outcome has been targeted by the year 2021.

The government, particularly the Prime Minister office, is working in cooperation with the UNDP to utilize ICTs tools to increase socio-economic development by the year 2021, consists of four pillars: (i) Developing human resources for the twenty-first century, (ii) Connecting citizens in ways that is most meaningful, (iii) Taking services to citizen's doorsteps, and (iv) Making the private sector and market more productive and competitive through the use of ICTs [29]. Although the growth of e-government in Bangladesh is very slow considering the world e-government development ranking. However, the government has still a very positive approach to make e-government a successful one with increased efficiency and effectiveness of the administration.

5 Discussion

Application of e-government, especially in developing countries, seems that just like many other management doctrine, has spread through simulation or hype [19]. Moreover, still in most parts of the world e-government has been considered as the means of ICTs installation. The concept is persisting in same fashion even though the potential changes have been recommended by scholars in the mainstream of e-government application. Eventually, it is very difficult to get benefit from ICTs without proper administrative changes. Therefore, changes are required both in the strategies and the actions for an effective and efficient government administration.

Government is an institution that has some specific goals to be performed for the betterment of its citizen through its administrative mechanisms. Although the main focus of government functions is between the government and its citizen, there are other important bodies to maintain strong communication for the utmost benefits from e-government. Seifert [33] in a study named Congressional Research Service (CRS) has outlined that in order for the success of the main purpose of e-government the interaction process should be maintained between government to government (G2G), government to business (G2B), government to citizen (G2C), and government to employee (G2E). However, it is very necessary to see how this communication is maintained or why.

If the communication is developed for the control of local administrative bodies by the central authorities then it would be a mistake in overall success of e-government [2, 19]. Moreover, the government particularly its citizen will be loser financially as well. The whole invested money will be wasted without sufficient outcomes. This scenario has happened in the first ICTs policy 2002 of Bangladesh government. The government has initiated ICTs policies with strong hope that they would be able to make a democratic government atmosphere. However, nothing remarkable development has been seen after a specific time frame of the initiated policy. Moreover, under the same administrative condition the government announced a new policy with new hopes. The only noticeable change is that two new committees have been appointed to find a new way of investing more money.

The visible landmark, since the massive ICTs application in the government of Bangladesh administration, are different phases of creating the task forces, policies, action plan, Acts, visions, etc. However, the main action plan has remain unchanged and persist in same manner as has been in the old administrative system. After the failure of first ICTs policy, the government has announced new policy to make a transparent, responsible, accountable government through the skilled human resources, enhanced social equity, and especially through public-private partnership. However, in order to succeed all the goals, a strong and well trained management is very necessary that is unfortunately missing in Bangladesh. In most cases it has been noticed that there are very limited training facilities provided by the government and the most training centers are based only in the capital city, Dhaka [34]. Therefore, local bodies, mainly related to the implementation of government functions, are not gaining the required training and the ultimate goal of e-government remain unseen.

Moreover, the application of ICTs into government administration has brought some terminological changes. However, it is very difficult to say that terminology can be effective without any substantial administrative changes. The administration practiced traditional system for long time, hence due to lack of attitudinal change, the application of ICTs into mainstream government administration has changed the way of old administration into the fast method of that old system. For example, if we go through the hierarchical model of traditional governance system we would see that the application of ICTs only changed nothing more than from a paper based communication to an online communication system. However, the main target of e-government is not to fasten the process of communication between administrative mechanisms. Moreover, the seamless communication between government administrations with its stakeholders, especially with citizens, has been considered as the main target of e-government applications.

The traditional administrative system is vertical in communication with the management and stakeholders. However, the main target of e-government is to maintain horizontal communication [35] system where staff can work freely and share their thoughts without fear moreover stakeholders can participate in the decision making process of the government and its administration. Simultaneously, seamless services do not mean the services from government administration for the citizen and other stake holders. Moreover, in order to be matured enough for the success of e-government, technological setup i.e. web, e-mail, portal should be used and both-way communication process should be established.

With the traditional management system the administration can never be effective and efficient in installing e-government and gaining benefits from it even if the government spent huge amount of money. Before start-up the process of e-government, government should decide the expected benefits they are going to achieve. Moreover, the specific planning systems should be identified for the overall success. Without proper plan and strategies the implementation cannot be made in proper way and successful outcome is impossible. Governments all over the world, before going for any plan, should set the strategies and the outcomes in a prudent manner. In order to benefit from any application, three most important factors, such as the strategies, implementation, and outcomes should be treated with equal priorities.

6 Conclusion

Administration has been considered as most important part of government operations where the success of e-government is dependent on proper functionalities by the administrative bodies. The way of operating administrative functionalities are considered as administrative approach. The government of Bangladesh has taken policies and strategies for the success of e-government. However, e-government success is not possible without the substantial administrative changes. Moreover, the administrative effectiveness and efficiency cannot be gained with the traditional administrative approach. Eventually, the government strategies should take into serious consideration to cope with the actual demand of e-government.

References

1. Anttiroiko A-V, Narasimhalu AD (2013) Innovative public managers' work book. University of Tampere, Finland. https://www.academia.edu/3839557/Innovative_Public_Managers _Work_Book
2. Amoretti F (2007) Digital international governance. In: Antttiroiko A-V, Malkia M (eds) Encyclopedia of digital government. Information Science Reference, Hershey, pp 365–370
3. Ahmed MU, Khan MAH (2016) E-government approaches to facilitate the process of democracy in the administration of Bangladesh: rhetoric or reality. In: Trends, prospects, and challenges in Asian e-governance. IGI Global, Hershey. doi:10.4018/978-1-4666-8.ch007
4. Bhuiyan SH (2010) Modernizing Bangladesh public administration through e-governance: benefits and challenges. Gov Inf Q 28(2011):54–65
5. Saeed S, Reddick CG (2013) Human-centered system design for electronic governance. IGI Global, Hershey. doi:10.4018/978-1-4666-3640-8
6. Serban M, Stefan RM, Ionescu EI (2014) Information protections—security, clustering and e-governance. In: 21st international economic conference, Sibiu, Romania
7. Kassen M (2014) Globalization of e-government: open government as a global agenda; benefits, limitations and ways forward. Inf Dev 30(I):51–58
8. Zanelle and Massen (2011) Strengthening citizen agency and accountability through ICT. Public Manag Rev 13(3):363–382
9. Heeks R, Bailur S (2006) Analyzing e-government research: perspectives, philosophies, theories, methods, and practice. Gov Inf Q 24(2007):243–265
10. Brown D (2005) Electronic government and public administration. Int Rev Admin Sci 71(2):241–254
11. Bhuiyan SH (2009) E-government in Kazakhstan: challenges and its role to development. Public Organiz Rev. doi:10.1007/s11115-009-0087-6
12. Ghorbani A, Sarlak MA (2011) Barriers of e-commerce in export. Academic Lambert, Germany

13. Sarlak MA, Ghorbani A (2012) E-government: concepts, theories, applications. Publication of Knowledge Reference, Tehran, pp 51–118. (In Persian)
14. Sarlak MA, Hastiani AA, Dekhordi LF, Ghorbani A (2009) Investigating on e-commerce acceptance barriers in dried fruits producing-exporting companies of Iran. World Appl Sci J 6(6):818–824
15. Dehkordi LF, Sarlak MA, Pourezzat AA, Ghorbani A (2012) A comprehensive conceptual framework for the e-government realization. Aust J Basic Appl Sci 6(8):50–64
16. Saeed S, Bajwa IS, Mahmood Z (2015) Human factors in software development and design. IGI Global, Hershey
17. Saeed S, Bamarouf YA, Ramayah T, Iqbal SZ (2017) Design solutions for user-centric information systems. IGI Global, Hershey
18. Asaduzzaman M, Rahman AKMM (2011) E-governance initiatives in Bangladesh: some observation. Nepal J Public Policy Gov xxix(2):42–54
19. Khan MAH, Anttiroiko A-V (2014) Democratizing digital Bangladesh: designing national web portal to facilitate government-citizen interaction. In: Anthopoulos LG, Reddick CG (eds) Government e-strategic planning and management: practices, patterns and roadmaps. Springer, New York, pp 245–261
20. Jain A (2004) Using the lens of Max Weber's theory of bureaucracy to examine e-government research. In: Proceedings of the 37th Hawaii international conference on system sciences. Temple University, Philadelphia
21. Newman J (2001) Modernizing governance: new labour, policy, and society. Sage, London
22. Ghosh RA, Glott R, Krieger B, Robles G (2002) Free/libre and open source software: survey and study. University of Maastricht, International Institute of Infonomics
23. Layne K, Lee J (2001) Developing fully functional e-government: a four stage model. Gov Inf Q 18(2):122–136
24. Baum CH, Di Maio A (2000) Gartner's four phases of e-government model. http://www.gartner.com. Accessed 28 Jan 2008
25. Hiller JS, Belanger F (2001) Privacy strategies for electronic government. The Pricewaterhouse Coopers Endowment for The Business of Government, Arlington. http://www.businessofgovenment.org/pdfs/. Accessed 28 Jan 2008
26. Wescott C (2001) E-government in the Asia-Pacific region. Asian J Pol Sci 9(2):1–24
27. Siddiqui K (2006) Towards good governance in bangladesh: fifty unpleasant essays. The University Press, Dhaka
28. Talukdar MRI (2009) Rural local government in Bangladesh. Osder, Dhaka
29. Khan MAH, Alam SMS (2012) E-governance in the developing world: an overview on Bangladesh. Int J Inf Commun Technol Human Devel 4(4):39–51
30. Ministry of Science and Information and Communication Technology (2008) Bangladesh ICT roadmap (draft). The Government of Bangladesh, Dhaka
31. Chandan Md. SK (2015) A new Bangladesh: Bangladesh's ICT sector is a glaring example of what can be achieved if the government goodwill and a skilled workforce, work together. Daily Star. http://www.thedailystar.net/a-new-bangladesh-17482
32. UNDP Bangladesh (2008) E governance and development projects: quarterly progress report (January–March 2008). UNDP, Bangladesh
33. Seifert JW (2003) A primer on e-government: sectors, stages, opportunities, and challenges of online governance. Congressional research service: the library of congress
34. UNESCAP (2014) Training program in ICT for development to be launched by UN in Bangladesh. http://www.unescap.org/news/training-program-ict-development-be-launched-un-bangladesh. Accessed 15 Feb 2015
35. Hanna NK (2009) E-government in developing countries. Information Policy. http://www.i-policy.org/2009/01/egovernment-in-developing-countries.html. Accessed 20 Feb 2013

Chapter 7
Agile Collaborative Architecture for the Development of E-Government Services in Romania: Electronic Public Procurement Case Study

Marian Stoica, Marinela Mircea, and Bogdan Ghilic-Micu

Abstract When speaking about electronic government, Romania is giving a special attention to relations between government and organizations. The main reason is the fact that private organizations are the driving force of economic growth. On the other hand, are two principles of public procurement: more attention to transparency and efficient use of public funds. SEAP (Public Procurement Electronic System) as G2B eGovernment solution was gradually developed starting 2002, offering numerous benefits. Still, it does not solve all the problems and challenges of the procurement process. This chapter offers a general view of the current state of the public procurement in Romanian organizations, highlighting the strengths and weaknesses of SEAP. Also, we present solutions for improvement of public procurement process, both from legislative and technological perspective. Special attention is given to a performant collaborative system that helps solve challenges of procurement, both on national and international level. Modern approaches like: Service Oriented Architecture, Business Intelligence, Business Rules, Business Process Management, Cloud Computing and others are used to create an agile architecture for development of G2B e-procurement services.

Keywords Electronic public procurement • Business process management (BPM) • Business rules (BR) • Service-oriented architecture (SOA) • Business intelligence (BI) • Cloud computing • Collaborative system • E-procurement • Enterprise architecture (EA) • Knowledge management (KM)

M. Stoica • M. Mircea (✉) • B. Ghilic-Micu
Department of Economic Informatics and Cybernetics, The Bucharest University of Economic Studies, Bucharest, Romania
e-mail: marians@ase.ro; mmircea@ase.ro; ghilic@ase.ro

© Springer International Publishing AG 2018   117
S. Saeed et al. (eds.), *User Centric E-Government*, Integrated Series in Information Systems 39, DOI 10.1007/978-3-319-59442-2_7

1 Introduction

A support element for implementation of basic processes in public institutions is public procurement. In the current context, the use of information and communications technology is a must, considering the level of expenditures, complexity vulnerability and importance of operations, the responsibility involved by public procurement and the need to align to European requirements.

The Romanian Public Procurement Electronic System (SEAP) was gradually developed starting in 2002. SEAP was built to provide transparency in achieving goals, prevent corruption (through use of electronic means) and support the European exchange of information about public institutions. In 2006 a new version of SEAP was launched, aligned to the new regulations in the field and allowing all kind of public procurement procedures allowed by Romanian legislation, aligned to the European one. SEAP is an integrated system, built on a high availability architecture, which ensures a high level of security. It is a mix of proprietary and open source technologies, according to global trends in designing complex information systems.

The new way of doing public procurement is an important driving factor for integration in e-business: it is an element included in the suite of applications required to implement the concept of "e-government"; it includes the use of internet in administration and the dialog between administration, organizations and citizens; facilitates the change to a paper-less administration, without bureaucracy; ensures information confidentiality and legislative compliance to the status of electronic signatures.

SEAP provides numerous benefits, like: increased transparency, reduced costs, facilitates the development of electronic commerce, reduces time-consuming activities, increases the efficiency of local and central administrations, allows easy auditing of public procurement processes, and provides a high security and trust framework for public funds management activities. The success of the current national electronic system for public procurement is highlighted by the published statistics (Fig. 7.1).

The transition process towards an ideal public procurement electronic system in Romania has faced challenges brought in by the legislative modifications to the Government Emergency Enactment OUG 34/2006. Some of the most significant

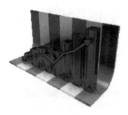

Registered Contracting Authorities/Suppliers:	15,476/68,256
Published Notices/Request For Quotation Invitations:	293,768/361,793
Notices Sent To OJEC:	145,562
Published Catalog Products:	564,530
Published Requests For Quotation/Direct Aquisitions:	89,415/8,829,820
Awarded Aquisitions Total:	175,774,884,921.23 RON

Fig. 7.1 Published statistics for SEAP (according with www.e-licitatie.ro)

challenges in the transition process are: resistance to transfer of information and services to online environment, dispersed procurement activities, lack of institution level procurement management, lack of monitoring and control systems on the system beneficiary's end, lack of inter-organization collaboration regarding procurement. Also, the procurement process is influenced by lots of internal and external factors like: diverse requests, changes in preferences, diversity of funding sources and necessities, changes in legislation, interaction with providers and existing problems within informational flows.

Political, legislative and technological challenges and problems (during 2006–2015) require a reform in national legislation and the creation and use of a collaborative performant system that will ensure transparency and efficiency of the public procurement process (national strategy in public procurement 2015–2020). The information system must be based on an agile architecture that uses modern approaches (like SOA, BI, BPM, BR, KM) as support in solving integration challenges and helps solve current problems.

2 Current State of Public Procurement in Romanian Institutions

Public procurement system in Romania has two components (institutional and legislative) and currently undergoes a transition process towards a performant collaborative system for public procurement, aligned to European legislation. The **institutional component** comprises specific institutions that contribute to regulation and oversight of public procurement contract adjudication (Fig. 7.2):

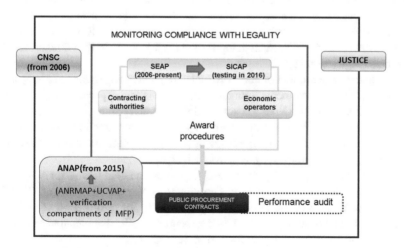

Fig. 7.2 Institutional component

- National Public Procurement Agency (ANAP), founded in 2015 as public institution, with juridical personality, subordinated to the Public Finance Ministry (MFP) [1]. ANAP took over the attributions, activity, jobs and personnel from National Authority for Regulation and Monitoring of Public Procurement (ANRMAP founded in 2005), from the Unit for Coordination and Verification of Public Procurement (UCVAP founded in 2006 under the Public Finance Ministry) and from departments that verify public procurement within regional general divisions of public finances.
- National Council for Solving Complaints (CNSC) founded in 2006 as independent jurisdictional-administrative organism;
- SEAP, that functions according to OUG 34/2006 with all subsequent modifications and additions regarding public procurement process using and managing all activities through electronic means. SEAP is managed by the Agency for Romania Digital Agenda (AADR) and is currently one of the most used government systems. SEAP will be replaced by SICAP (Collaborative Informatics System for a performant environment of Public Procurement), which will be launched for national testing starting in August 2016.

Between 2006 and April 2015 the institutional component was confronted with distributed functions fragmented and redundant between several institutions with key competences in public procurement: ANRMAP, UCVAP, CNSC, AADR, Romanian Court of Accounts and Audit Authority, Competition Council—control activities; Appeal courts—instances with competencies in solving complaints against decisions of CNSC (second body for solving complaints). Also, the institutional component was concentrated on procedural aspects, detrimental to efficient use of funds. Due to this situation, in 2015 ANAP was established.

The **legal component** comprises the legislative package that regulates adjudication of public procurement contracts, public works concessions contracts and service concessions contracts available on ANAP site. Currently there are 52 normative acts that directly regulate public procurement in Romania. Figure 7.3 shows modifications to Romanian legislation during 2006–2015, without including abrogated legislation [1].

Due to the large number of normative acts, frequent changes, lack of transparency and efficiency of investments, numerous complaints and especially lack of project sustainability, in 2015 ANAP has authored the national public procurement legislation, aligned to the European one. Current strategy is presented in a document that proposes actions defining the government policy regarding the reformation of the national public procurement system in 2015–2020.

In this context, public procurement becomes the main tool for unblocking economic growth on European level. Through prime minister Decision no. 218/2014 regarding setting up of the inter ministry committee for reformation of legislative and institutional framework for public procurement, Romanian government has created an operative work frame for system reformation.

National strategy for public procurement, passed on 27.10.2015 is structured on five chapters that tackle the major challenges identified, adequate action directions

The number of annual legislative changes in public procurement									
2006	2007	2008	2009	2010	2011	2012	2013	2014	2015
Primary legislation									
3	1	2	3	3	2	1	3	2	1
Secondary legislation									
2	1	1	2	1	1	1	1	0	0
Tertiary legislation									
0	0	0	2	1	2	6	2	0	0

Fig. 7.3 Public procurement legislation dynamics during 2006–2015

to reform the system, as well as a series of support documents that describe the identified situations. Each chapter provides an action plan with clear deadlines, responsible institutions, and foreseen impact and performance indicators [1].

The identified problems are analyzed in detail in this strategy, which integrates solutions to correct: the legislative framework, institutional system deficiencies, public procurement process, strengthening of administrative capacity of contracting authorities, monitoring and oversight. The proposed measures target mainly an increased efficiency, effectiveness, economy, with integrity and responsibility.

The general objective of the national strategy is *improvement of the public procurement system in Romania, through implementation of the new European directives into national legislation, reformation of institutional framework and continued functionality of the system.* In order to achieve the general objective, the strategy seeks to achieve the following specific goals [1]:

- A new legislative package, flexible and coherent, passed in February 2016;
- Consolidation of ANAP, from functional and operational points of view, so it can coherently fulfil the tasks stipulated in the strategy;
- Consolidation of the remedy and complaint system through dedicated legislation;
- Development of a professional evolution within the system for the personnel responsible for public procurement;
- Fight corruption through increased use of electronic means for procurement procedures and prevent conflicts of interests through the prevention system.

The new legislation (law 98/2016 regarding public procurement) brings more transparency, since all procurement will take place exclusively online, through SEAP (and soon through the new SICAP system). Already some of the procurement procedures take place exclusively online, and until 2018 all procedures will be carried online [2].

2.1 Public Procurement Electronic System (SEAP)

The e-licitatie application, operational since 2006, was appreciated on international level, repeatedly receiving awards and mentions as "good practice". Also, since January 1, 2007, the www.e-licitatie.ro portal has become OJS eSender, meaning it is the point that sends electronic announcements to the European Union Official Journal [3].

SEAP is an open and transparent system that provides access to public funding contracts. It is a centralized system that facilitates meeting of offer and demand on national level, providing economic operators fast and easy access to requests from contracting authorities. By registering in a single system and choosing various search criteria (CPV code—Common Procurement Vocabulary, contract type, procedure type etc.) SEAP sends alerts to economic operators with opportunities that are added to the system.

Strategic implications of the system are important both for government, and for the business environment. Legal regulations aim to create a global market, where public and private sectors can do business in a simple, efficient, transparent and correct manner, market size being very important (Fig. 7.4). For example, in 2013 the value of goods, works and services bought with public funds was 13.3% of Romanian GDP, of which 9.46% (14,250 million Euros) form state budget and ~3.87% (5,491 million Euros) from European funds and other sources [1]. Also, the ANAP president highlighted the importance of regulations because public procurement totals 15 billion Euros, over 10% of Romanian GDP [4].

SEAP is permanently updated, according to legal regulations, but also by offering new features that support both public and private sector. For example, following the passing of new methodological normative for implementation of public/sectorial/framework procurement contract award, starting on 08.06.2016, SEAP provides new features like:

- Market consultation, as preliminary step in public procurement;
- Documentation on how to generate, fill in DUAE as Unique European Procurement Document both for contracting authorities and economic operators as users of SEAP;
- The possibility to publish Annual Public Procurement Plan/biannual excerpts from Annual Public Procurement Plan;
- Technical ability to upload intermediary reports during the public procurement process etc.

Also, awarding procedures may be initiated, including the simplified procedure, which can take place in one or two stages; awarding documentation includes new sections like contracting strategy and declaration of decision positions within contracting agency that organizes the awarding procedure.

The government supports contracting authorities and economic operators through a demo version of SEAP available at http://www.demo.e-licitatie.ro:8080/. Also, it monitors the system information that may influence economic activities (Fig. 7.5).

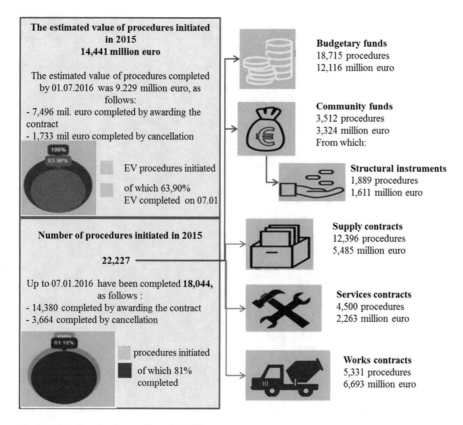

Fig. 7.4 Market size (according with [5])

SEAP provides numerous benefits, but according to studies carried out, current awarding procedures in Romania are inefficient, hurdled by bureaucracy barriers and do not target the efficient use of funds, which is a cause of low absorption rate and corrections to European funds financing [1].

2.2   SEAP-SICAP: Moving to a Full Electronic Public Procurement Solution

As a starting point in this transition, we propose an approach built on the model of a complete electronic procurement process. Developed in an agile manner, this model involves the three SCRUM methodology specific phases: pre-game, game and post-game. In the context of public procurement, the game is the actual procurement procedure, which leads to the generic model shown in Fig. 7.6.

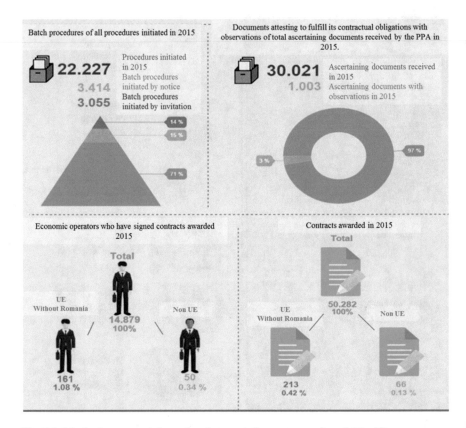

Fig. 7.5 Monitoring system information that may influence economic activities [5]

Fig. 7.6 Generic agile model
for e-procurement

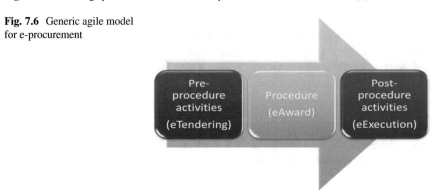

In the context of public procurement, the pre-game phase (*eTendering*) must include specific activities to facilitate the exchange of information between the electronic system and participating actors in the procurement procedure (contracting authorities, economic operators, public institutions involved). These specific

Fig. 7.7 eTendering features in SEAP

information activities may be grouped in a specialized module—*eDocumentation*. This phase must also provide features to enroll/authenticate in the electronic system, through another specialized module—*eSubmission*. At the end of pre-game phase, participants must be able to choose/decide the type of public procurement through a dedicate module—*eAuctions*.

Romanian SEAP implements about 80% of the pre-game specific activities (Fig. 7.7—print screen from SEAP). This is achieved through options *Notices* (for publishing documentation, asking questions/receiving answers through SEAP). Also, SEAP provides features to verify compliance to contracting authorities' criteria compare offers and compute scores for them, description and use of formulas.

SEAP completes the first phase of the agile electronic public procurement model with the feature called *AwardPocedures* (Fig. 7.8—print screen from SEAP), through which participants may decide on the type of procedure to be performed. The next step of the proposed model is the actual electronic public procurement procedure through the game phase (*eAward*).

The post-game phase (*eExecution*) of the generic agile eProcurement model involves activities related to public procurement contract management and progress (order management, bills, payment orders, addendums etc.), which currently are not implemented in SEAP. This is why AADR considers a priority the implementation of Open Contracting Data Standard in SEAP, as an instrument to increase transparency of public procurement; this is a feature of the project developed on European funding—SICAP. Open Contracting Data Standard is available in SEAP starting with August 2016 [3]. This involves providing (in a processable format—

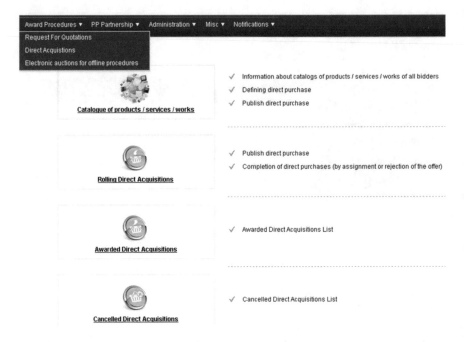

Fig. 7.8 Award procedures feature in SEAP

JSON) the following data: information about procurement planning, information related to the contracting/procedure initiating authority, information related to contract implementation (contract phase, description of contract phase, phase deadline, contract status, contract related documents, list of contract related expenses), information related to payments made for a contract (transaction date, source of money/transaction, payer, payment beneficiary, information about addendums, modifications of the contract, reasons for rejecting the addendums).

SEAP provides a series of features and comes to support the legislation by providing a central hub for procurement on national level, transparency, search and reporting features, the possibility to take advantage of opportunities to buy/sell, a space where offer and demand can meet etc. In order to implement the principle of efficient use of public funds, SEAP must be used together with other modern technological solutions.

Unfortunately, SEAP also has some shortcomings. For example, it is not designed to conduct calculations and reports regarding cost-efficiency or cost-benefits indicators [6], does not allow advanced searches and searching is slowed down by the need to input a CAPTCHA code. Even more, the file format is not standardized for multi-criterial searches and there are no management modules for contracts, payments, orders, statistical analysis.

The analysis of the national public procurement system has led to identification of a series of shortcoming that have lead, over time, to inefficient use of public funds, bureaucratic barriers and a lack of responsibility, numerous complaints that led to prolongation of procedures or even cancelling them, low use of electronic means, financial corrections and low absorption of European funds.

Considering existing problems (detailed in [1]), the current goal is to develop a performant environment for public procurement aligned with European Union requirements and current legislation regarding public procurement. SICAP provides increased efficiency of public services through administrative services provided via modern electronic means, which are efficient, effective and easily accessible, based on interoperability paradigms, security and traceability, in order to create services for citizens, juridical persons and public administration [3].

The new SICAP system comes to help solve the problems of SEAP, increase the automation of public procurement and its management and the efficiency of public procurement activities. SICAP has advanced search specifications, preliminary consultation of market, a payment module and automated activation of pre-payments, a dedicated module for public procurement, uses intelligent forms and provides online training for users (according to SEAP). SICAP will have an intuitive interface, starting with registration in the system, so it will be easy to use by contracting authorities, economic operators and institutions involved in regulating, verifying and monitoring public procurement, which will be interconnected with the system.

SICAP will have an extended reporting and statistics service, through which all actors in public procurement will be able to generate reports that will help create a better general view both on own procurement as well as all procurement activities that take place in a given time frame. Also, the reports can be exported from SICAP in editable formats to be processed and interpreted. There will also be a series of statistics regarding public procurement in Romania available to the public.

The public procurement contracts module in SICAP will allow, both for contracting authorities and economic operators, managing all types of contracts and addendums signed as result of public procurement procedures performed through the system. Also, SICAP will provide extended web services for interoperability.

Another goal is to interconnect SICAP and informatics system of CNSC, so that ANAP can access all the data required for monitoring activities and access aggregated decisions issued by CNSC for public procurement procedures.

3 Agile Architecture for Development of E-Government Services in Public Procurement (G2B)

Considering the problems and challenges facing a general public procurement process, there is a need for an agile architecture that adapts fast to legislative changes and ensures efficiency of the process itself. Using an agile architecture, based on modern technological solutions that lead to decreased costs and increased flexibility, is a critical solution required to meet the challenges of the current business environment and knowledge society.

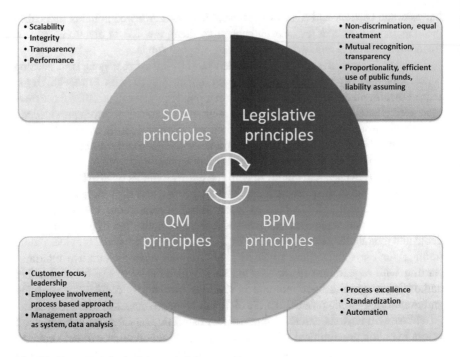

Fig. 7.9 Examples of principles underlying an agile procurement process

The proposed architecture includes modern technological solutions (SOA, Cloud Computing, BPM, BR, Knowledge Management, BI) that will lead to achieving government objectives (in general) and public institutions objectives (in particular): (1) increased savings; (2) increased quality of provided services/goods/works; (3) increased capitalization of opportunities in procurement process. The architectural solution must be built in such a way that it is based on a series of principles, like: legislative principles, SOA principles, BPM principles and principles of quality management (QM), in order to improve the procurement process and increase its agility (Fig. 7.9).

An agile architecture, oriented on services may provide numerous benefits to the public procurement system, allowing a reduced complexity and increased flexibility of business processes. In order to meet the increased organizational needs, quality standards and increased funding available to public institutions, the architecture must integrate specific informatics systems like Business Intelligence for Procurement. A combined use of BPM and BR with SOA and BI leads to agility and efficiency.

The use of ICT (Information and Communication Technology) must not be a purpose by itself, but must be aligned to institution/government strategy. ICT solutions used in the procurement process must be permanently adapted to current legislation, recommendations of legit bodies, management of procurement risk, internal procedures and quality management policy. Additionally, creation of an infrastructure that combines SOA and BPM principles, quality management and legislative principles leads to operational efficiency and agility in public procurement process.

There are frequent changes in public procurement, especially due to permanent changes in legislation. Also, there are integration and interoperability issues due to market size and the need to use different IT platforms/solutions on government level. Government applications are not easy to change over time because many times the business logic is buried deep in the system.

SOA is recognized by researchers and practitioners as an architecture that provides flexibility to frequent market changes. SOA allows decoupling, extraction, migration combination and reuse of software components to implement and support public sector procedures and flows [7]. Also, SOA allows separation of data from processes and user interface. Additionally, SOA provides interoperability and reuse of various software components that can be executed on different platforms.

In public procurement process, the operations of each involved party may be exposed as web services in a service oriented architecture. Orchestration and choreography may be used to provide an open approach, standardized to connect web services in order to create high level business processes [8]. Sustainability and advantages of SOA in e-government process, and especially in e-procurement, are recognized both by researchers and practitioners, SOA being used more and more in e-government processes.

Cloud Computing: With ever increasing ICT demands and limited resources, Cloud Computing offers a new model of providing, on demand, common configurable computation resources. Even if Cloud Computing is best suited for small and medium organizations, the solution may be successfully used in creating a national level agile architecture for public procurement services. Use of cloud computing solutions requires rigorous analysis of institutional necessities and selection of those service models (IaaS—Infrastructure as a Service, PaaS—Platform as a Service, SaaS—Software as a Service) and development models (private cloud, community cloud, public cloud, hybrid cloud) that lead to achieving government objectives.

The large volume of data processed on national level makes the use of cloud computing advisable for storing data. Migration of data, services and processes to cloud platform must be performed based on well-defined models/strategies. Each migration model has specific objectives to be achieved, according to organization policies, information control and security [9]. Infrastructures, security characteristics, norms, rules and policies are critical elements of the most successful e-procurement solutions based on cloud [10].

BPM is frequently used in government solutions, being recognized as having an important role in collecting data related to electronic government systems, simplification of complex processes, automation and optimization of work flows. Also, BPM is a central element of service oriented application development [11]. Thus, each business process is modelled as a set of tasks individually processed, implemented as services. SOA exposes the services and BPM helps automate the process, by calling the services. The combination of SOA, cloud computing and

BPM may generate a synergic construction to ensure the success in implementing agile eProcurement systems.

In order to have a dynamic system, that answers quickly to frequent changes, mainly of legislative nature, system reengineering must be performed without major changes in implementation, instead modifying (where possible) the business rules. **BR** are used more and more in development of informatics systems, providing flexibility and adaptability to internal and external changes of the environment. It is important to use BR in an agile architecture because [12]: they can be reused, allows fast changes in the system, support making decisions in real time.

In order to provide flexibility in implementation remodeling, business rules will be described in separate modules. According to [13], business logic implementation in separate modules leads to big advantages, like:

- It is well designed and the business logic module is transparent to business users;
- It allows adaptation of business rules to frequent changes;
- It reduces duplicates, meaning that if the IT department decides to change an ETL (Extract, Transform and Load) or BI instrument, business rules implementation does not change;
- It allows inter-functionality, large scale IT usability and business rules management.

Additionally, many times one only needs to change the processes or business rules. For example, there may be new regulations or business strategies that modify only the business rules, without requiring changes in the business processes (changing the minimum threshold for some procurement procedures, for example). Also, there are situations where changes in system implementation are required (like changing the work flows), which do not involve changes on business rules. In both cases, separation of business rules helps a faster implementation of changes in the system. Modelling the business rules on various levels of abstraction may be achieved by integrating a BRM (Business Rule Management) module in the public procurement architecture.

The public procurement system involves the existence of a large volume of data that must be analyzed in order to increase the system efficiency. The analysis of large volumes of data regarding expenses from public money, calculation of performance indicators, evaluation and classification of offers, management of public procurement contracts and procedures lead to the need to use a specific G2B electronic government BI solution. The BI solution must provide procurement features, like: forecasts of future needs and required quantities, evaluation of persons in charge of procedures and finding indicators to measure the efficiency of using public funds, evaluation of providers, and calculation of performance indicators.

The features of BI in public procurement may be grouped in three categories (Fig. 7.10): intelligent procurement (extraction of information about providers, contract object—goods/services/works, procurement activities, support for making intelligent decisions), portfolio management (practices/templates for sale, demand forecasts, centralization and management of procurement plans) and performance

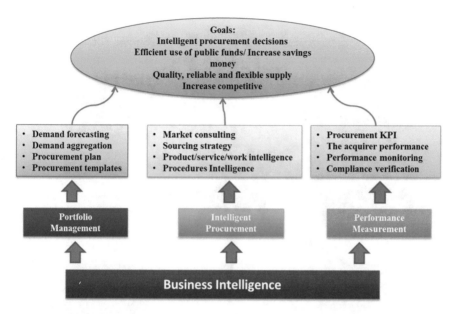

Fig. 7.10 Overview of business intelligence components for public procurement

management (procurement monitoring, verification pf compliance to legislation, measure the efficiency of procurement, compute performance for buyer) [14].

In order to combine business processes with business rules, BI and SOA, a modelling stage is required before creation of the system. In this stage public procurement elements must be described in a structured or formalized manner. In this stage business rules that govern business processes must be analyzed. Mircea and Andreescu [15] presents a case study in public procurement that showcases the use of BI, BR and SOA as support to achieve organization goals. The paper highlights the links between BR and BI, presents BR patterns, and stages of creating a public procurement dedicated BI: (a) Identify Goals; (b) Identify performance quantitative indicators for public Acquisitions; (c) Describe each indicator as a completely specified business rule; (d) Publish business rules service.

The knowledge based society leads to challenges in using knowledge as key factor in achieving business competitiveness. An important role goes to Knowledge Management. A knowledge base in Romanian public procurement has been accumulating (Fig. 7.11) in recent years on national level, representing important sources for making intelligent decisions on G2B market. The knowledge base consists both of explicit knowledge (easy to manage, consisting of documents, data bases, used to make decisions) and silent knowledge.

In public procurement explicit knowledge include mainly legislative regulation regarding public procurement and norms for application of legislation. Also, in order to increase efficiency, good practices and procedures must be recorded. Silent knowledge, which belongs to persons involved in public procurement and their

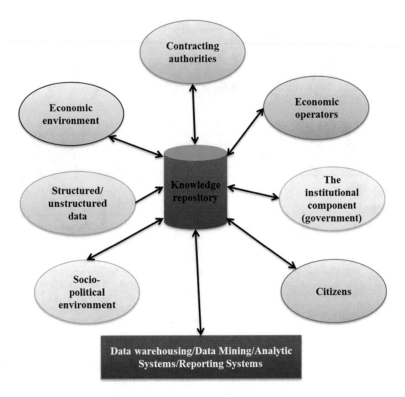

Fig. 7.11 Knowledge management system

experience in this field are hard to define and transfer. The experience, qualifications and competencies of buyers may be obtained during recruitment phase [16].

An agile architecture for public procurement must allow for adaptability to policies and legal regulations ensure the link between parties involved in procurement and interoperability with their systems. It must include systems, hardware and data that allow changes in public procurement processes. Starting from the technological solutions discussed above, Fig. 7.12 presents an example of combining them in order to create an agile architecture for public procurement process.

Creating and using an agile architecture for public procurement process does not guarantee its success. The success of public procurement depends on a series of factors like: IT infrastructure quality, size of organization culture, knowledge management, quality of structural, processual and functional organization, quality in organization and management, quality in system and technology etc. All these factors are very well detailed in [17].

Building a successful and performant public procurement system is a vital element in the development of G2B and achieving economic capitalization on national and international level. The approach must be exhaustive, regarding the three dimensions of the enterprise architecture: business architecture, technological architecture and informational architecture.

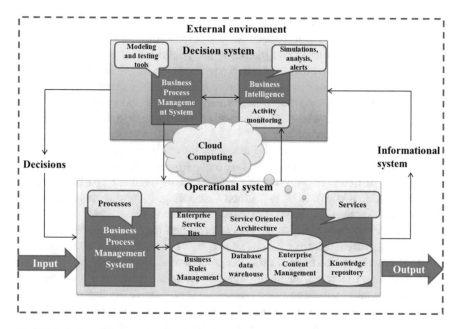

Fig. 7.12 Agile architecture for eProcurement system

4 Conclusions

This chapter is the result of significant experience accumulated by the authors in Romanian public procurement and specific information technologies for development of agile architectures and systems. Beyond the current state of public procurement in our country, in this chapter we have synthetized the research directions and proposed solutions to improve general public procurement systems, with focus on Romanian system. Even the Romanian authorities, represented by authorized institutions, admitted that the Romanian electronic public procurement system (SEAP) is not complete and fully compliant to the legislation at the time this case study was elaborated. This is why, starting with August 2016, a new electronic system for public procurement it was released in 2017 May for testing and general use. The new system, at least on declarative level and design specifications (at this time the platform is available at http://sicap.e-licitatie.ro/pub), provides real features for full unfolding of electronic public procurement.

We must also note that Romanian legislation in public procurement was updated and aligned with the European one, which again calls for a change in the approach towards eProcurement. The European trend is to simplify the norms, procedures and methodologies used for public procurement. This is a result of the relatively low absorption of European funds in the member state (especially the newest members). Without even touching the aspects of European policies in public procurement, we must note that one of the European Union goals is to promote investments in countries that became members after 2003 (among which is Romania, member since January 1, 2007). Investments require procurement, and when the funds come from the European Union (therefore are public funds) public procurement is recommended. Beyond these aspects, the main reason for the frequent changes in public procurement is the drive to make procedures more transparent. Unfortunately, too much desire for transparency may easily lead to breaking the principles of public procurement (equal treatment, non-discrimination, proportionality, efficiency in spending public funds etc.).

Avoiding such mistakes may be achieved by implementing electronic public procurement systems based on agile, safe and performant technologies. From this perspective, this chapter proposes this kind of solutions, using specific elements of BPM, BRM, KM, BI, SOA and Cloud Computing. Proposing this architecture for general e-business systems, but customized for eProcurement, comes from accumulated experience, including system problems that we faced during public procurement procedures. Even more, this proposal envisages a fully electronic public procurement process, from drafting the procurement documentation to unfolding the procurement contract, including specific features for contract management, order and bill management and electronic payment through eBanking means.

This chapter may be a beginning of a "state of the art" of public procurement in Romania, built on the current SEAP, with high expectations from the new SICAP. The research may be continued with evaluation of the new Romanian e-procurement solution from the perspective of the proposed agile architecture and the extent to which SICAP provides participants to public procurement process with opportunities to capitalize and exploit the success factors identified in this case study.

References

1. ANAP (2015) Agenția Națională pentru Achiziții Publice, Strategia națională în domeniul achizițiilor publice. http://anap.gov.ro/web/wp-content/uploads/2015/12/Strategia-Nationala-Achizitii-Publice-final.pdf. Accessed 20 July 2016
2. InfoEst (2016) Din 2018, achizițiile publice se vor face numai online. http://www.argument-cs.ro/content/din-2018-achizi%C5%A3iile-publice-se-vor-face-numai-online. Accessed 20 July 2016
3. AADR (2016) Agentia pentru Agenda Digitala a Romaniei, Sisteme operate. https://www.aadr.ro/sisteme-operate_0_25.html. Accessed 20 July 2016
4. AGERPRES (2016) Pușcaș (ANAP): Noul sistem de achiziții publice, SICAP, va fi supus testării în perioada 27–31 iulie 2016. http://www.agerpres.ro/economie/2016/06/21/puscas-anap-noul-sistem-de-achizitii-publice-sicap-va-fi-supus-testarii-in-perioada-27-31-iulie-2016-10-43-27. Accessed 20 July 2016
5. ANAP (2015) Agenția Națională pentru Achiziții Publice, Sinteza raportului de activitate pe 2015. http://anap.gov.ro/web/wp-content/uploads/2015/12/Prezentare-sinteza-raport-de-activitate-ANAP-2015.pdf. Accessed 20 July 2016
6. ZIARE (2015) Raport SAR. http://www.ziare.com/afaceri/stiri-afaceri/raport-sar-5-dovezi-ca-sistemul-electronic-de-achizitii-publice-este-o-mascarada-1350133. Accessed 20 July 2016

7. Oracle (2016) Oracle igovernment: modernize and integrate operations to transform services, http://www.oracle.com/us/industries/046094.pdf. Accessed 20 July 2016
8. Patra MR, Dash RK (2006) Suitability of service oriented arhitecture for e-procurement. In: Bhattacharya J (ed) Technology in government. https://books.google.ro/books?id=0BIJ69iZyZ0C&pg=PA32&lpg=PA32&dq=service+oriented+architecture+in+e-procurement&source=bl&ots=Tx37F26tP0&sig=GOIe3aWWr3RHTaSDzSO8_SOjjVg&hl=ro&sa=X&ved=0ahUKEwjBw6rN4vXNAhXLBcAKHZUiB4YQ6AEIIDAB#v=onepage&q=service%20oriented%20architecture%20in%20e-procurement&f=false, Accessed 20 July 2016
9. Mircea M, Ghilic-Micu B, Stoica M (2011) Combining business intelligence with cloud computing to delivery agility in actual economy. J Econ Comput Econ Cyb Stud 45(1):39–54
10. Wang H-I (2012) The planning of the architeture of a public e-procurement environment under the cloud—the case of Taiwan. J Global Bus Manag 8(2):134–143
11. Behara GK (2006) BPM and SOA: a strategic alliance. http://www.bptrends.com/publicationfiles/05-06-WP-BPM-SOA-Behara.pdf. Accessed 20 July 2016
12. Corradini F, Polzonetti A, Riganelli O (2009) Business rules in e-government applications. Electron J e-Gov 7(1):45–54
13. Blasum R (2007) Business rules and business intelligence. DM Review Magazine. http://www.dmreview.com/issues/20070401/1079638-1.html. Accessed 20 July 2016
14. Chia CL, Hong LC (n.d) Business intelligence in government procurement. https://www.dsta.gov.sg/docs/publications-documents/business-intelligence-in-government-procurement.pdf?sfvrsn=0. Accessed 20 July 2016
15. Mircea M, Andreescu A (2009) Using business rules in business intelligence. J Appl Quant Methods 4:382–393
16. Wyrwicka M, Staniszewska A, Guszczak B (2014) Knowledge management in public procurement. Res Logist Prod 4(2):179–187
17. Eskandarian M, Marthandan G, Malarvizhi CA, Tehrani SZ (2016) Quality in E-procurement success. Int J Manag Inf Syst 20(3):73–86

Chapter 8
User Centric Services Under the Web 2.0 Era. Coproduction, Execution and Efficiency of Public Services

Manuel Pedro Rodríguez Bolívar

Abstract Public agencies are being pressured for innovation, driving service delivery towards a more personalized, outcome-driven, participative, efficient and collaborative model. This paper captures the perception of policymakers responsible of strategies for e-government in local governments about the influence of Web 2.0 technologies on: (a) the design and coproduction of public services; (b) the easy access to services and the problem solving in the execution of public services; and (c) the evaluation of public services and the improvement of efficiency and accountability. To answer these research questions, an e-survey was sent to policymakers responsible of strategies for e-government in large Spanish local governments. Findings indicate that Web 2.0 technologies are seen as simple adaptations of offline behaviour in public services, which fail to generate meaningful interaction with citizens. It responds to the "representation" strategy, which is focused on the "push" tactic in which no interactions are allowed and a means of "crowdsourced democracy" is produced.

Keywords Web 2.0 technologies • Public services • Policymakers • Local governments

1 Introduction

A recent demand-side survey performed by the European Commission [1] has put emphasis on the need to address the needs and concerns of citizens as well as on the need of more communicative actions to inform those that are unaware of what public services are available on line. In fact, public administrations are being pressured for innovation, driving service delivery towards a more personalized, outcome-driven, participative, efficient and collaborative model [2, 3]. So, public

M.P. Rodríguez Bolívar (✉)
Faculty of Business Studies, Department of Accounting and Finance, University of Granada, Granada, Spain
e-mail: manuelp@ugr.es

© Springer International Publishing AG 2018   137
S. Saeed et al. (eds.), *User Centric E-Government*, Integrated Series in Information Systems 39, DOI 10.1007/978-3-319-59442-2_8

administrations are now moving to scenarios in which citizens are involved in both public services creation and the use of public e-services [4]. Also, public administration is monitored regarding the performance of the delivery of public services with the aim at improving efficiency [5] and raising levels of accountability.

In addition, citizens demand participation offers via the Internet and mobile applications, a demand that will promote the use of Information and Communication Technologies (ICT) in public participation [6]. This way, governments have sought to engage citizens through the incorporation of Web 2.0 technologies[1] into the governmental workplace, which have been seen as effective tools to promote public goals [9]. The implementation of these technologies is changing the roles played by citizens, who will no longer be mere 'end-users', but will become partners and co-creators of information and services [10, 11], which promotes to put citizens into the heart of the value chain [12], and expecting them to provide insight and knowledge and thus improve public services.

The use of Web 2.0 technologies could help governments to involve citizens in the coproduction of public services making them more user centric, friendly and efficient. Having Web 2.0 tools available and being used more widely will help governments to better identify the collective public value while still enabling them to respond to individual preferences [13]. These new developments put pressure on government organizations to innovate in their dealings with citizens, introducing new competition for 'nodality' in social and informational networks [14, 15] and offering the potential for 'coproduction' and even 'co-creation' of government services [16].

Nonetheless, despite the great significance of the future implementation of Web 2.0 technologies in public administration and calls for studies to analyse the impact of legal, institutional, and political challenges regarding the use of ICT in local governance [17], little research has been conducted in the field of public administration to analyse the use of these technologies with the aim at examining the capacities that Web 2.0 technologies provide to governmental actors and stakeholders in transforming public services into user centric services and user evaluation of these services.

This analysis is especially relevant in local governments because they are an important subject for the study of social media and interactivity because of traditions of citizen participation at the local level [18] and the tradition of these governments to use more mechanisms that permit direct citizen involvement, in part because they are more manageable at that scale [19] as well as they provide a wide variety of services [20]. Inside local governments, the perception of policymakers responsible of e-government is of great interest taking into account not only their significant role in the policy-making process within local government, but also their direct

---

[1]In this paper, Web 2.0 should be viewed as a networked platform, spanning connected devices to encourage collaboration, in terms of the creation, organization, linking and sharing of content [7, 8]. Thus, it is related to the technical platform on which social media applications are built to create and exchange user-generated content.

involvement in the possible implementation of Web 2.0 technologies in public sector delivery.

Therefore, this chapter contributes to the current debate on Web 2.0 technologies and its implication for the coproduction of user centric services, aiming at identifying the perceptions of policymakers responsible of e-government in local governments about the influence of Web 2.0 technologies on: (a) the design and coproduction of public services; (b) the easy access to services and the problem solving in the execution of public services; and (c) the evaluation of public services and the improvement of efficiency and accountability. To achieve this aim, a questionnaire was designed and sent to all policymakers responsible of e-government in large Spanish municipalities (those with a population of over 50,000 inhabitants) in order to capture their perceptions to answer each one of the research questions posed in this chapter.

The chapter is organised as follows. The next section is addressed to analyse the coproduction of public services under the Web 2.0 technologies era, proposing some research questions to be analysed in this paper. Then, an empirical research is performed obtaining the policymakers' perceptions regarding the participation of citizens in the delivery and problem solving of public services. Finally, this paper highlights the main conclusions and discussions of the empirical results and answer the research questions posed previously.

2 Coproduction of Public Services Under the Web 2.0 Technologies Era

The advent of social media using Web 2.0 technologies has opened up unprecedented new possibilities of engaging the public in government work and has changed the public's expectations about how government work should be done [21–23]. Indeed, social media applications provide channels not just for mass dissemination but also for mass production and collaboration [24], which can transform public administration services, enabling the development of better policies and eliminating data silos [25] see Table 8.1.

This way, Web 2.0 technologies have the potential to change the way government delivers services and its relationship with the public. Among the several ways that Web 2.0 technologies can provide added value to the delivery of public services are the possibility of citizens' engagement and collaboration with the government in the design and coproduction of public services with the aim at achieving services more personalized, faster, easier to use and deliverable, as well as the provision of a development tool for internal staff that offers higher productivity than the Web alone can provide [28].

Potential benefits of this engagement with citizens also include the improvement of the citizen-government relationship, and enhanced policy implementation [29]. In this regards, citizen-sourcing can strengthen the relationship between citizens

Table 8.1 Differences between Government 1.0 and Government 2.0

	Direct and Orthodox government	Transformational government
Dimension	Government 1.0	Government 2.0
Operating model	• Hierarchical	• Networked
	• Rigid	• Collaborative
		• Flexible
New models of service delivery	• One-size-fits-all	• Personalized
	• Monopoly	• Choice-based
	• Single channel	• Multi-channel
Performance	• Input-oriented	• Outcome-driven
	• Closed	• Transparent
Decision-making	• Spectator	• Participative

Source: Author based on Deloitte [26] and Taylor [27]

and government, and may boost trust and confidence in government [30] helping government to obtain legitimacy and political support to adopt new policies or test novel objectives [31].

Also, regardless the citizen participation approach, with the help of Web 2.0 technologies, governments could capture citizens' needs and, then, customize services based on personal preferences and needs [32], which would largely enable users' needs to be met [33], and it is a means to enrich citizens' substantive knowledge of issues, broaden their understanding of key actors and the government's role, and hone their civic skills in using governance tools [29]. Finally, Web 2.0 technologies may boost innovation of information and service production modes converting citizens in "makers and shapers" of policies and decisions [29].

Essentially, these new technologies empower the individual to voice opinions and share thoughts on important issues [34]. This way, these technologies are putting pressure on governments to innovate in their dealings with citizens, offering the potential for 'coproduction' and even 'co-creation' of government services [16]. This way, citizens will no longer be mere 'end-users', but will become partners and co-creators of information and services [11], which promotes to put citizens into the heart of the value chain [12], and expecting them to provide insight and knowledge and thus improve public services. Governments must now strengthen their capacity to assess the needs of users and involve user groups through the use Web 2.0 technologies in order to engage users in the production of policies and to forge collective initiatives and interaction [35]. In this regards, a push towards government coproduction of services with citizens has been very clear in behavioural public policy fields, the 'nudge' territory of changing life choices [36].

Despite previous comments regarding the advantages of using Web 2.0 technologies in governments, we cannot ignore potential threats to user privacy and security [37]. Also, while the potential impact of social media technologies on the functioning of government is expected to be "profound," it will come with "challenges in the areas of policy development, governance, process design, and conceptions of democratic engagement" [38]. Indeed, the use of social media introduces a number of policy problems, such as the interpretation of the information shared in networks or the loss of significant control over the content and applications [39]. Therefore, it would be relevant to know if policymakers are prone to implement Web 2.0 technologies with the aim at involving citizens in the design and coproduction of public services. The first research question is therefore:

RQ1. Do policymakers think that the use of Web 2.0 technologies improves the citizen engagement in the design and coproduction of public services?.

On the other hand, a growing number of public policy tasks involve "wicked problems" that are ill-defined, difficult to respond to, require specialized knowledge, involve a large number of stakeholders, and carry a high potential for conflicts [40]. Indeed, even more interventionist European governments acknowledge that government-only interventions are unlikely to be successful [16] and the implementation of Web 2.0 technologies by government has become an expression of the recognizant that conventional governments are unable to address society's challenges alone.

In this regards, evolving Web 2.0 applications will demand a new environment of collaborative culture within government agencies and organizations [7]. Such novel approaches of connecting with citizens through Web 2.0 technologies create conditions for improving transparency and fostering innovation [41]. Indeed, Web 2.0 technologies have the potential to share knowledge and enable problem solving in the network [42].

Despite previous comments, little is known about how Web 2.0 technologies can affect to the ease of access to reaching public services and to knowledge-sharing purposes. Therefore, it could be relevant to focus research on the use of Web 2.0 for this access and the resolution of problems in the execution of public sector services. This way, the second research question is:

RQ2. Do policymakers think that Web 2.0 technologies promote easy access to public services and problem solving?

Finally, according to the second eGovernment Action Plan [43], governments will use eGovernment to increase their efficiency and effectiveness and to constantly improve public services in a way that caters for users' different needs and maximizes public value [43]. This way, policymakers looking for public service cuts could be prone to implement Web 2.0 technologies, which could lead to new interest in Digital Era Government type models [16]. In fact, with public spending reductions squeezing public services at all levels, the strategies adopted by public agencies have been aimed at achieving higher levels of on-line service uptake and at developing public e-services [44, 45], as well as obtaining the anticipated cost efficiencies [27].

Accordingly, local governments are increasingly embracing Web 2.0 technologies to encourage the use of means of bidirectional communication to change how they interact with stakeholders and to become more efficient in their response to stakeholders' demands, thus providing the greater efficiency and accountability demanded [46, 47]. Nonetheless, whether or not citizens actually participate online, a municipal presence on social networks may convey the message that government is more responsive, open, and democratic, by allowing citizens to express their views via this channel [48]. Therefore, the last research question is:

RQ3. Do policymakers think that Web 2.0 technologies enable the evaluation of public services and the improvement of efficiency?

3 Policymakers' Perceptions About the Use of Web 2.0 Technologies for User Centric Services in Spanish Local Governments

3.1 Sample Selection

Social networks are becoming increasingly important to local governments due to the long tradition of citizens' participation at the local level [49]. Indeed, local governments tend to use more mechanisms that permit direct citizen involvement [19], in part because they are more manageable at that scale—see also Briggs [50] and Sirianni [51]. Furthermore, local governments are a prime target for public sector reforms [52], especially the largest cities, which have generally been at the forefront in the adoption of innovations in e-government [32, 53] and the greater complexity involved for public sector delivery [54]. Finally, the quantity and variety of services delivered by these administrations are very comparable.

This paper is part of a wider research undertaken in Spanish local governments, taking into account the legislative reform policies applied to administrative structures in Spain in the 1990s [55], the managerial devolution process implemented in this country [56] and the rapid introduction of new technologies by these local governments, which has been fostered by new legislation in this respect in recent years. Thus, the Information Society Services and E-Commerce Act (No. 34/2002) guaranteed access to government information, while the Local Government Modernization Act (No. 57/2003) promoted the use of new technologies in order to enhance participation and communication with citizens and enhance interaction with municipal authorities. Finally, the Electronic Access to Public Services Act (No. 11/2007) guaranteed the access of all citizens to online public services and the rights of all citizens to interactive communication with the government. As a result of these legislative measures, all levels of public administration were required to develop a wide range of Web-delivered services.

According to recent studies, 61% of Internet users in Spain make use of social networks to chat with friends or organizations as well as to generate content, which could indicate that Spanish Web users are sufficiently familiar with these new technologies and could make use of e-services if local governments introduced Web 2.0 applications.

Therefore, the present empirical study is based on a sample of large Spanish municipalities, defined as those with a population of over 50,000 inhabitants, together with municipalities that are provincial capitals, regional capitals or in which the headquarters of regional institutions are located. In total, 148 Spanish municipalities meet these conditions, and account for over 50% of the total population of Spain [57].

Of the 148 municipalities that comprised the survey sample, seven stated that neither had experience of Web 2.0 nor dedicated human resources to this area. Therefore, the questionnaire was sent to 141 local governments and 47 complete replies were received from policymakers (minimum response rate: 33.33%). Nonetheless, some policymakers of local governments responded to some items without finishing the full e-survey. In consequence, for some questionnaire items, the response rate exceeded the above-mentioned minimum (see Tables 8.2, 8.3 and 8.4 in the analysis of results—see Annex).

According to Roscoe [58], a sample size between 30 and 500 is considered satisfactory. By contrast, a high number of responses could be also damaged to obtain a good picture of the perceptions of the sample policymakers due to the problem of saturation. Data saturation is reached when there is enough information to replicate the study when the ability to obtain additional new information has been attained, and when further coding is no longer feasible [59]. Nonetheless, there is no one-size-fits-all method to reach data saturation with many authors proposing different figures and methodologies [60] because study designs are not universal and there are numerous factors that can determine sample sizes in qualitative studies [60]. Indeed, the point of saturation is a rather difficult point to identify and of course a rather elastic notion and depends on the research skills of the researcher [60, 61]. This way, the research undertaken in this paper has taken the saturation as the guiding principle for the qualitative data collection, which is necessary in a qualitative research like this [60], obtaining data from a random sample of policymakers that come from sample municipalities with different characteristics like size of the municipality, Web 2.0 technologies used, political factors in the municipality and so on. This way a good overall picture of the perceptions of the policymakers have been obtained in our results.

3.2   Questionnaire Design

This paper is part of a wider research focused on the use of Web 2.0 technologies for citizen engagement in public services. Data were obtained by sending a link to perform an e-survey, and this was sent to the policymakers of all the local authorities studied, via email. The contact details were obtained from the Spanish central government's website. The global questionnaire of the research contained a total of 75 questions including the reasons for using Web 2.0 technologies, the advantages of using Web 2.0 technologies for public services, the technological innovation of public services with the use of Web 2.0 technologies, the improvement of efficiency in public sector delivery with the use of Web 2.0 technologies, the legitimacy of government in the use of Web 2.0 technologies and so on.

For the purpose of the analysis in this paper, we focus our efforts in analysing 15 questions covering the following issues: design and coproduction of public services (in Table 8.2 in Annex—five questions); advantages of using Web 2.0 technologies for access to services and resolution of problems (in Table 8.3 in Annex—five questions); the evaluation of public services and the improvement of efficiency (Table 8.4 in Annex—five questions).

Policymakers were addressed in this survey taking into account not only their significant role in the policy-making process within local government, but also their direct involvement in the possible implementation of Web 2.0 technologies in public sector delivery. In fact, recent research has confirmed that policymakers usually act as "leaders" and "interpreters of the societal trends" by defining the general policies for the continuous innovation of the service provision in the public sector [62]. Before the e-survey was sent out, every policymaker in the sample population was contacted and asked to participate in the study, after being informed of the study goals and of what was required by the questionnaire.

Two draft versions of the survey were pre-tested on a selected group of stakeholders. First, the research team drafted a preliminary version based on the conclusions of previous research in the field of Web 2.0 technologies, justifying the items selected on the e-survey. All these items were based on prior research with the aim at capturing perceptions of sample policymakers regarding the use of Web 2.0 technologies for participating in the design and coproduction of public services (five items—items 1.1 and 1.2 for design of public services and items 1.3, 1.4 and 1.5 for coproduction of public services), regarding the introduction of Web 2.0 technologies to achieve an easier access to services and to solve problems in the execution of public services (five items—items 2.1 and 2.2 for the ease of access to public services and items 2.3, 2.4 and 2.5 for resolution of problems in the execution of public services) and their perception about use of Web 2.0 technologies for the evaluation of public services and the improvement of efficiency (five items—items 3.1 and 3.2 for the evaluation of public services, items 3.3 and 3.4 for analysing the efficiency of public services and item 3.5 for analysing the improvement of accountability).

In the second phase of questionnaire design, the initial text was presented to two specialists on Web 2.0 technologies and to ten policymakers, to ascertain their opinions on: (a) the understandability of the questionnaire; (b) the clarity of the questions posed and possible ambiguities; (c) the possible inclusion of other questions relevant to the study aims. The comments and suggestions made were analysed and, when considered appropriate, incorporated into the text of the questionnaire.

Local governments provided an institutional response to the questionnaire, one that was non-personal and non-subjective. A single liaison officer was appointed in each case, this being the person in the organization who was responsible for implementing new technologies on public services. The institutional response was supervised and supported by the policymakers of each local government. Moreover, the possibility of clarifying any remaining doubts was offered before completing the questionnaire and thus we may be reasonably sure that the questions measured the intended constructs.

Based on prior studies on attitude analysis [63], the respondents were asked to describe their degree of agreement with each statement on a five-point Likert scale (ranging from strongly disagree, "1" to strongly agree, "5"). Although the Likert scale has some limitations, such as its inability to approximate intervals of ordinal data [20] and its closed response format [64], it was used in this research due to its suitability for attitude studies [65, 66]. Also, a 5-point scale can alleviate the psychological distance between categories [67] and, as observed by Norman [66], the closed nature of the Likert scale avoids the need to draw inferences about differences in the underlying, latent characteristic, without this invalidating the conclusions drawn.

After the questionnaire was completed, each item was analysed separately using the median and the mode of the responses because it has been proved to be useful in order to analyse data obtained using Likert scale [68].

3.3   Analysis of Results

RQ1. Do policymakers think that the use of Web 2.0 technologies improves the citizen engagement in the design and coproduction of public services?

Table 8.2 in Annex collects the information collected from policymakers regarding the improvement of citizen engagement in the design and coproduction of public services with the use of Web 2.0 technologies. As it can be seen, policymakers think that Web 2.0 technologies could mainly help to collect information from citizens regarding their preferences and needs of public services (see median and mean scores of item 1.1 in Table 8.2). It could make to obtain well-targeted public services (see median and mean scores of item 1.2 in Table 8.2), which could help governments to better decide how to design the services for the citizenry.

By contrast, results indicate that policymakers are not prone to the active participation of citizens in the design or coproduction of public services. Indeed, respondents indicate that citizens should not be encouraged to participate in the generation of content or information about public services (see median and mean scores of item 1.3 in Table 8.2), perhaps due to the additional "noise", destructive behaviour by users or the manipulation of content by interested parties and privacy infringements [69]. These issues could make policymakers to stop the effective involvement of citizens in the coproduction of public services.

By contrast, policymakers think that Web 2.0 technologies could foster the collaboration with citizens in the delivery of public services (see median and mean scores of item 1.4 in Table 8.2), although the experience in public services before their final implementation is not seen essential for respondents (see median and mean scores of item 1.5 in Table 8.2). In fact, policymakers did not show interest in promoting spaces or tools where citizens could use public services as a trial prototype before their final implementation. It means that policymakers only think relevant to involve citizens to capture their needs but not to test whether these needs have been met.

In brief, results indicate that, according to policymakers' perceptions, Web 2.0 technologies could be the means to collect information and to collaborate with the government but not the means of citizens to actively participate in the design and coproduction of public services.

RQ2. Do policymakers think that Web 2.0 technologies promote easy access to public services and problem solving?

Results shown in Table 8.3 in Annex indicate that Web 2.0 technologies could facilitate the access of citizens to all public services (see median and mean scores of item 2.1 in Table 8.3), as well as the reduction in time on obtaining the public services (see median and mean scores of item 2.2 in Table 8.3). Therefore, it seems that policymakers think that Web 2.0 technologies could help to make public services more available for the citizenry.

In addition, according to the results, policymakers think that Web 2.0 technologies could help them to collect suggestions of citizens to enhance the quality of public services and the information about them (see median and mean scores of item 2.3 in Table 8.3). This result seems to be contrary to that in which they think that citizens should not participate in the generation of content and information about public services (see item 1.3 in Table 8.2). Nonetheless, the difference between these results lies in the active (item 1.3) or passive (item 2.3) attitude of citizens in the execution of public services.

This way, it seems that policymakers are prone to collect information about the public services from citizens but no participation of citizens is encouraged by them. In addition, they are not prone to use the knowledge, skills and talent of the population to help them in solving problems in the execution of public services (see median and mean scores of item 2.4 in Table 8.3) or to use tools like Wikis to create knowledge to solve problems in the delivery of public services (see median and mean scores of item 2.5 in Table 8.3).

Thus, no active participation is fostered by governments. Respondents seem to indicate that the use of Web 2.0 technologies could only be helpful for information disclosure and for putting available public services. So, Web 2.0 technologies seem only to be used as a means for communication and crowdsourcing which involves the use of technology to foster the exchange of information and ideas among participating agents.

RQ3. Do policymakers think that Web 2.0 technologies enable the evaluation of public services and the improvement of efficiency?

As it can be seen in Table 8.4 in Annex, policymakers think that Web 2.0 technologies could be used as tools for evaluating the efficiency and transparency of public services (see median and mean scores of item 3.1 in Table 8.4) but they are not relevant for improving the quality of public services (see median and mean scores of item 3.2 in Table 8.4).

In addition, according to the policymakers' perceptions, Web 2.0 technologies can be used to improve efficiency of public services because these technologies allow the reduction in costs and the increase in revenues (see median and mean scores of item 3.3 in Table 8.4). Also, these technologies allow the better allocation of financial resources (see median and mean scores of item 3.4 in Table 8.4) because, among other reasons, governments can be led to meet the citizens' needs directly in an electronic way since governments can capture the data necessary to achieve this aim (see median and mean scores of item 1.1 in Table 8.2).

Finally, respondents indicate that Web 2.0 technologies should be used for disclosing information regarding the performance of the government in public sector delivery. This way, local governments could accomplish better their duty of accountability (see median and mean scores of item 3.5 in Table 8.4).

Therefore, respondents think that Web 2.0 technologies could help to improving efficiency but also accountability. According to our results, these technologies could be used, firstly, as a means of collecting the need of citizens regarding public services and, later, these technologies could help to disclosing information about them and to putting them available in an electronic way. All these actions make public services to achieve a better efficiency because they are driven to meet citizens' needs, and cost cutbacks and higher revenues are achieved. Also, the higher volume of information disclosed could help citizens to evaluating better the accountability of the government.

4 Conclusions and Discussions

Citizen participation is not always good for efficient and effective government decision making. It may entail poor decisions and a significant expenditure of resources that could be used elsewhere to achieve better on-the-ground results [70]. Nonetheless, the use of innovative participation technologies can reduce administrative costs and raise instrumental benefits, reinvigorating the frequently criticized public hearing [71]. In this regard, the advent of Web 2.0 technologies has allowed the two-way communication and rich data exchange among different actors for purposes of communication to the network, knowledge exchange, and problem solving [42]. These technologies have raised expectations in citizens and other stakeholders about the quality, availability, and effectiveness of public services and these stakeholders are demanding tailored services [72, 73].

Nonetheless, findings indicate that sample policymakers seem to think that Web 2.0 technologies should mainly play the role of simple adaptations of offline behaviour in public services, which fail to generate meaningful interaction with citizens, because they do not offer active participation to involve citizens in the design, coproduction or problem solving in public services. This finding does not confirm prior literature that indicates that social media could be related to solving specific problems and/or coproducing a specific good or service [74]. In contrast, our findings confirm recent research which points out that the desires and expectations of the citizens and public sector differ significantly [6]. Our findings show that policymakers do not simply reject the idea of additional public participation in the generation of content of information about public services (see median and mean scores of item 1.3 in Table 8.2); rather, they are restrained in terms of a desire for more public participation in the delivery of public services.

Therefore, why to use Web 2.0 technologies? Recent research has indicated that the use of Web 2.0 technologies in public sector is positively related to satisfaction and perceptions of public sector trustworthiness, because they are used to convey less detailed information than other forms of e-government such as e-government websites [75]. The main purpose from this point of view could be to increase trust in government operations by providing more frequent and transparent online information, which makes government to accomplish better its duty of accountability (see median and mean scores of item 3.5 in Table 8.4).

This way, Web 2.0 technologies can be seen as a means of "crowdsourced democracy" because it is used or thought to be used as a means of communication and crowdsourcing of collected information regarding public services, but their use is limited to a passive role of citizens. Recent research has indicated that importance of online platforms in crowdsourcing can have a consistent impact on services delivery system in local public administration [76]. Our findings confirm previous comment, because sample policymakers think that Web technologies could be relevant to collect information about citizens' needs, to foster the effective collaboration between citizens and governments in the delivery of public services, to disclose information regarding public services, to put them available in an electronic way and to serve as an instrument to evaluate efficiency and accountability of local governments. It describes the "representation" strategy in the use of Web 2.0 technologies pointed out by Mergel [77], which is focused on the "push" tactic in which no interactions are allowed. This way, this new form of representation can be seen as the lowest degree of online engagement and is oftentimes misinterpreted as true citizen participation.

Nonetheless, recent research [62, 78] and international organisations [79] have indicated that public innovation, focused on service innovation, may generate complex processes of social change that will eventually lead to the emergence of new modes of public governance [62], taking their underpinnings in the Networked Governance model [80]. Therefore, it seems that ICT can be used to support and enable bureaucratic practices in favour of government reforms and service delivery improvements [81].

In fact, Web 2.0 technologies should enhance the ability of citizens to democratically engage with political discourse and decision-making and hence influence meaningful change in public policy with the aim at achieving citizen-centric e-governance [82]. Citizen centric e-governance argues for "we government", meaning that citizens work collaboratively with government and promote real and meaningful change together [83]. In fact, governance is not about what governments do but about the outcomes of interactions between all actors in the public domain [84]. This way, according to Reddick et al. [82] citizen-centric e-governance aims to explain the postulated theoretical relationships between political efficacy and civic engagement, and fosters citizens to take power and engage themselves actively and democratically to influence public affairs and policy.

So, based on the use of Web 2.0 technologies, citizens should be encouraged to play a more active role to become more and more able to influence the rate and direction of innovation and often coproduce it. This is especially relevant at the local level of government, because these governments hold key positions in the development of digital spaces for civic participation in the issues that directly impact citizens' everyday lives [85]. In addition, cities around the world are ever increasingly piloting new technologies to become "smart" by providing data for new management platforms, informing authorities, businesses, and citizens with relevant information and evidence to make informed decisions regarding policies and daily life activities [86]. The engagement of citizens in all the steps of smart city initiatives have been identified as key challenges in the successful scaling up of the smart city initiatives in the pioneering cities in America and Europe [87].

But, why not to involve citizens in an active participation in the design, coproduction and problem solving in the delivery of public services? Recent research has demonstrated that technology, organisation, and environment factors including perceived benefits, perceived security risks, compatibility, and degree of formalisation are important predictors of social media impact in local government [88]. In this regards, the implementation of Web 2.0 technologies make policymakers to potentially fear the loss of power and influence through greater public participation [89, 90], which could lead to a defensive reaction toward greater public participation. Perhaps, the existence of a clear regulatory framework for the activities related to social networks or the establishment of a process to combat unauthorized or fraudulent postings could mitigate this risk and could make policymakers to be more prone to the effective involvement of citizens in the coproduction of public services.

In addition, the defensive reaction of policymakers could be due to the fear that their control will be weakened [91]. Perhaps this is the result of the current inexperience of local governments in Spain in managing social media tools, in providing public sector services with Web 2.0 technologies and in the way of interaction with individuals through these technologies [92]. Indeed, experience has been shown to be a highly significant factor for networking and network management [93] and, in Spain, we are viewers of the early stage in the development and implementation of social media tools into governments. Therefore, future research should analyse if experience in using Web 2.0 technologies for the delivery of public services could be a main factor to solve this defensive reaction shown in our study by sample policymakers.

On another hand, do citizens really want to interact with government and discuss all important (local) public affairs?. Prior research has demonstrated that citizens wish to participate in public affairs [94] but their participation depends on the different conceptions of democracy they have [95], on the need to perceive advantages (cost savings, less time to contact with government, etc.) for their e-participation [96] and on the organizational capacity of the government to be transparent and innovative [97]. Also, recent research has demonstrated that the information quality characteristics, i.e., accuracy and completeness, and the channel characteristics, i.e., convenience and personalization, have also significant effects on citizens' intentions to use e-government [98]. Thus, the improvement of the government capacity and the existence of educational programs to "create" good citizens could be key aspects to foster a higher participation of citizens in public affairs [99]. Educating for democratic citizenship is possible but educational choices we make have consequences for the kind of society we ultimately help to create [99].

In brief, local governments must make greater efforts to improve their relational strategies regarding the use of Web 2.0 technologies in providing public services. These technologies could be good tools for citizen engagement in public policies and in the delivery of public services, but the technology has not yet changed the interactions considerably. In fact, our findings demonstrate that policymakers do not consider them as the main channel for citizen participation. A recent research undertaken by Díaz-Díaz and Pérez-González [100] have found that several elements are required: the determination and involvement of the government, a designated community manager to follow up with the community of users, the secured privacy of its users, and a technological platform that is easy to use. Also, citizens' willingness to participate in public affairs should be built by governments, firstly improving their organizational capacity, second with educational programs to foster deliberative actions and, finally, with the implementation of tools to disclose information for taking informed decisions and for making citizens to perceive advantages about their participation (collective or personal advantages of their participation). The questions are: are there only technical and organisational issues necessary to implement Web 2.0 technologies for citizen participation? Or is it a cultural change needed to include these technologies as a main vehicle for citizen participation in the delivery of public services?. These questions remain without answer and future research should contribute to answer them.

Acknowledgments

This research was carried out with financial support from the Regional Government of Andalusia (Spain), Department of Innovation, Science and Enterprise (Research project number P11-SEJ-7700).

Annex

Table A.1 Design and coproduction of public services with the use of Web 2.0 technologies

Questionnaire	Frequency	Response rate (%)	Median	Mean	Mode	Standard deviation	Maximum	Minimum
1.1. Web 2.0 technologies improve the communication between public administrations and stakeholders, and to better identify the needs of public services	53	37.59	4	3.38	4	1.06	5	1
1.2. Web 2.0 technologies enable the design of well-targeted public services to meet the needs of end users	49	34.75	4	3.71	4	1.08	5	1
1.3. Citizens may participate in the generation of content and information about public services.	53	37.59	3	3.15	4	1.20	5	1
1.4. Web 2.0 technologies foster the effective collaboration between citizens and governments in the delivery of public services	54	38.30	4	3.67	4	0.95	5	1
1.5. Web 2.0 technologies allow the development and promotion of tools and spaces where user can proof new online public services before their general availability	52	36.88	3	2.75	3	1.10	5	1

Table A.2 Ease of access to public services and resolution of problems with the use of Web 2.0 technologies

Questionnaire	Frequency	Response rate (%)	Median	Mean	Mode	Standard deviation	Maximum	Minimum
2.1. Web 2.0 technologies facilitate the access of citizens to all public services	50	35.46	4	3.72	4	0.97	5	1
2.2. Web 2.0 technologies reduce time on obtaining public services	55	39.01	4	3.95	5	1.22	5	1
2.3. Web 2.0 technologies allow the collection of suggestions from citizens regarding public services, which enhances the quality of public services and the information about them	53	37.59	4	3.96	5	1.14	5	1
2.4. The local government opens up a problem or activity for resolution or co-execution by citizens in order to tap into the unique skills, talents, and knowledge of the population	54	38.30	3	3.13	4	1.20	5	1
2.5. Wikis allow the creation of knowledge to solve problems in the delivery of public services	51	36.17	3	3.24	4	1.07	5	1

Table A.3 Evaluation and efficiency of public services with the use of Web 2.0 technologies

Questionnaire	Frequency	Response rate (%)	Median	Mean	Mode	Standard deviation	Maximum	Minimum
3.1. Web 2.0 technologies facilitate citizens to evaluate the efficiency and transparency of public services	47	33.33	4	3.74	4	0.99	5	1
3.2. Web 2.0 technologies offer citizens the means to evaluate the quality of public services	50	35.46	3	3.18	3	1.00	5	1
3.3. Web 2.0 technologies promotes the cut of the costs and the increase of financial resources in the delivery of public services	49	34.75	4	3.61	3	1.15	5	1
3.4. Web 2.0 technologies enable the better allocation of financial resources	48	34.04	4	3.77	4	1.10	5	1
3.5. Governments use Web 2.0 technologies to disclose proactive information with the aim at making transparent the performance achieved by the government to improve its accountability	48	34.04	4	3.92	4	0.85	5	2

References

1. European Commission (2013) Public services online. 'Digital by default or by detour'. Assessing user centric eGovernment performance in Europe–eGovernment Benchmark 2012. http://ec.europa.eu/digital-agenda/sites/digital-agenda/files/eGov%20Benchmark%202012%20insight%20report%20published%20version%200.1%20_0.pdf
2. International Development Association (IDA) (2011) Information and Communication Technology Agency of Sri Lanka (ICTA), vol 3, Colombo, Sri Lanka
3. Peedu G (2011) Enhancing public service user experience in information society. Master Thesis, Tallinn University, Estonia
4. Asgarkhani M (2005) The effectiveness of e-service in local government: a case study. Electron J e-Government 3(4):157–166
5. El-Haddadeh R, Weerakkody V, Al-Shafi S (2013) The complexities of electronic services implementation and institutionalization in the public sector. Inf Manag 50(4):135–143
6. Wagner SA, Vogt S, Kabst R (2016) How IT and social change facilitates public participation: a stakeholder-oriented approach. Gov Inf Q 33(3):435–443
7. Chang AM, Kannan PK (2008) Leveraging Web 2.0 in government. IBM Center for the Business of Government, Washington, DC
8. O'Reilly T (2007) What is Web 2.0: design patterns and business models for the next generation of software. Commun Strateg 65:18–37
9. Rowe G, Frewer L (2005) A typology of public engagement mechanisms. Sci Technol Hum Values 30(2):251–290
10. Johnston E, Hansen D (2011) Design lessons for smart governance infrastructures. In: Ink D, Balutis A, Buss T (eds) American Governance 3.0: Rebooting the public square? National Academy of Public Administration, Washington, DC
11. Huijboom N, Van den Broek T, Frissen V, Kool L, Kotterink B, Nielsen M, Millard J (2009) Public services 2.0: the impact of social computing on public services. Institute for Prospective Technological Studies, Joint Research Centre, European Commission. Office for Official Publications of the European Communities, Luxembourg
12. Tuomi I (2002) Theory of innovation: change and meaning in the age of internet. Oxford University Press, Oxford
13. Hui G, Hayllar R (2010) Creating public value in E-government: a public-private-citizen collaboration framework in Web 2.0. Aust J Public Adm 69(suppl 1):S120–S131
14. Escher T, Margetts H, Petricek V, Cox I (2006) Governing from the centre? Comparing the nodality of digital governments. In: Annual meeting of the American Political Science Association, Philadelphia, PA, 31 Aug–4 Sept 2006
15. Hood C, Margetts H (2007) The tools of government in the digital age. Palgrave, Basingstoke
16. Margetts H, Dunleavy P (2013) The second wave of digital-era governance: a quasi-paradigm for government on the Web. Philos Trans R Soc A:1–17
17. Sandoval-Almazan R, Gil-Garcia J (2012) Are government internet portals evolving towards more interaction, participation, and collaboration? Revisiting the rhetoric of E-government among municipalities. Gov Inf Q 29(suppl 1):S72–S81
18. Berry J, Portney K, Thomson K (1993) The rebirth of urban democracy. Brookings Institution Press, Washington, DC
19. Peters BG (2001) The future of governing. University Press of Kansas, Lawrence
20. Russell CJ, Bobko P (1992) Moderated regression analysis and Likert scales: too coarse for comfort. J Appl Psychol 77(3):336–342
21. Chun S, Shulman S, Sandoval-Almazan R, Hovy E (2010) Government 2.0: marking connections between citizens, data and government. Information Polity 15:1–9
22. Lathrop D, Ruma L (2010) Open government: collaboration, transparency, and participation in practice. O'Reilly, Sebastopol
23. McDermott P (2010) Building open government. Gov Inf Q 27(4):401–413

24. Benkler Y (2006) The wealth of networks: how social production transforms markets and freedom. Yale University Press, New Haven
25. Klein P (2008) Web 2.0: reinventing democracy. CIO Insight Magazine, pp 30–43
26. Deloitte (2008) Change your world or the world will change you. The future of collaborative government and Web 2.0. Deloitte & Touche LLP and affiliated entities, Quebec
27. Taylor JA (2012) The information polity: towards a two speed future? Inf Polity 17(3/4):227–237
28. Accenture (2009) Web 2.0 and the next generation of public service. Driving high performance through more engaging, accountable and citizen-focused service. http://www.majorcities.eu/generaldocuments/pdf/accenture_public_service_web_2_dot_0_in_public_service_3.pdf. Accessed 1 June 2011
29. Nam T (2012) Suggesting frameworks of citizen-sourcing via Government 2.0. Gov Inf Q 29(1):12–20
30. Parent M, Vandebeek CA, Gemino AC (2005) Building citizen trust through e-government. Gov Inf Q 22(4):720–736
31. Tyler TR (2006) Why people obey the law. Princeton University Press, Princeton
32. Ho ATK (2002) Reinventing local governments and the e-government initiative. Public Adm Rev 62(4):434–444
33. Bonham G, Seifert J, Thorson S (2001) The transformational potential of e-government: the role of political leadership. In: Fourth Pan European international relations conference, University of Kent, September 2001
34. Abdelsalam HM, Gamal S, Reddick CG, Saeed S (2013) Web 2.0 applications' use and perception for research collaboration in Egyptian public universities. Int J Services Technol Manag 19(1–3):99–119
35. OECD (2010) Denmark: efficient e-Government for smarter service delivery. OECD Publishing. http://dx.doi.org/10.1787/9789264087118-en
36. Thaler M, Sunstein C (2009) Nudge: improving decisions about health, wealth and happiness. Penguin, London, p 2009
37. Faraz SH, Tanvir SH, Saeed S (2012) A study on privacy and security aspects of Facebook. Int J Technol Diff 3(4):48–55
38. Bertot JC, Jaeger PT, Munson S, Glaisyer T (2010c) Social media technology and government transparency. Computer 43(11):53–59
39. Graells-Costa J (2011) Administración colaborativa y en red. El profesional de la información 20(3):345–347
40. Koppenjan J, Klijn E-H (2004) Managing uncertainties in networks. Routledge, London
41. Meijer A, Thaens M (2010) Alignment 2.0: strategic use of new internet technologies in government. Gov Inf Q 27(2):113–121
42. Welch EW (2012) The rise of participative technologies in government. In: Transformational government through eGov practice: socioeconomic, cultural, and technological issues. Emerald Group Publishing, Bingley, pp 347–367
43. European Commission (2010) The European eGovernment Action Plan 2011–2015. Harnessing ICT to promote smart, sustainable & innovative Government. Communication from the Commission to the European Parliament, the Council, the European Economic and Social Committee and the Committee of the Regions. European Commission, Brussels
44. Queensland State Archives (2010) Recordkeeping and Web 2.0. Survey report. Queensland State Archives, Sunnybank Hills
45. Reggi L, Scicchitano S (2011) European Regions Financing Public e-Services: the Case of EU Structural Funds. Working Papers 1110, University of Urbino Carlo Bo, Rome
46. Redell T, Woolcock G (2004) From consultation to participatory governance? A critical review of citizen engagement strategies in Queensland. Aust J Public Adm 63(3):75–87
47. Leighninger M (2011) Using online tools to engage – and be engaged by – the public. IBM Center for The Business of Government, Washington
48. Hibbing JR, Theiss-Morse E (2002) Stealth democracy: Americans' beliefs about how government should work. Cambridge University Press, Cambridge

49. Oates WE (1972) Fiscal federalism. Harcourt Brace Jovanovich, New York
50. Briggs XS (2008) Democracy as problem solving: civic capacity in communities across the globe. MIT Press, Cambridge
51. Sirianni C (2009) Investing in democracy: engaging citizens in collaborative governance. Brookings Institution Press, Washington, DC
52. Ter Bogt HJ, Van Helden GJ (2000) Management control and performance measurement in Dutch local government. Manag Account Res 11(2):263–279
53. Moon MJ (2002) The evolution of e-government among municipalities: rhetoric or reality? Public Adm Rev 62(4):424–433
54. Torres L, Pina V, Acerete B (2005) Gauging E-government evolution in EU municipalities. J Syst Cybern Inf 3(6):43–54
55. Gallego R, Barzelay M (2010) Public management policymaking in Spain: the politics of legislative reform of administrative structure, 1991-1997. Governance 23(2):277–296
56. Bastida FJ, Benito B (2006) Financial reports and decentralization in municipal governments. Int Rev Adm Sci 72(2):223–238
57. Spanish National Statistics Institute (SNSI) (2014) Internet document. http://www.ine.es/inebmenu/mnu_padron.htm. Accessed 1 June 2014
58. Roscoe JT (1975) Fundamental research statistics for the behavioural sciences, 2nd edn. Holt, Rinehart and Winston, New York
59. Fusch PI, Ness LR (2015) Are we there yet? Data saturation in qualitative research. Qual Rep 20(9):1408
60. Mason M (2010) Sample size and saturation in PhD studies using qualitative interviews. Forum Qual Soc Res 11(3)
61. Bernard HR (2012) Social research methods: qualitative and quantitative approaches. Sage, Thousand Oaks
62. Scupola A, Zanfei A (2016) Governance and innovation in public sector services: the case of the digital library. Gov Inf Q 33(2):237–249
63. Collison D, Lorraine N, Power D (2003) An exploration of corporate attitudes to the significance of environmental information for stakeholders. Corp Soc Responsib Environ Manag 19(4):199–211
64. Hodge DR, Gillespie D (2003) Phrase completions: an alternative to Likert scales. Soc Work Res 27(1):45–55
65. Matell MS, Jacoby J (1971) Is there an optimal number of alternatives for Likert Scale Items? Study I: reliability and validity. Educ Psychol Meas 31(3):657–674
66. Norman G (2010) Likert scales, levels of measurement and the "laws" of statistics. Adv Health Sci Educ 15(5):625–632
67. Wakita T, Ueshima N, Noguchi H (2012) Psychological distance between categories in the Likert scale comparing different numbers of options. Educ Psychol Meas 72(4):533–546
68. Bertram D (2007) Likert scales. Department of Computer Science, University of Calgary. http://poincare.matf.bg.ac.rs/~kristina/topic-dane-likert.pdf. Accessed 28 June 2014
69. Osimo D (2008) Web 2.0 in government: why? and how? Institute for Prospective Technological Studies, Joint Research Centre, European Commission. Office for Official Publications of the European Communities, Luxembourg
70. Irvin RA, Stansbury J (2004) Citizen participation in decision making: is it worth the effort? Public Adm Rev 64(1):55–65
71. Moynihan DP (2003) Normative and instrumental perspectives on public participation citizen summits in Washington, DC. Am Rev Public Adm 33(2):164–188
72. Bowden A (2005) Knowledge for free? Distributed innovation as a source of learning. Public Policy Adm 20(3):56–68
73. Carter L, Bélanger F (2005) The utilization of e-government services: citizen trust, innovation and acceptance factors. Inf Syst J 15(1):5–25
74. Brabham DC (2013) The four urban governance problem types suitable for crowdsourcing citizen participation. Citizen E-participation in urban governance: crowdsourcing and collaborative. Creativity, pp 50–68

75. Porumbescu GA (2016) Linking public sector social media and e-government website use to trust in government. Gov Inf Q 33(2):291–304
76. Sumra KB, Bing W (2016) Crowdsourcing in local public administration: importance of online platforms. Int J Public Adm Digital Age 3(4):28–42
77. Mergel I (2013) Social media adoption and resulting tactics in the U.S. Federal Government. Gov Inf Q 30(2):123–130
78. Rodríguez Bolívar MP (2015) Governance models for the delivery of public services through the Web 2.0 technologies a political view in large Spanish Municipalities. Soc Sci Comput Rev 35(2):203–225
79. European Union (2013) European public sector innovation scoreboard 2013. A pilot exercise. European Union, Belgium
80. Benington J, Hartley J (2001) Pilots, paradigms and paradoxes: changes in public sector governance and management in the UK. In: International research symposium on public sector management, Barcelona
81. Cordella A, Tempini N (2015) E-government and organizational change: reappraising the role of ICT and bureaucracy in public service delivery. Gov Inf Q 32(3):279–286
82. Reddick C, Chatfield AT, Brajawidagda U (2017) Increasing policy success through the use of social media cross-channels for citizen political engagement. In: Proceedings of the 50th Hawaii international conference on system sciences, Jan 2017
83. Linders D (2012) From e-government to we-government: defining a typology for citizen coproduction in the age of social media. Gov Inf Q 29(4):446–454
84. Rodríguez Bolívar MP (2016) Characterizing the role of governments in smart cities: a literature review. In: Smarter as the new urban agenda. Springer, New York, pp 49–71
85. Freeman J (2016) Digital civic participation in Australian local governments: everyday practices and opportunities for engagement. In: Social media and local governments. Springer, New York, pp 195–218
86. Albino V, Berardi U, Dangelico RM (2015) Smart cities: definitions, dimensions, performance, and initiatives. J Urban Technol 22(1):3–21
87. Degbelo A, Granell C, Trilles S, Bhattacharya D, Casteleyn S, Kray C (2016) Opening up smart cities: citizen-centric challenges and opportunities from GIScience. ISPRS Int J Geoinf 5(2):16
88. Sharif MHM, Troshani I, Davidson R (2016) Determinants of social media impact in local government. J Org End User Comput 28(3):82–103
89. Bertot JC, Jaeger PT, Hansen D (2012) The impact of polices on government social media usage: Issues, challenges, and recommendations. Gov Inf Q 29(1):30–40
90. Picazo-Vela S, Gutiérrez-Martínez I, Luna-Reyes LF (2012) Understanding risks, benefits, and strategic alternatives of social media applications in the public sector. Gov Inf Q 29(4):504–511
91. Brainard LA, Derrick-Mills T (2011) Electronic commons, community policing, and communication. Adm Theory Praxis 33(3):383–410
92. Meijer AJ, Koops BJ, Pieterson W, Overman S, Tije S (2012) Government 2.0: key challenges to its realization. Electron J e-Government 10(1):59–69
93. Edelenbos J, Klijn EH, Steijn B (2011) Managers in governance networks: how to reach good outcomes? Int Public Manag J 14(4):420–444
94. Neblo MA, Esterling KM, Kennedy RP, Lazer DM, Sokhey AE (2010) Who wants to deliberateand why? Am Polit Sci Rev 104(03):566–583
95. Bengtsson Å, Christensen H (2016) Ideals and actions: do citizens' patterns of political participation correspond to their conceptions of democracy? Gov Oppos 51(02):234–260
96. Zheng Y, Schachter HL (2016) Explaining citizens' E-participation use: the role of perceived advantages. Public Org Rev 1–20. https://link.springer.com/article/10.1007/s11115-016-0346-2
97. Grimmelikhuijsen SG, Feeney MK (2016) Developing and testing an integrative framework for open government adoption in local governments. Public Administration Review. http://onlinelibrary.wiley.com/doi/10.1111/puar.12689/abstract

98. Venkatesh V, Thong JY, Chan FK, Hu PJ (2016) Managing citizens' uncertainty in E-government services: the mediating and moderating roles of transparency and trust. Inf Syst Res 27(1):87–111

99. Westheimer J, Kahne J (2004) Educating the "good" citizen: political choices and pedagogical goals. Pol Sci Politics 37(02):241–247

100. Díaz-Díaz R, Pérez-González D (2016) Implementation of social media concepts for e-Government: case study of a social media tool for value co-creation and citizen participation. J Org End User Computing 28(3):104–121

Part III
User Centric E-Government

Chapter 9
Towards User Centric E-Government

Madeeha Saqib and Asiya Abdus Salam

Abstract Governmental organizations play an important role in any society to offer services to their citizens. Digital media has transformed the conventional government administration into e-government. However, the successful adoption to e-government systems by citizens is still a bigger challenge. User centered design approach focuses on involving citizens in the design of e-government systems. In this chapter, we re-emphasize the need for user centric e-government to motivate e-government researchers to use this approach in the design of e-government systems for better user acceptance.

Keywords E-Government • User centred design • User centric e-government

1 Introduction

Technology has transformed operations of modern day work environments more efficient and effective. E-government is broadly defined as use of technology in delivering governmental services by any governmental organization [cf. 1–3]. The success of e-government systems is dependent on appropriate technological systems provided by governments and citizens' acceptance of these systems. The governments operations are not uniform globally and same is the case with the skills of citizens, which makes designing e-government systems very specific in each organizational setting. It has been observed that many e-government projects fail since they are not appropriated according to the needs and skills of end users. To enhance the acceptance of e-government systems, users' work practices need to be analyzed deeply and e-government systems need to take these work practices into consideration during system design. Recent emergence of social media has also opened new avenues for e-government [cf. 4–8]. Social media not only brings

M. Saqib (✉)
Abasyn University, Islamabad, Pakistan
e-mail: madeeha.saqib@gmail.com

A. Abdus Salam
Imam Abdur Rahman Bin Faisal University, Dammam, Saudi Arabia

S. Saeed et al. (eds.), *User Centric E-Government*, Integrated Series in Information Systems 39, DOI 10.1007/978-3-319-59442-2_9

161

in more transparency in societies but also provides citizens an opportunity to participate effectively in policy making [cf. 9–13]. In this chapter, we discuss user centred e-government approach and emphasize e-government researchers to use this in their system design approaches.

2   User Centric E-Government

User centered design is a specialized design approach where end users play an active role in the design process of software artifacts [cf. 14, 15]. The shell of user centric system design approach is involving the end users in the system design to take human factors into account to increase the technology acceptance [cf. 2, 16]. The user centered design has different emerging themes such as participatory design, usability engineering and interaction design. E-government systems need to adopt user centric methodologies in the development process to involve end users [cf. 17, 18]. E-government adoption is not uniform among all the governments and the implications of designing e-government systems become more evident especially in the developing countries where the impact of digital divide is more evident. Khan et al. identified the challenges for developing countries in fostering user centric e-government infrastructures and conclude that technical skills are not the core skills required by end users to effectively use e-government systems [19].

Along with the involvement of users in design process, usability evaluation is also an important concept in human computer interaction domain. Usability can be defined as the degree of easiness in effective interaction among users and computer systems [cf. 20–23]. Wang et al. believe that core determinant of success of e-government system is based on easy information access by end users and they present a model to evaluate the e-government websites to understand the reasons of success or failure of users in locating desired information [24]. Usable e-government systems enable users to carry out their tasks efficiently. Donker-Kuijer et al. has presented heuristics for e-government web applications, which will enable developers to quickly evaluate the usability of their e-government systems [25]. There have been similar research projects to evaluate usability of e-government systems in different geographical regions e.g. in United Kingdom [cf. 26–29], Spain [cf. 30], Romania [cf. 31], Hungary [cf. 32], Korea [cf. 33], Saudi Arabia [cf. 1, 34, 35], Pakistan [cf. 36–38] and so forth. These research projects advocate for more rigorous usability studies of e-government systems to better design such systems in future.

Another challenge faced by e-government systems is to include every citizen rather than excluding who have hindrances in using technological systems to formulate an inclusive society [cf. 20, 39, 40]. The concept of universal access in usability engineering advocates for designing usable systems providing equal accessibility irrespective of age, gender, skills, and physical abilities of end users. Huang presented different recommendations to make e-government websites accessible for disable users based on his empirical research on Taiwan's center government website [41]. Jaeger has investigated the federal e-government websites in US to identify the accessibility of disable citizens and provide recommendation for better accessibility [42].

3   Conclusion

Despite these contributions, there is a need to enrich the body of knowledge to document best practices and more case studies on involving users in design of e-government systems. With the emergence of web 3.0 applications the need to tailor e-government systems as per user needs has become more evident [cf. 43, 44]. Despite the e-government adoption by different governments, there is a need for more rigorous measures to enhance the performance of e-government infrastructures [45–47]. Tcheir et al. believe that despite the adoption of e-government systems the service quality for citizens has not improved [48]. It is very important to measure the effectiveness of e-government systems for continuous improvement of service delivery to citizens. Alanezi et al., propose that quality of e-government can be measured by seven key factors which are website design, reliability, responsiveness, security/privacy, personalization, information, and ease of use [49]. The involvement of users in design process can improve the performance of e-government delivery due to better alignment of e-government systems and work practices of citizens.

References

1. Al-Khalifa HS (2010) Heuristic evaluation of the usability of e-Government websites: a case from Saudi Arabia. In: Proceedings of the fourth international conference on theory and practice of electronic governance. ACM, pp 238–242
2. Bertot JC, Jaeger PT, McClure CR (2008) Citizen-centered e-government services: benefits, costs, and research needs. In: Proceedings of the 2008 international conference on digital government research. Digital Government Society of North America, pp 137–142
3. Golden W, Hughes M, Scott M (2003) The role of process evolution in achieving citizen centered e-government. In: AMCIS 2003 Proceedings, p 100
4. Bonsón E, Royo S, Ratkai M (2015) Citizens' engagement on local governments' Facebook sites. An empirical analysis: the impact of different media and content types in Western Europe. Gov Inf Q 32(1):52–62
5. Hong S, Kim SH (2016) Political polarization on twitter: implications for the use of social media in digital governments. Gov Inf Q 33(4):777–782
6. Kavanaugh AL, Fox EA, Sheetz SD, Yang S, Li LT, Shoemaker DJ, Xie L (2012) Social media use by government: from the routine to the critical. Gov Inf Q 29(4):480–491
7. Oliveira GHM, Welch EW (2013) Social media use in local government: linkage of technology, task, and organizational context. Gov Inf Q 30(4):397–405
8. Wei J, Xu J, Zhao D (2015) Public engagement with firms on social media in China. J Inf Sci 41(5):624–639

9. Bertot JC, Jaeger PT, Grimes JM (2010) Using ICTs to create a culture of transparency: E-government and social media as openness and anti-corruption tools for societies. Gov Inf Q 27(3):264–271
10. Gandía JL, Marrahí L, Huguet D (2016) Digital transparency and Web 2.0 in Spanish city councils. Gov Inf Q 33(1):28–39
11. Linders D (2012) From e-government to we-government: defining a typology for citizen coproduction in the age of social media. Gov Inf Q 29(4):446–454
12. Porumbescu GA (2016) Comparing the effects of e-government and social media use on trust in government: evidence from Seoul, South Korea. Public Manage Rev 18(9):1308–1334
13. Stamati T, Papadopoulos T, Anagnostopoulos D (2015) Social media for openness and accountability in the public sector: cases in the Greek context. Gov Inf Q 32(1):12–29
14. Abras C, Maloney-Krichmar D, Preece J (2004) User-centered design. In: Bainbridge W (ed) Encyclopedia of human-computer interaction. Sage, Thousand Oaks 37(4): 445–456
15. Saeed S, Bamarouf YA, Ramayah T, Iqbal SZ (2017) Design solutions for user-centric information systems. IGI Global, Hershey
16. Saeed S, Bajwa IS, Mahmood Z (2015) Human factors in software development and design. Springer, Cham
17. Saeed S, Reddick CG (2013) Human-centered system design for electronic governance. IGI Global, Hershey
18. Verdegem P, Verleye G (2009) User-centered E-Government in practice: a comprehensive model for measuring user satisfaction. Gov Inf Q 26(3):487–497
19. Khan GF, Moon J, Rhee C, Rho JJ (2010) E-government skills identification and development: toward a staged-based user-centric approach for developing countries. Asia Pacific. J Inf Syst 20(1):1–31
20. Becker SA (2005) E-government usability for older adults. Commun ACM 48(2):102–104
21. Chou JR, Hsiao SW (2007) A usability study on human–computer interface for middle-aged learners. Comput Hum Behav 23(4):2040–2063
22. Fernandez A, Insfran E, Abrahão S (2011) Usability evaluation methods for the web: a systematic mapping study. Inf Softw Technol 53(8):789–817
23. Nielsen J (1994) Usability engineering. Elsevier, New York
24. Wang L, Bretschneider S, Gant J (2005) Evaluating web-based e-government services with a citizen-centric approach. In: HICSS'05. Proceedings of the 38th annual Hawaii International Conference on IEEE System Sciences, Jan 2005, pp 129b
25. Donker-Kuijer MW, de Jong M, Lentz L (2010) Usable guidelines for usable websites? An analysis of five e-government heuristics. Gov Inf Q 27(3):254–263
26. Barnes SJ, Vidgen R (2004) Interactive e-government: evaluating the web site of the UK Inland Revenue. J Electron Commerce Org 2(1):42–63
27. Kuzma JM (2010) Accessibility design issues with UK e-government sites. Gov Inf Q 27(2):141–146
28. Ma HYT, Zaphiris P (2003) The usability and content accessibility of the e-government in the UK. In: Proceedings of human computer interaction international conference, Greece
29. Soufi B, Maguire M (2007) Achieving usability within e-government web sites illustrated by a case study evaluation. In: Symposium on human interface and the management of information. Springer, Berlin, July 2007, pp 777–784
30. Criado JI, Carmen Ramilo M (2003) E-government in practice: an analysis of web site orientation to the citizens in Spanish municipalities. Int J Public Sector Manage 16(3):191–218
31. Colesca SE, Dobrica L (2008) Adoption and use of e-government services: the case of Romania. J Appl Res Technol 6(3):204–217
32. Szeróvay K (2011) Usability of e-Government websites, evaluation of the Hungarian e-Government portal. In Proceedings of COFOLA 2011
33. Lee S, Kim BG, Kim JG (2007, July) Accessibility evaluation of Korean e-government. In: International conference on universal access in human-computer interaction. Springer, Berlin, pp 73–78

34. Abanumy A, Al-Badi A, Mayhew P (2005) e-Government Website accessibility: in-depth evaluation of Saudi Arabia and Oman. Electron J e-Gov 3(3):99–106
35. Al-Nuaim H (2011) An evaluation framework for Saudi e-government. J e-Gov Stud Best Pract 2011:1–12
36. Saeed S, Malik IA, Wahab F (2013) Usability evaluation of Pakistani security agencies websites. Int J E-Politics 4(3):57–69
37. Saeed S, Shabbir S (2014) Website usability analysis of non profit organizations: a case study of Pakistan. Int J Public Adm Digit Age 1(4):70–83
38. Saeed S, Wahab F, Cheema SA, Ashraf S (2013) Role of usability in e-government and e-commerce portals: an empirical study of Pakistan. Life Sci J 10(1):8–13
39. Johnson R, Kent S (2007) Designing universal access: web-applications for the elderly and disabled. Cogn Technol Work 9(4):209–218
40. Phang CW, Li Y, Sutanto J, Kankanhalli A (2005) Senior citizens' adoption of e-government: In quest of the antecedents of perceived usefulness. In: HICSS'05. Proceedings of the 38th annual Hawaii international conference on IEEE System sciences, Jan 2005, pp 130a
41. Huang CJ (2003) Usability of e-government web-sites for people with disabilities. In: Proceedings of the 36th annual Hawaii international conference on IEEE system sciences, 2003
42. Jaeger PT (2006) Assessing Section 508 compliance on federal e-government Web sites: a multi-method, user-centered evaluation of accessibility for persons with disabilities. Gov Inf Q 23(2):169–190
43. Baker DL (2009) Advancing e-government performance in the United States through enhanced usability benchmarks. Gov Inf Q 26(1):82–88
44. Hendler J (2009) Web 3.0 emerging. Computer 42(1):111–113
45. Choudrie J, Ghinea G, Weerakkody V (2004) Evaluating global e-government sites: a view using web diagnostics tools. Academic Conferences International
46. Sigwejo AO (2015) Evaluating e-government services: a citizen-centric framework. Doctoral dissertation, Cape Peninisula University of Technology
47. Sigwejo A, Pather S (2016) A citizen-centric framework for assessing e-government effectiveness. Electron J Inf Syst Dev Countries 74
48. Teicher J, Hughes O, Dow N (2002) E-government: a new route to public sector quality. Manag Serv Qual 12(6):384–393
49. Alanezi MA, Kamil A, Basri S (2010) A proposed instrument dimensions for measuring e-government service quality. Int J u-and e-Service Sci Technol 3(4):1–18

Chapter 10
Enacting Digital Government Services for Noncitizens: The Case of Migration Services

Luz Maria Garcia-Garcia and J. Ramon Gil-Garcia

Abstract Historically, e-government approaches have focused on citizens as the most important audience for government information and services. This focus is appropriate for most traditional public services. However, a large number of service users are noncitizens, including, for example, people applying for immigration services. Theoretically and practically, there are interesting differences between government services targeted to citizens and migration services. Some of these differences are due largely to the rules and laws that apply in each case, but there are also differences related to the fact that the majority of users of migration services are not citizens and they are very diverse in many respects. For instance, in the case of noncitizens the audience and their needs can be as broad as their different nationalities and different contexts they reside in. This chapter identifies and explains some of these differences and also a few similarities. It considers the variables from Fountain's technology enactment framework and includes some additional environmental conditions based on a previous extension of that initial model, applying them to the case of immigration services for border workers in the south of Mexico. Based on this analysis, this chapter suggests a preliminary reinterpretation of the technology enactment framework and highlights the differences between e-government services for citizens and for noncitizens, in order to propose a discussion about a group of users that has not been thoroughly analyzed in the literature, but which is important for scholars and practitioners to consider.

Keywords Digital government • Noncitizens • Migration services • Migration management • Border workers • Mexico • Web portal

L.M. Garcia-Garcia (✉)
Universidad de la Sierra Sur, Guillermo Rojas Mijangos S/N, Cd. Universitaria, Miahuatlán de Porfirio Díaz, Oaxaca, Mexico
e-mail: luz2g@yahoo.com.mx

J.R. Gil-Garcia
University at Albany, State University of New York, Albany, NY, USA

© Springer International Publishing AG 2018   167
S. Saeed et al. (eds.), *User Centric E-Government*, Integrated Series in Information Systems 39, DOI 10.1007/978-3-319-59442-2_10

1 Introduction

The terms *citizen-centered* and *user-centered* e-government have been used synonymously in the literature to refer to the user orientation of e-government projects. In fact the two terms are often used interchangeably in articles, which might refer to citizen-centered e-government in their titles, but they use the terms users and citizens interchangeably in the actual content of the articles [1]. However, in this work, we want to emphasize the difference between users and citizens. A user can be any individual or group, but the term citizen implies a specific political status. A citizen is a subject with rights and obligations, while a user can be a citizen of the nation that offers the service or may be a citizen of another country. We argue that these differences are important in conceptualizing e-government and its successful implementation.

In addition, it seems that there is more e-government literature related to citizens. To illustrate this, the theory that defines e-government considers the relationship between government and citizens. One approach defines e-government as the interactions with several stakeholders: government to citizens (G2C), government to business enterprises (G2B), government to government (G2G), and some scholars even talk about government to employees (G2E) [2]. Most of the time, e-government theories focus on government services that are aimed at citizens, not to more general users, such as individuals from foreign nations.

It is often assumed that e-government is only for citizens, with little attention to e-government services that are provided to individuals from other countries. This discussion becomes more relevant when e-government is implemented in government agencies that do work specifically for domestic and foreign users, such as migration services. Foreigners are not within the category of citizens; therefore, we should consider e-government for noncitizens as an important, distinct phenomenon. This term could create confusion though, as immigrants are not citizens in the host country, but they are citizens in their country of origin. There is likely to be a debate about how to label the target audience for e-government services: citizens, noncitizens, or the more inclusive term of users. The contribution of this book chapter to the literature, however, is to start a discussion about citizenship as a defining feature of e-government and to consider the relationship between e-government and immigration services, since this subject has clearly been underdeveloped.

Based on the technology enactment framework [3] and including some environmental conditions based on a previous extension to that initial model [4], this chapter reviews the technology enactment framework and reinterprets this model in relation to services for noncitizens. This reinterpretation aims to be a methodological and theoretical tool for the study of e-government initiatives, not only for citizens, but also noncitizens. The model will be illustrated using the case of immigration services in the south of Mexico [5] and will include descriptions of the following variables and their interrelationships: (1) organizational structures and processes, (2) institutional arrangements, (3) enacted technology, (4) results, and (5) environmental conditions [4].

2 The Technology Enactment Framework

The technology enactment framework [3] explains how a given technology is implemented within a government agency. Broadly speaking, technology enactment is understood as the perception, design, implementation, and use that organizations and individual users give to technology.

The technology enactment framework is based on institutional theory, as technology is adapted from institutional arrangements maintained by organizations. That is why technology enactment varies according to the different organizational factors and institutional arrangements in each organization. The technology enactment framework features a socio-technical approach, as neither technology nor its implementation within an organization is previously determined, but rather the actors decide how to incorporate it according to traditional ways of behaving. The technology enactment framework uses institutionalism to explain the impact that formal and informal institutions have on the adoption of information technologies [3, 6, 7]. The technology enactment framework consists of five constructs: institutional arrangements, organizational forms and structures, objective information technologies, enacted technology, and outcomes.

In the case of institutional arrangements, institutions are understood as constraints on choice and they frame how those constraints operate during technology adoption. Fountain [3] describes how, in the process of technology incorporation, the actors implement the new information and communication technologies (ICT) in ways that reproduce, strengthen, and institutionalize socio-structural mechanisms, even when such implementations lead to irrational and suboptimal use of technology. The actors enact technology by trying to follow the traditional networks, routines, frames, and patterns within the organization.

A different way to operationalize Fountain's institutional arrangements [3] is to classify them in three groups. The first one is formal institutions such as laws and regulations, budgetary processes, and government agencies' autonomy. The second group relates to culture, the value system, and informal institutions. Finally, the third group are the macro institutional arrangements, such as the institutional relationship between government and the IT industry or international governmental agreements [7].

Another construct is the organizational forms and structures, including bureaucracy in the form of hierarchy, communication methods, rules, and interorganizational networks. The most frequent organizational variables in scholarly analyses are organizational structure (organization's size, hierarchical structure, centralized or decentralized authority allocations), human resources, marketing, financial resources, feedback mechanisms, and technological infrastructure.

According to Fountain, there are two ways of conceiving technology—objective and subjective. Objective technology refers to technology as it is conceived: hardware, software, internet, and telecommunications. Whereas subjective technology is the actual use of that technology by individuals, without taking into consideration whether the technology's capacity is fully realized.

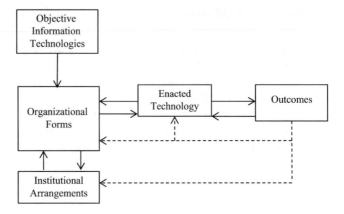

Fig. 10.1 Technology enactment framework (adopted from [3])

Enacted technology is the perception, design, and use of objective technologies. The new information technologies are enacted, one finds the meaning of them, and they are designed and used through existent organizational and institutional arrangements, with their own logics and internal trends. These multiple logics are inserted in operational routines, performance programs, bureaucratic policies, regulations, cultural beliefs, and social networks, as shown in Fig. 10.1.

A great deal of technology used in e-government services is provided through a website that users can access; in that sense, the enacted technology includes the website's technical specifications, which are usability, functionality, and accessibility. The three approaches are seen as key factors to user-centered e-government evaluations [8]. Usability is whether users can easily access and navigate the website [9–11]. Accessibility has to do with the website's universal access, particularly for those with visual, auditory, and/or motor disabilities [8, 12–16]. It also considers potential social inequalities, including language proficiency [17] or even material limitations such as access to the internet, hardware, and software. Finally, the outcomes of technology enactment, according to Fountain [3], are unpredictable and variable. Therefore, the effect of ICTs on the government will be profoundly influenced by local organizational, political, and institutional logics in often unexpected ways. For outcomes in the government context, accountability, transparency, cost reduction, time reduction, and enhancement of services are all considered in the government-citizen relationship.

In addition to Fountain's original constructs, scholars have added environmental conditions as a theoretical construct of technology enactment, which has been applied in other models [4]. In the case under discussion in this chapter, the environment is fundamental to understanding the user conditions when interacting with e-government, and we examine some of the case's broader economic, political, and social factors. Economic factors are one of the most influential forces for enhancing e-government use. In developing countries, an e-government project's success is related to that country's economic status, because it is directly related to the government budget, but also because many people do not have access to Internet and, therefore, cannot use online services easily. In fact, the spread of the internet, e-commerce, and e-government are significantly influenced by the availability of wealth, measured by GDP per capita in a country or region [18]. Consequently, countries with more financial resources have larger programs for e-government website services.

Political factors are also crucial for the success of information systems [19, 20]. Bolgherini [21] argues that political and administrative traditions play an important role in e-government, pointing out that only when an e-government policy has political support will it also have a good chance of success. Therefore, e-government policy must be part of a larger, more politically-centered project with a long-term goal. Political factors include the political party of the elected leaders, citizens' political orientation, and the percentage of votes for each party in recent elections. Talking about social factors, these are useful to understand the context and conditions surrounding the user, which influence whether the user has the skills and capacities to use the information as presented on government websites. The concept of the digital divide considers gaps in individual skills for digital literacy, the resources available to individuals (computers and internet access), and the potential impact of socio-demographic characteristics: gender, age, level of education, and income [22–26].

The technology enactment framework offers an explanation about technology adoption and use within government and the possible outcomes. In Fountain's approach [3], the user's perspective is not included explicitly and is separate from the organizational perspective. This chapter, however, focuses on the user, including noncitizens, in the case of migration services for border workers in the south of Mexico.

3 Context: Migration of Border Workers in the South of Mexico

In Mexico, the phenomenon of migration consists of emigrants, immigrants, and transmigrants. In this case, we are interested in the documented immigrants who come from Guatemala and cross the southern Mexican border in order to work, which requires them to have a relationship with the Mexican government. These workers cross the border in order to harvest coffee in one of the poorest regions of Mexico. Most of these workers are men, mainly between 20 and 34 years old, some of them speak an indigenous language, some are illiterate, and the majority have only completed 6 years of school at best. It is with this backdrop that this chapter presents the delivery of electronic services for noncitizens from divided social conditions.

Mexico's southern border is 1149 km long and sits next to Guatemala and Belize. It is not physically visible like the US-Mexico border in the north, but there are natural borders, like the Suchiate River, separating Mexico and its neighbours.

As a result, the border is extremely porous as it lacks the natural infrastructure and authorities to patrol it. In addition to formal border crossing points, there are hundreds of informal pedestrian and vehicle crossings, in addition to the frequent raft crossings on the Suchiate. This border was historically disputed by Mexico and Guatemala at the end of the nineteenth Century, particularly the Soconusco region in Chiapas. Finally, the two countries signed a deal in 1882 declaring this border belonged to Mexico [27, 28]. From then on, the dynamic there is one of a cross-border region with important commercial exchanges and population movements, mainly due to Guatemalan workers crossing for employment in the agricultural sector of the border state of Chiapas. The Guatemalans have crossed the border to work in the coffee states since the end of the nineteenth Century, although Mexican authorities did not track migration flows at that time [29].

Migration to Mexico changed in the 1980s. Due to armed conflicts in Central America, greater numbers of migrants came to Mexico from that area; migration ceased being solely for labor and switched to refugee migration. The Mexican Commission for Refugee Aid (COMAR) was created in 1980 and it began to operate in the border state of Chiapas to manage Guatemalan refugee flows. The large refugee population made it necessary to register these Central American citizens and to somehow legalize their stay in Mexico.

At the end of the 1990s, a series of reforms in migration management at the southern border of Mexico began to record foreigners seeking work or engaging in other lawful activities (visiting their relatives, going shopping) at the border. The first record of agricultural workers was done through a collective list that employers presented, which included the names of the agricultural workers who would be hired. In 1993, the National Institute of Migration (INM) was created, which is a technical body dependent on the Secretary of the Interior and which implements the secretary's migration policy. In 1997, the Institute set about registering all Guatemalan workers individually by means of the Agricultural Visitor Immigration Form (FMVA), which was a paper document. It included some restrictions—they could only have a job in Chiapas, exclusively in the agricultural sector—and it was only given to Guatemalans. This immigration form was valid from 1997 to 2008.

Migration management in the southern border received greater attention from the Mexican government during the 2000–2006 presidential administration, particularly in 2005 when new plans were created to discuss migration policy in the south of the country [30]. The newly proposed plans would include legal, procedural, and technical changes that would take into account the unique context of the Mexican southern border. In addition to updating immigration laws and increasing border security, the plans called for an upgrade to the migration services infrastructure to modernize and automate entry and exit at the border. A new information system, the Integral System of Migratory Operation (SIOM), was designed to be used in all southern border states and included capabilities for migration flow tracking, issuance of temporary work visas, and identity verification. These technical improvements were accompanied by updates to the documentation required for border crossings.

In 2008, the Border Worker Visitor Card (TVTF) was created, which had an ID format and expanded the employment categories from the agricultural field to other areas, such as construction and hospitality services. In addition, workers were now allowed in the states of Chiapas, Tabasco, Campeche, and Quintana Roo. The TVTF is valid for 1 year and workers can come in and out of the country whenever they wish [31]. To obtain a TVTF, Guatemalan workers must present a written job offer signed by the employer, three photos of themselves, and have paid the fee (approximately US$18). The Guatemalan workers must go to any of the seven points of entry at the southern border, a migration officer checks their documents and interviews them, and after that the officer checks the SIOM and submits the resolution. If approved, the worker's biometric data is registered: fingerprints, iris, signature, and digital photo. Finally, they are given the Border Worker Visitor Card.

Beginning in October 2009, revisions were made to the migration process and the INM developed a new information system: the Electronic System for Migration Processes (or SETRAM). In 2010, not only were there important reforms in regulation, but also greater ICT adoption in order to improve the tracking of migration flows. The principal administrative reform was the publication of the Manual of Criteria and Migration Procedures in which INM issued newer and simpler immigration forms, as well as an electronic application procedure. Among the technical aspects this modernization implemented were updates to computer equipment, the SIOM re-engineering (including revisions to the "Central Biometric Engine" that scans and stores workers' irises, fingerprints, and photos), and the creation of SETRAM's biometric identification technology that allows INM to verify the identity of individuals regardless of whether they are carrying paper documentation.

Part of the INM's procedures to complete immigrant workers' documentation is the use of the information systems SIOM and SETRAM. The use of these information systems for document processing is important because of the number of people who are granted this working visa. From 2008 to 2014, an average of 23,734 Guatemalans received a TVTF each year. However, from the user's perspective, migration management and the information systems only provide them with information. The actual process to obtain the Border Worker Visitor Card has to be done in person.

Life in the cross-border region between Mexico and Guatemala has a long history in which the citizens of these two nations had family and other relationships even before their borders were defined and the region was divided into two countries. In spite of the establishment of a legal border, the economic dynamic in that area has continued to function, but the conditions of interaction have become more complex as time passes and have been accompanied by a rise in problems such as crime and violence.

One of the resources Guatemalan border citizens have had is that they can work in the Soconusco region between Mexico and Guatemala. This access to workers has helped companies in the region, mainly the coffee industry, as they require a cheap labor force. Since the entry of Guatemalan workers has long been part of the economy of the region, and it has contributed to both countries' economic stability, it justifies the existence of this complex migration process. These workers' registration and documentation allows them to exercise their working rights and legally secure their stay in Mexico. In a case like this one, noncitizens are important stakeholders who require quality government services that are easy to access and ensure their personal safety.

4 An Application and Preliminary Reinterpretation of the Technology Enactment Framework for Noncitizens

This work aims to be used as a guide for the electronic administration of migration services, shifting the citizen-centered approach into the context of noncitizens. There is complexity in immigration services, because when we talk about the "user" as a non-citizen, the possibilities for the potential user's profile are broad and the challenges for personalized attention are major, since the aims of migration can be very diverse: work, tourism, or business. Furthermore, migrants may come from different nations, where local conditions may have an effect on the procedure they follow. For instance, some countries may be experiencing political and social conditions such as armed conflicts, the operation of organized crime, or even terrorism that influence access to migrant services, whereas other countries that are not experiencing these events may have fewer constraints on access. Plus, the profile of the immigrant him- or herself may be very different from that of the citizens. For instance, speaking a different language may pose a challenge since some immigration services websites do not have translation options to universal languages such as English. Another aspect is being comfortable with technology; some users are familiarized with it, whereas others are not. These access barriers represent a relevant problem that can lead to an applicant's misunderstanding of the procedure and slow down the process.

In this case, we selected Fountain's framework [3] and applied it to the migration management approach and services described here, emphasizing the differences and similarities between citizen and non-citizen users (Fig. 10.2). Focusing on this application, we will start by describing what happens with the original constructs of the technology enactment framework, to which we have added the analysis of environmental conditions as a variable.

4.1 Organizational Processes and Structures

In this case, the organizational processes can vary between a citizen and a non-citizen. Within the organizational structure of government, there are areas and positions specifically designed to assist with immigration. In general terms, citizens and noncitizens encounter different organizations within government, thereby leading them to have different experiences of organizational structure and processes.

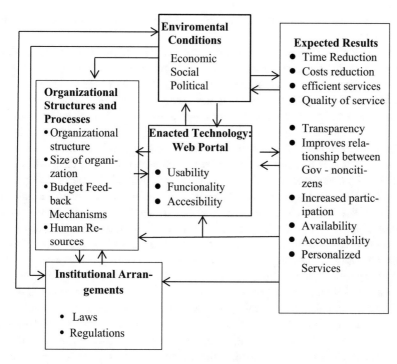

Fig. 10.2 Enacting digital government services for noncitizens

The size of the organization is another variable that may present interesting similarities and differences in terms of its effect on online migration services. It is related to the size of the migration flow, with the number of entry points to the country, and even with the foreigners' mobility. That means that there are borders where the economic and social dynamics cause the need for more facilities and staff, which is similar to other government services. Linked to the size of the organization, there are the human resources that can change, including something as simple as the number of people who work in the migration department. Training can also be different, leading to differences in the staff's understanding of regulations and the need for additional training when a new information system is introduced. The processes that an organization's staff follow may also vary according to each of the migration conditions of the users. In addition, other types of training in foreign languages to communicate with the users or cultural knowledge of other countries are likely necessary.

In the organization there is a specific budget for the activities related to immigration. Apart from this budget, there are external funds coming from other sources, including those from international agreements signed with the purpose of increasing border security or communicating and exchanging information with international security agencies. The ICT budget can therefore come from different sources, not all of them domestic, which is not necessarily the case for other government services.

The feedback mechanisms are understood as the recommendations, suggestions, or comments that the users of the services provide that can then be used to improve service. In the user-centered approach, feedback is a key aspect to achieving success. Feedback mechanisms include satisfaction surveys or any other section of a website that can be used to leave comments or complaints about each of the processes. If these sections do not exist, then the users' perspective is never captured. A user-centered approach assumes that the information systems and websites are designed according to the needs and interests of users. However, it is not clear whether the opinions of citizens and noncitizens will be equally taken into consideration and in the case of migration services there are not clear feedback mechanisms. Finally, not only can citizens provide their opinions about the service, but they could also vote to re-elect the current government—or not. This is not the case for the noncitizens, who do not have voting rights or any other political means to voice their interests, needs, and opinions about government information systems and services.

With regards to marketing, the advertising and diffusion of the migration services for citizens and foreigners may vary. For citizens, there are more communication opportunities thanks to proximity and there is a wide range of resources such as broadcasting, billboards, and adverts in airports and bus or train stations, whereas for foreigners, marketing resources are mostly focused on the internet. ICT infrastructure is no necessarily different for citizens and noncitizens, but the information systems must be adequate for immigration, with certain modules in the system to assist immigration processes or foreigners' arrivals, which goes beyond a web page. For example, technology enables biometric identification (which has become necessary due to the environmental conditions related to border security) and that biometric information is found on identification cards such as visas and work permits. The level of security and identity verification for migration services is high when compare to other government services.

4.2   Institutional Arrangements

Institutional arrangements are understood as laws or regulations and there are important differences between the rules applicable for citizens and noncitizens. In the case of migration management, most of the rules apply to foreigners only. There are laws and norms established for each type of process depending on the conditions of the migrants and their country of origin. Therefore, the rules indicate how to perform procedures, which has also been incorporated into ICTs. There are a series of laws that apply to immigrants. These laws determine how migration management should proceed, from constraints or conditions to enter the country to duration of stays, fees, visas, or other types of permissions. These constraints depend on the immigrants' nationality, reasons for immigrating, length of residence, and many other aspects.

Migration policy is considered as an institutional aspect. It changes according to migration flows and a series of conditions related to the background of an applicant, such as economic, political and social aspects. That is the case of the border in the south of Mexico; the migration policy for some migrant groups was nonexistent until the number of undocumented immigrants was so high that it drew more attention and better recordkeeping began. Ten years later, during another federal administration, efforts were made to create a migration policy for the southern border in the context of a change of government and different social and economic conditions.

At the same time, migration policy modifies organizational processes. The organizational structure, the size of the organization, its resources, and its infrastructure change according to the actions that the government takes around immigration. Since some international agreements are linked to international security, they may also have an effect on the entry policies for immigrants. Therefore, the effect of institutional arrangements on organizational structures and processes also exists for migration services, but some rules vary for different foreigners, even if they are applying for the same service, and there are also some additional rules that need to be carefully considered such as international agreements.

4.3   Enacted Technology

In theory it may seem that technical matters are not closely related to citizenship, however, technology is influenced by the organizational variables and by institutional arrangements, which, at the same time, are influenced by the environmental conditions that will indirectly modify the use of technology. And since technology is placed in an institutional context in which a set of cultural and cognitive elements, values, and rules are related, then when that technology is adopted it will make sense in the place where it is enacted. For those who are outsiders of that institutional context, technology is adopted differently and, therefore, understood differently.

For instance, in the beginning, the technical features of websites could be indistinguishable for citizens and noncitizens. It is likely, however, that some citizens may have an easier time accessing certain services because the technology will be introduced in particular institutional and cultural contexts, and it will be understood inside those contexts. In the case of citizens, a government website, from their perspective, would be easier to navigate and more usable, because they speak the same language and are immersed in the same culture. Use of that site becomes more difficult when users are not native to the country and therefore cannot easily understand what the processes are, taking into account that not all websites have translations and that the cultural context could be very different. Furthermore, the structure of the page can be similar to other governmental pages that citizen users have previously used, making the design and the location of its elements more familiar. While the technical rules of accessibility require websites to meet certain standards, the degree to which accessibility is achieved can vary with the interest and the will of a government organization, regardless of the rules established by the law. The context and social conditions of immigrants are often unknown and can vary widely, as we previously said, making it difficult to adapt the technical elements to that population.

4.4   Results

Results are where we see the largest difference between citizens and noncitizens. In general, the outcomes of government services for citizens can have a series of advantages such as time and cost savings or better communication between government and citizens, among other potential benefits. In contrast, for the noncitizens results are determined by what the legislation states, by the country they come from, and by the constraints related to the specific purpose for migration. One of the main advantages of e-government is time savings. However, in the case of migration services, the differentiated application of rules and the additional security concerns mean that most websites only provide information, but do not allow transactions; therefore, users normally need several face-to-face visits to government offices. Therefore, time and cost savings are not as clear as in other government services designed for citizens.

Another potential benefit of e-government is that it improves the relationship between government and citizens, according to the majority of the literature. In the relationship between government and noncitizens, however, the government has fewer incentives to seek a better or more direct relationship. One of the typical ways to improve the relationship between government and citizens is through participation. However, participation is generally understood as citizens contributing to the improvement of a service or public policy, but this role is not clear for noncitizens and migration services websites rarely have multiple participation mechanisms. Another area in which e-government can provide improvements is in transparency and accountability. In the case of citizens, they have the right to transparency in governmental actions, whereas for noncitizens these rights are not as clear, and sometimes are even invalid, depending on the legal framework of a specific country. The same happens with accountability; it is the government's duty to be held accountable to the citizens, but not necessarily to noncitizens, arguably because they do not pay taxes and do not hold voting rights.

In practice it is easier to create personalized services for citizens rather than for noncitizens. Citizens and companies from the host country usually need the same types of processes and services in relation to migration. These services will be very few for citizens (such as a permit to hire a foreigner in a small business), plus users' profiles are more or less homogeneous (same language, same culture). In general, the relative homogeneity helps to design highly functional websites and information systems for citizens, irrespective of the type of service and the policy domain. It also helps to include more participation and feedback mechanisms that truly reflect a user-centric approach. In contrast, noncitizens have a variety of profiles, with different types of processes, applicable laws and regulations, different cultures, multiple and diverse countries of origin, and different admission conditions.

4.5   Environmental Conditions

With regards to economics, the situation for citizens and foreigners may also vary. Some users come from countries where there are better economic conditions, but others come from countries where the economic conditions are much worse. The economic conditions are aspects that influence most immigrants, positively or negatively. Based on the country of origin, if the economic conditions are unfavorable, it is likely there will be more migration flows. This volume of migration also can lead to greater visibility of those migration flows, which can lead to changes in the dynamics of the approach to migration management and create constraints in the destination country.

On the other hand, the social conditions of noncitizens and citizens of a country may be similar or vastly different. It may be possible that some noncitizens have better opportunities and capabilities for the use of ICTs than the citizens themselves, whereas other foreigners have less capability. In the most developed countries, people will have the opportunity to speak more than one language and greater access to the internet or different technologies, while in underdeveloped countries the opportunities would be more limited. In the case of the border between Mexico and Guatemala, the environmental condition of armed conflict led to a change in the regulations for migration and its associated records. The social conditions of crime and organized crime have also initiated the use of biometric identification. In economic terms, citizens that cross to work in a poor region such as the south of Mexico are likely to be poorer and their distance in the digital divide will be even greater.

5   Conclusions

Migration is omnipresent around the world and it is forecasted that in the future it will increase, from voluntary migrations (work, study, family) to forced migrations (refugees, displacement). That is why it is important to consider migration management as a government task that requires revision and constant adaptation to the environmental conditions and circumstances, including the use of emergent information technologies. Through the case of the border workers in the south of Mexico, we have shown some of the differences between services for citizens and services for noncitizens. Most of the variables of the technology enactment framework were modified or reinterpreted in order to consider how the aims, the background, and the results affect the way services are managed for noncitizens.

However, in most cases the reinterpretation refers only to the details of the indicators and specific circumstances and not to fundamental changes to the constructs and overall hypothesized relationships.

There are greater similarities in organizational processes, although there are specialized areas of migration services. And, even when the information systems could be considered the same, the system modules and their rules vary for different noncitizen users. The institutional arrangements are also different for citizens and noncitizens, particularly in terms of additional international rules and the differentiated application of certain laws and regulations. Regarding technology, it can be stated that both have the same aspects, however, the technical features and the usability and usefulness of the systems may differ due to differences in culture and skills. For instance, to make it easier for a noncitizen to use web pages, there should be translations or explanations of the processes that must be followed in more universal terms, which is not always easy to accomplish.

Another aspect that is different are the results, because a great deal of the expected results or benefits of e-government do not take noncitizens into account, such as improvement of the relationship between the government and citizens, transparency or accountability, increases in participation, and personalized services. Many of these potential benefits rest on strong assumptions about the nature of the relationship between government and users, which are normally thought of as citizens. One of the main constructs that change in the migration management context is the environmental conditions. It is important to consider that for noncitizens there is a very different context from that of citizens, which can be related to how the websites and information systems are used and the success of certain government services and programs in national and cultural contexts.

Finally, this reinterpretation of Fountain's framework aims to provide a useful example to remind practitioners and academics that the services for noncitizens should not only consider the standards for citizens, but also all the conditions that surround the noncitizens' reality and their environment. Considering all these variables will help to develop information systems and digital services that would be more appropriate for different users, including noncitizens.

References

1. Alsagheir H, Ford M, Nguyen A, Hexel R (2009) Conceptualising citizen's trust in e-Government: application of Q methodology. Electron J e-Gov 7(4):295–310
2. Hiller JS, Bélanger F (2001) Privacy strategies for electronic government. In: Abramson MA, Means GE (eds) E-govermment 2001. Rowman and Littlefield Publishers, Lanham, pp 162–198
3. Fountain J (2001) Building the virtual state. Information technology and institutional change. Brookings Institution Press, Washington, DC
4. Gil-García JR (2012) Enacting electronic government success. An integrative study of government-websites, organizational capabilities and institutions. Springer, New York

5. Garcia-Garcia LM, Gil-Garcia JR, Gómez V. Citizen-centered e-government: towards a more integral approach. In: Proceedings of the 15th Annual International Conference On Digital Government Research, DG.O '14. ACM, New York, 2014, pp 339–340
6. Gil-Garcia JR, Pardo T (2005) E-government success factors: mapping practical tools to theoretical foundations. Gov Inf Q 2:187–216
7. Seok-Jin E (2010) The institutional dimension of e-Government promotion: a comparative study on making business reference model (BRM) in the U.S. and Korea. National Center for Digital Government, p 37
8. Bertot J, Jeager P (2006) User-centered e-government: challenges and benefits for government Web sites. Gov Inf Q 23:163–168
9. Carvajal MY, Saab J (2010) Lineamientos y metodologías en usabilidad para gobierno en línea. Programa Gobierno en línea, Manual para la implementación del decreto 1151. Ministerio de Tecnologías de la información y las comunicaciones
10. Gant D, Gant J, Johnson CL (2002) State web portals: delivering and financing E-service, The Price waterhouse Coopers Endowment Business of Government
11. Hassan Y, Fernandez F, Lazza G (2004). Diseño web centrado en el usuario: usabilidad y arquitectura de la información "Hipertext.net", núm. 2, 2004. Recuperado de http://www.hipertext.net
12. King N, Ma TH-Y, Zaphris P, Petrie H, Hamilton F (2004) An incremental usability and accessibility evaluation framework for digital libraries. In: Brophy P, Fisher S, Craven J (eds) Libraries without walls 5: the distributed delivery if librarian and information services. Facet, London, pp 123–131
13. DiMaggio P, Hargittai E (2001). From the digital divide to digital inequality: studying internet use as penetration increases. Center for Arts and cultural policy studies. Working paper series # 15
14. Snead J, Bertot JC, Jeager PT, CR MC (2005) Developing multi-method, literature and user-centered evaluation strategies for digital libraries: functionality, usability, and accessibility. Proc Am Inf Soc Sci Technol 42(1). doi:10.1002/meet.14504201161
15. McClure CR (2002) Information policy-based indicators to assess U.S. federal Websites: methods and issues. In: Stein J, Kyrillidou M, Davis D (eds) Proceedings of the 4th Northumbria international conference on performance measure in libraries and information services. Association of Research Libraries, Washington, DC, pp 145–154
16. Jeager P, Matteson M (2009) e-Government and technology acceptance: the case of the implementation of section 508 guidelines for websites. Electron J e Gov 7(1):87–98
17. Jeager PT (2003) E-government around the world: Lessons, challenges, and future directions. Gov Inf Q 20:389–394
18. Ifinedo P (2011) Factors influencing E-government maturity in transition economies and developing countries: a longitudinal perspective. The data base for advances in information systems 42, 4 Nov 2011
19. Jansen A (2011) E-Government-just a matter of technology? In: Proceedings of the 44th Hawaii international conference on system sciences, 2011
20. Gronlund A, Horan T (2005) Introducing E-Gov: history, definitions, and issues. Commun AIS 15:Article 39
21. Bolgherini (2006) The technology trap and the role of political and cultural variables: a critical analysis of the E-Government policies. XX IPSA World Congress, 2006
22. Hargittai E (2002) Second-level digital divide: differences in people's online skills. First Monday, [S.l.], apr. ISSN 13960466. doi:10.5210/fm.v7i4.942. Available at: <http://firstmonday.org/ojs/index.php/fm/article/view/942/864>. Accessed 27 Jul. 2014
23. Gil-Garcia R, Helbig N, Ferro E (2006) Is it only about internet Access? An empirical test of a multi-dimensional digital divide. In: Wimmer MA et al (eds) EGOV. Springer, Berlin, pp 139–149

24. Ferro E, Gil-García R, Helbig N (2008) Digital divide and broadband access: the case of an Italian Region. In: Dwivedi YK, Papazafeiropoulou A, Choudrie J (eds) Handbook of research on global diffusion of broadband data transmission. IGI Global, Hershey, pp 159–175. ISBN: 978-1-59904-851-2 [Estados Unidos]
25. Gauld R, Goldfinch S, Horburgh S (2010) Do they want it? Do they use it? The demand -side of e-government in Australia and New Zealand. Gov Inf Q 27:177–186
26. Bélanger F, Carter L (2009) The impact of the digital divide on E-Government use. Commun ACM 52(4):132–135
27. Castillo MA (2006) México: caught between the United States and Central America. Migration Information Source. Recuperado de: http://www.migrationinformation.org/feature/display.cfm?ID=389
28. Álvarez S (2010) Frontera sur chiapaneca: el muro humano de la violencia. Análisis de la normalización de la violencia hacia la migración indocumentada en tránsito en el espacio fronterizo Tecún umán-Ciudad Hidalgo-Tapachula-Huixtla-Arriaga (Tesis de maestría inédita). Universidad Iberoamericana, México, D.F
29. Ángeles H (2010) Las migraciones internacionales en la frontera sur de México. In: Alba F, Castillo M, Verduzco G (Coord.) Los grandes problemas de México III, Migraciones Internacionales, Colmex, México
30. INM (2005) Propuesta de Política Migratoria Integral en la Frontera Sur de México, 2nd edn. Centro de Estudios Migratorios, México
31. Lineamientos para trámites y procedimientos migratorios (2012) DOF

Chapter 11
The 'engage' System: Using Real-Time Digital Technologies to Support Citizen-Centred Design in Government

Brian Cleland, Jonathan Wallace, and Michaela Black

Abstract Much of the literature on citizen-centric e-government focuses on the evaluation and classification of systems, while relatively little research exists on methods to ensure that such systems are designed around unmet user needs. This chapter focuses on the use of a specific ICT-based tool for citizen-centred service design within Northern Ireland. The 'engage' system is a novel technology for user research developed by Ulster University and commissioned by a variety of public sector clients to support the development of new policies and services. The 'engage' platform is examined in the context of the wider trend towards user-centred design and digital transformation in government. The relative advantages and disadvantages of the system are analysed in light of alternative user research methods and tools currently in use in the public sector. Lessons from real-world trials over a period of approximately 5 years are discussed, and implications for the future adoption of user research technologies in the public sector are explored.

Keywords e-Government • Digital government • e-Participation • User research • User-centred design • Citizen-centric

1 Citizen-Centred Service Design in e-Government

Policy and research interest in the impact of technology on the structure and function of the public sector has continued to grow in recent years [1, 2]. At the same time, there has been an increasing demand for more citizen-centred public services. Links have been drawn between these two trends, with some experts speaking of

B. Cleland (✉) • J. Wallace
School of Computing and Maths, Ulster University, Northern Ireland, UK
e-mail: b.cleland@ulster.ac.uk

M. Black
School of Computing and Intelligent Systems, Ulster University, Northern Ireland, UK

© Springer International Publishing AG 2018   183
S. Saeed et al. (eds.), *User Centric E-Government*, Integrated Series in Information Systems 39, DOI 10.1007/978-3-319-59442-2_11

Discussion Groups / Tables

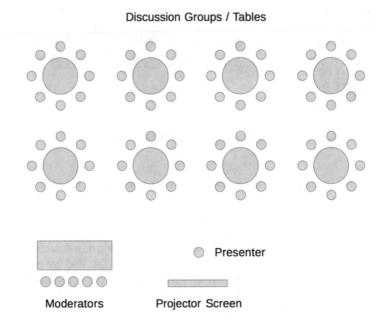

Fig. 11.1 Typical room layout for an eTM/engage workshop (from Galbraith et al. [46])

the demand for citizen-or user-centred e-government [3–5]. Despite this alignment, there has been relatively little exploration of how technology can be used to support user-centred service design. In this chapter we will investigate one example of how digital tools can support user-centred design in the public sector, and consider the implications for future adoption of such technologies.

1.1 Overview of e-Government

The move towards internet-based services in the private sector has increased demand for similar forms of interaction with government. Edmiston [6] argues that citizens now expect the same service standards and levels of satisfaction in their dealings with the public sector. The promise of e-government is "more efficient, transparent and accessible public services" [7]. As a research field, e-government is relatively young [8], and has generally been multidisciplinary in character [9]. Some experts argue that the field is showing some signs of maturity, and alternative labels have been suggested, including "transforming government", "online government", and "digital government". Irani et al. [7] point out that it is not yet clear whether e-government should be considered a field in its own right, or is more properly understood as a subset Public Administration or Information Systems research, or even as an intersection of these two disciplines.

According to Welch et al. [10], research on e-government addresses how the public sector can use online information exchange and deliver services relevant to the needs of citizens, businesses, and other government bodies. Others have suggested that e-government promises efficiency and process improvement within government alongside enhanced public services [11, 12]. Irani et al. [7] highlight the need to identify effective strategies, practices and processes in order for e-government to become broadly adopted. In addition, the benefits, challenges and organisational change requirements of each e-government project must be understood in relation to its specific context [13]. It should also be noted that the benefits of e-government, such as better transparency and higher quality services, come at a significant cost to the public sector [14], and that the uptake of e-services by citizens may sometimes present a challenge [15].

A review of the literature by Irani et al. [7] observed that while earlier research tended to emphasise the challenges of e-government delivery (e.g. [12, 16–18]), later studies were more likely to address questions of diffusion and adoption (e.g. [15, 19–21]).

1.2 Citizen-Centred e-Government

Early discussions of citizen-centred e-government by Chen [5] suggested that e-government had arrived at an important turning point, as progress was slower than many had hoped [22, 23] and that its potential was not being fulfilled [24]. Digital interactions with government were still relatively rare, with the exception of a few popular examples such as driver licence renewals and online filing of taxes. According to Scott [25], e-participation had an even lower level of uptake, following an examination of US-based municipal authority websites. Despite these issues, the continuing global trend towards online services in the private sector has created an expectation that governments will follow suit.

Chen [5] argues that the tension between expectations and delivery has encouraged experts to question existing research assumptions. Alternative perspectives have been proposed, critiquing standard linear models of e-government maturity [16, 22, 26]. Chen [5] proposes that such innovators are characterised by their ability to deviate from the linear model of progress. Citing the UN report on e-government [27], he suggests that the research should focus on citizen-centric services as "the ideal manifestation" of e-government. The implication is that government information needs to be shared across internal silos, organisations, and sectors [28]. Furthermore, service users should not be required to have knowledge of the internal structures of the public sector. On the contrary, government agencies should be interconnected in order to enhance their efficiency and effectiveness. Chen [5] illustrates this point with the example of 311, a single phone number which connects users to non-emergency services in many parts of the United States and Canada.

1.3   Engagement and Digital Government

More recently, many practitioners have been using the term "digital government" to describe the transformative impact of technology on the public sector. This has been reflected to some degree in the literature. One example is Janowski [29], who presents a model of digital government evolution which proposes that the concept tends towards greater complexity, contextualisation and specialisation over time, mimicking the evolutionary processes one finds in culture and society. Janowski's model has four stages: Digitization (Technology in Government), Transformation (Electronic Government), Engagement (Electronic Governance) and Contextualization (Policy-Driven Electronic Governance). Evidence for the model is provided by an analysis of the digital government research published between 1992 and 2014 in Government Information Quarterly. The author also describes a Digital Government Stage Analysis Framework to explain the evolutionary process.

In the context of this chapter we are particularly interested in the Engagement Stage. According to Janowski, this stage is intended to transform the relationships between government and non-government institutions, including citizens, businesses, and the voluntary sector. Some of desired outcomes include the promotion of the knowledge-based economy, enhanced civic participation, and better access to government information and services. Janowski argues that the Engagement Stage dovetails with the more general trends towards Digital by Default and Open Government, and thus should enable greater transparency, accountability and trust between government and external actors. This stage builds on the earlier Digitisation and Transformation stages, facilitating improved interactions and collaborations internal and external organisational boundaries.

Examples of activities typically carried out during the Engagement Stage include: increasing adoption of e-services by citizens (e.g., [30–32]); growing levels of civic engagement and participation (e.g., [33, 34]); more open, transparent and accountable government (e.g., [35–37]); and increased trust and cultural transformation (e.g., [35, 38]).

1.4   Digital Government Exemplars

We have described how e-government research has developed in recent years and examined where engagement might fit in terms of the evolution of digital government. However, as Brown [39] points out, while maturity models can be useful to understand global behaviours they are less effective in explaining the behaviour of individual organisations. We will therefore take a closer look at two exemplars commonly cited in research and policy literature—the UK and US governments.

1.4.1 UK Government

Brown et al. [40] explore the example of the UK's Government Digital Strategy, outlining how the public sector might realise the government's concept of "digital-by-default" services. The authors point out that the term "digital" might be best understood as a vision of new organisational practices and values, highly focused on user needs, with an emphasis on speed, agility and flexibility. While technology is often the catalyst for such changes, digital transformation is not restricted to technical innovations. The aims include services that can respond quickly to changes in policy and user expectations, reduced costs and increased efficiency, as well as the exploitation of novel technologies.

A key part of this digital transformation strategy has been the establishment and growth of the Government Digital Service (GDS), a new agency that is designed to grow digital capacity in the heart of the public sector. GDS has been charged with developing the vision for digital government in the UK, as well as implementing key changes and new online services. One of the architectural principles that the GDS team are working towards is "Government as a Platform" (GaaP), which envisions a suite of shared e-services and digital standards to be implemented across government. GDS are also extremely vocal about the central importance of user needs to service design. Thus the first of their ten Design Principles is "Start with needs", which they explain means "user needs not government needs" [41]. From April 2014 it was mandated that all new public services must meet the GDS digital design standards in full [40].

1.4.2 US Government

In the US, an important catalyst for digital transformation was the Presidential Innovation Fellows programme, launched by President Obama in early 2012 with the aim of saving lives, reducing the burden on taxpayers and enhancing private sector job growth. A key aspect of the programme was the hiring of private sector innovators to bring experience of agile and user-centred design methods to apply [42]. Of the over 700 people who applied, 18 were eventually appointed as Fellows. During the last 6 months of Obama's first term, small innovation teams were effective in making bidding processes 12 times more competitive and reduced contract costs by 30%. They also developed a range of tools for making government services easier to find and use, and enabled US citizens to access their personal health data.

As awareness grew of what had been achieved, demand for Fellows also increased. Working alongside the General Services Administration, the White House created a completely new agency—called 18F—to promote wider adoption of successful practices that had originally been championed in the Presidential Innovation Fellows programme. 18F has since established a strong reputation for innovation and leadership in open collaborative networks in the US public sector [43].

Around the same time as 18F was being established, the US government launched its much-heralded Healthcare.gov website in October 2013. It's aim was to provide access to information and services associated with the Affordable Care Act, but the site failed to work from the start. Drawing on private sector skills and Presidential Innovation Fellows, the White House created a small team of experts to correct the problem. By April 2014 the site was operating properly and eight million citizens had been signed up for health insurance. Following the high-profile success of the rescue operation (including a Time magazine cover feature), the White House decided to create the US Digital Service, partly modelled on the UK Government Digital Service. This organisation works within the Office of Management and Budget to support other public sector agencies to design, develop and deploy online services [42].

Strong links exist between the UK and US government initiatives, with the US in many instances emulating practices that originated in the UK Government Cabinet Office. Common themes emerge when looking at both programmes side-by-side, such as the emphasis on recruiting external talent into Government, the adoption of agile processes and the focus on user needs. While it is too soon to speculate on the long-term impact of these initiatives, the overall level of public investment suggests a significant commitment to creating a fundamental organisational shift.

1.5   The Purpose of This Chapter

From the preceding analysis, it seems clear that e-government is about a broader transformation of government, and not simply about adopting new technologies. It is about evolving culture and practice, introducing new approaches such as agile development, and focusing on user needs [44]. This focus on the user applies not just to online activities, but to everything that government does. Despite the link between digital transformation and citizen-centrism, there is a marked lack of attention being paid to how technology can enable better user-centred design. This may be due in part to the fact that engagement happens only in the later stages of e-government [29]. In the rest of this chapter we will examine one particular example of how technology can support effective user engagement.

2   The Use of 'engage' in the Design of Citizen-Centred Services

The *engage* e-participation system has its origins in the PARTERRE project, which was funded by European Framework 7's Competitiveness in Innovation Programme (CIP). One of the core goals of the project was to pilot a number of workshops—called "Electronic Town Meetings" (eTMs)—across the partner countries, in order to address a variety of public policy issues. These pilots were designed to determine the viability of the eTM framework, which comprised a specific technical framework and methodology based on small group discussions. Ultimately, the aim was to analyse the effectiveness of the eTM as a tool for engaging with communities of "lead users" [45, 46] in the context of developing public policy. Ulster University, as one of the partners in the PARTERRE project, was responsible for piloting the eTM framework within Northern Ireland.

2.1   The engage Methodology

The eTM methodology was implemented in Northern Ireland in the following manner. Each eTM is a workshop-style event, typically coordinated with members of a particular stakeholder network. These members normally invite other stakeholders to attend an event to discuss a matter of importance to the network. At the start of each event, a short introduction to the topic is provided to the entire room of participants, which can number from 20 to 150. The room is then organised into small round-table discussion groups, which then discuss typically 3–5 sub-topics related to the overall theme of the workshop. Each discussion is normally 15–30 min in length. Instant minutes of each group's conversation are taken by table facilitators, using wirelessly networked tablet computers. In another part of the room, a team of domain experts collects and reviews the comments in real-time, clustering emerging issues, removing duplication and identifying conflicting perspectives.

The system also allows polling so that participants can select their preferred option from multiple alternative opinions. Comments, themes and polling results can be visualised on a projector screen, and feedback is given to the room at regular intervals during the event. An "instant report" is also generated in parallel with the discussion, and is available for distribution as soon as the workshop is completed. This report summarises the aims of the debate, the process which has been undertaken and the key results of the work [46] (11.1).

2.2   Technical Implementation

The design of the engage system is deliberately focused on the needs of users who hold regular consultative and participative events. For this reason, the system is intended to be unobtrusive to workshop participants, highly interactive and responsive to group discussions, and easy for table facilitators and event organisers to use. It is also designed to minimise the workload for organisers pre- and post-event. Thus, setting up the equipment before the event and taking it down after the event can be done quickly by one or two individuals in under an hour.

These requirements are enabled by the strategic use of specific technologies. Thus, mobile devices with bluetooth keyboards can be quickly deployed to a large number of tables and connected to a wireless network without worrying about either power or ethernet cabling. The use of off-the-shelf tablets provides familiar, user-friendly controls for table facilitators and other participants. Node.js, a software framework for building real-time applications, is used to allow the rapid capture of comments and voting data and to provide immediate visual feedback on a projector screen. By combining consumer hardware with open source software the entire system can be made available at a relatively small cost.

2.3   Application in Service and Policy Design

The use of the engage system as a policy tool consists of two main phases. The first phase was the PARTERRE project, during which it was deployed across Northern Ireland in a range of policy contexts. This initial phase included eight pilot events, which are described in Table 11.1. For each of these eTM pilots, the topic was identified by a representative of a specific community, who approached the project team with a request for an event. User-centred research methodologies were employed during the organisation and implementation of each eTM. The research team found high levels of interest and motivation among Lead Community Coordinators (LCCs), who were keen to professionalise the engagement process, make it more efficient and improve the outcome of the civic engagement [46]. LCCs can be defined as highly motivated experts who take a leadership role to connect user communities. The number of participants of each eTM pilot ranged from 40 to 50 per eTM, with a total of 380 participants across the eight cases. The pilot events took place over a period of approximately 12 months.

The second phase of engage deployment took place after the PARTERRE Project ended. The pilot events have successfully identified and catalysed a market for novel stakeholder engagement tools and methods, which lead to ongoing demand following the end of the research project. Due to strong research network links the majority of these additional workshops took place in collaboration with the public health sector. A range of strategy, policy and service design issues were addressed in 16 events which took place between 2014 and 2016. The specific event topics are detailed in Table 11.2 below.

3   Comparison of 'engage' with Other Approaches

In order to gain a deeper understanding of the context of the ongoing demand for the *engage* platform, six in-depth semi-structured interviews were carried with users of the system. These users included health sector managers and university staff who had co-organised and delivered engage events, and were selected for their ability to

Table 11.1 eTM pilot events in Northern Ireland under the PARTERRE project

Title	Objectives	Participant profile
Strategy for Allied Health Professionals (AHP) in Northern Ireland	Develop a comprehensive response to the DHSSPSNI consultation on AHP Strategy for Northern Ireland	Representatives from the AHP workforce and experts from related academic fields
Open Government—Making Open Data Real	To co-design a response to the public consultation on open data, and to influence public policy at regional and national level	Industry representatives, local and regional government, policy-makers, academics
Partnerships for Business Innovation—Engaging for Growth	To explore how businesses can be supported in innovation activities using partnerships models with academic and government stakeholders	Representatives from industry, trade associations, regional and local government, and academia.
Worklessness Within North Belfast	To engage stakeholders in North Belfast in civic debate on issues related to worklessness in their local communities	Community representatives, local and regional government, academics.
Maximising Social Value Through Public Sector Procurement	To improve understanding among stakeholders of how social value can be integrated within the commissioning process	Academics, charitable and voluntary sector, procurement practitioners, policy-makers
Innovation in Sustainable Construction and Energy Management	To consider implications of sustainable construction and energy management for industry and educators	SMEs, large corporates, academics, local and regional government
Brain-Computer Neural Interfaces	To improve understanding of the potential for BCNI to support people with neurological conditions who are living at home	Academic staff and students, occupational therapists
Embedding Telehealth in Care & Service Provision	To understand the future role of connected health technologies within the South Eastern Health and Social Care Trust	Clinicians, senior management

Table 11.2 Post-PARTERRE engage workshops

Date	Client	Topic
21 Feb 2014	Health and Social Care Board	Strategic Futures Workshop on eHealth and Care Strategy for NI
28 May 2014	BCS Health NI and HSCNI	Better Data Better Care
06 Jun 2014	Telecare Service Association	Best Practice Workshop on ECRs, Interoperability and Big Data
05 Sep 2014	European Connected Health Alliance	Exploring Engagement Between Academic, Business and Clinical
16 Sep 2014	Assoc. British Pharmaceutical Industry	Increasing collaboration with the Pharmaceutical Industry in NI
09 Dec 2014	Public Health Agency	Beyond 2015 Staff Engagement—Internal
10 Mar 2015	Public Health Agency	Beyond 2015 Staff Engagement—External
26 May 2015	Public Health Agency	Making Life Better in Partnership
19 Jan 2016	MAGIC Project	Pre-Commercial Procurement Stakeholder Engagement
21 Jan 2016	MAGIC Project	Pre-Commercial Procurement Stakeholder Engagement
16 Feb 2016	Public Health Agency	Electronic Clinical Health Record Benefits
07 Apr 2016	HOME SBRI	SBRI Stakeholder Engagement
12 Apr 2016	HOME SBRI	SBRI Stakeholder Engagement
16 May 2016	Public Health Agency	Research for Better Health & Social Care
15 Jun 2016	Health and Social Care NI	Domiciliary Care Workforce Review
22 Jun 2016	Ulster University	Employers Engagement Event

provide feedback on organisational drivers and barriers, usability issues, and policy impacts.

A key theme that quickly emerged was increasing organisational demand for stakeholder engagement, along with a growing expectation that policy and service design should be focused on user needs. In some cases, this was linked to a policy drive for greater openness and accountability. This trend in the Northern Irish public sector reflects the push for user-centred design that we observed in the context of digital government, which in turn suggests a deeper shift in public sector culture, permeating from the national down to the regional level. It also reflects the observation of [29], that the Engagement Stage of digital government evolution is often linked to the concept of Open Government.

In this context we will explore how user research is currently carried out by the leading digital transformation agencies, as well as public bodies in Northern Ireland.

3.1   Alternative User Research Methods

In the US and the UK, there has been a shift towards bringing technically skilled individuals and agile methodologies into government, accompanied by an increasing emphasis on user-centred design. In the case of 18F and GDS, each of these organisations have published online guides to agile development in the public sector. Within these guidelines, specific user research methods are suggested for adoption by government agencies. Both 18F and GDs divide the design process into four phases. 18F name the phases "Discover", "Decide", "Make", and "Validate", and categorise the research methods according to the appropriate design phase. GDS, on the other hand, name their development phases "Discovery", "Alpha", "Beta", and "Live", and while they note that "Different types of research are more appropriate depending on what phase of service development process you are in." [47], they do not provide specific guidance on when each method should be used (Tables 11.3 and 11.4).

In terms of research methods commonly used in the Northern Ireland public sector, our investigation of *engage* users revealed that the most frequently mentioned methods were interviews, focus groups, workshops and online surveys. Methods mentioned by interviewees were limited in variety compared to those listed by organisations like 18F and GDS. This is perhaps not surprising, given the difference in available resources and cultural focus between these high-profile digital transformation agencies and local organisations in Northern Ireland which are primarily focused on operational matters. Nevertheless, there was a consistent message from respondents that stakeholder engagement and citizen-centred service design were increasingly important.

Table 11.3 User research methods used by 18F

Discover	Decide	Make	Validate
Feature dot voting	Comparative analysis	Protosketching	Card sorting
KJ method	Content audit	Wireframing	Multivariate testing
Metrics definition	Design principles	Design pattern library	Usability testing
Design studio	Site mapping	Prototyping	Visual preference testing
Bodystorming	Task flow analysis		
Cognitive walkthrough	User scenarios		
Contextual inquiry	Affinity diagramming		
Heuristic analysis	Journey mapping		
User interviews	Mental modeling		
	Personas		
	Storyboarding		
	Style tiles		

Table 11.4 User research methods used by UK Government Digital Service

Method	Description
Evidence-based personas	A persona is a fictitious individual, based on a composite of the characteristics of a group of real users
User Journey Maps	A technique that helps teams to understand the full experience that users have throughout the lifecycle of the service
Eye tracking	
Unmoderated usability study	User attempts a task or series of tasks alone and the moderator observes in a separate room
Surveys	A survey is user research that includes a questionnaire
A/B and Multivariate testing	A/B tests are controlled experiments on the web. Show two randomly assigned groups of users different designs of a page
Remote user research	User research can be done over the phone or using a VoIP system. Can be done in conjunction with screen sharing
Pop-up research	Take questions and prototypes to where target users are likely to be, such as libraries, day centres and colleges
Depth interviews	Semi-structured conversation that help learning about users' needs. Ideal for exploring attitudes, aspirations and preferences
Community research panel	A group of pre-selected users who have agreed to participate in research activities on a regular basis
Ethnographic research	Ethnographic research is sometimes called contextual research or contextual inquiry
Affinity mapping	A technique for sorting large volumes of unstructured information, as a means of understanding patterns and themes
Card sorting	Helps to understand how users naturally organise different kinds of information. Can also be used for sorting user needs
Co-design	A co-design workshop involves getting users in the same room creating sketches/prototypes and generating ideas
Day in the life	Mapping someone's activity over a day, including what products and services they use at what time of day
Guided tour	Helps to understand what people actually do rather than their reported experience
Map your use	Can be used to understand a user's current use of services and their feelings towards them
Think aloud	A way of testing how users experience a service. Using a service while thinking aloud about what they are doing
Write a diary	

3.2 Alternative Tools and Technologies

There appear to be limited alternative technologies specifically tailored for citizen engagement—perhaps reflecting the fact the engagement happens at the later stages of e-government development according to Janowski's evolutionary model [29]. The UK's Government Digital Service provides a list of user research tools that it uses, which is given in Table 11.5 below. According to Northern Ireland users of the *engage* system, technology-enabled engagement was restricted to online surveys

Table 11.5 UK Government Digital Service user research tools

Tool	Description of usage
UserZoom	UserZoom is used for quarterly benchmarking of the usability of top tasks on GOV.UK. It also enables remote testing by external stakeholders
What Users Do	WhatUsersDo allows for rapid usability testing with people who are in their own home/work with their own computers. Teams can quickly and inexpensively conduct iterative usability testing at a feature based level. Teams can also able to see videos of user sessions
CRM	A CRM system is used to build and manage a panel of people who have agreed that they are interested in participating in user research
GoToMeeting	GoToMeeting supports moderated remote user research with users who are either too busy or otherwise unable to come into the lab, or when it important to talk to them in their own context
FluidSurveys	FluidSurveys are used to perform online surveys
OptimalWorkshop	OptimalWorkshop enables testing about information architecture and navigation, including card sorting and tree testing
Mental Models Template	GDS use a mental model template to structure discovery research data. A mental model skyline diagram can be generated using a Python script (CSV to Visio)

(which were widely used) and electronic voting systems (which were less common). The limited range of available technologies is somewhat surprising given that all respondents recognised an increasing demand for stakeholder engagement at the organisational level.

3.3   Where Does engage Fit Into Existing Practices?

According to Daae and Boks [48], user research methods can be divided into three categories, according to how information is collected: methods for communicating with users, methods for investigating what users do, and methods that both investigate what users do and communicate with users. This classification is illustrated with examples in Table 11.6. Within this framework the *engage* system would be most appropriately classified as a method for communicating with users.

It was clear from talking to *engage* users was that the system, which in many ways resembles a traditional roundtable workshop, fitted easily into familiar business practices. This is not surprising, given that Preece et al. [49] consider workshops to be one of the five basic data collection methods. All the respondents had taken part in such workshops before, and some had used them for stakeholder engagement in the past. In this sense, the system felt familiar to both organisers and participants and did not require a steep "learning curve". For organisers, the

Table 11.6 Three types of user research method (from Daae and Boks [48])

Methods for communicating with the user	Methods for investigating what the user does	Methods that include both investigation and communication
Interview	Observation	Applied ethnography
Focus group	Studying	Contextual enquiry
Survey	Documentation	
Verbal protocol	Video ethnography	
Conjoint technique	Shadowing	
Wants and needs analysis	User testing	
Card sorting	Empathic design	
Group task analysis	Culture-focused research	
Probes/diary study		

burden of preparing for an engage event was no greater than it might have been for a more traditional workshop. For participants, the process of engaging in a series of structured conversations was a familiar and comfortable activity.

3.4   Comparative Advantages of engage

User feedback from the PARTERE pilots was in general very positive, particularly in terms of the methodology [46, 50]. Stakeholders felt that participation levels were good, and that the quality of discussion and debate was high. An analysis of user responses showed that *engage* offered advantages over traditional workshops in a number of ways, which might be classified as "immediacy", "connectedness", "transparency", and "efficiency".

Immediacy—One of the frustrations that users expressed with traditional workshops was the delay between participating in a discussion and receiving a formal report of that discussion. Some users felt that this gap between contribution and feedback lead to a sense that such events were merely a "box-ticking" exercise, and that the lack of tangible outputs was a sign that their contribution would have little impact on actual policy or service design. For these users, the *engage* framework addressed this issue by allowing for real-time feedback during the event and for a final report to be distributed immediately after a workshop was completed. Thus "immediacy" appeared to be a significant source of value for many respondents.

Connectedness—Another benefit of the *engage* approach was the ability to connect multiple different discussion groups, and thus multiple perspectives, within the context of a wider shared conversation. One example given by a frequent user of the system was the facility to compare and contrast the views of different professional groups—for example, pharmacists and physiotherapists. The user pointed out that such groups inevitably have a different view of how services should be delivered and how value can be created for service users. By allowing conflicting perspectives to be surfaced and discussed, the user felt that it was possible to achieve a more robust consensus and thus a more effective overarching strategy.

Transparency—The value of transparency was raised by a number of users. In the context of *engage*, this meant the transparency of the process by which participant comments were converted into the final report and recommendations. One of the problems with a traditional paper-based workshop is that the delay between recording ideas and opinions on paper, and converting those statements into a final report is slow and opaque. By making feedback immediate and visible to all, users of the *engage* platform can see straightaway whether the outputs of the discussion are reflective of their inputs, thus enhancing trust and increasing user satisfaction.

Efficiency—A fourth major theme that emerged from interviews was that the *engage* framework was attractive to event organisers due to its ability to reduce their workload compared to conventional workshops. Stakeholders felt that relevant data was collected, analysed and distributed in a more timely and resource-efficient manner. It was suggested that *engage* workshops allowed for effective consultation at scale, making it significantly more cost-effective that running multiple interviews or focus groups.

3.5 Challenges of Wider Adoption

The *engage* methodology has a number of limitations in its current state. The level of engagement of participants depends to some degree on the skills of the individual table facilitator. Also, by their nature, roundtable discussions do not allow for the same level of in-depth analysis as one-to-one interviews. Nevertheless, the experience of the engage platform suggests that an acceptable level of participation can be created through the use of untrained facilitators, with a minimal technical introduction to the system.

Perhaps the largest methodological barrier is the need for trained event organisers, particularly with regard to the structuring of discussions and presentations. In particular, the correct wording of questions is critical to ensuring satisfactory outcomes [46, 50]. Defining effective questions is an important challenge that requires some experience in terms of what typically works, but also a specific understanding of the discussion topics and purpose of the engagement. At the moment, the need for trained event coordinators is a major contributor to the cost of using the system. Wider adoption is likely to be accelerated if this cost can be reduced through a training programme, or perhaps partial automation of core tasks.

A further challenge to the *engage* method is the need to have all participants in the same room at the same time. While this requirement supports high levels of engagement and inclusion for those in the room, it may occasionally exclude stakeholders who are unable to attend the event in person. In the context of health sector service design and policy development, this created a challenge for service users and carers. It is possible that this issue might be addressed in future through technical enhancements to facilitate remote participation.

There are a number of costs associated with the use of the system that may be addressed through technical improvements. For example, the price of hardware is continuing to come down over time. Another significant cost is the requirement for university staff to attend each event. This could be addressed by the provision of a cloud-based software model, accompanied by a suitable training programme for clients. Furthermore, from talking to users it became clear that further technical enhancements could increase the value of the system and reduce overheads. Specific examples could include increased automation of core tasks (including report generation), richer visualisation and analysis tools, and easier integration with social media.

One of the key messages from users is that significant obstacles to technology adoption exist in the public sector. Some concerns raised during user interviews included challenges relating to IT infrastructure, including the difficulty giving novel hardware and software systems access to public sector networks. These issues were associated primarily with security and resource concerns—i.e., getting access to IT staff who can enable integration, and justifying perceived risks to security.

Another issue, related to organisational culture, was ensuring that engagement activities had credible impacts. A number of stakeholders suggested that it was often the case that consultation was a "box-ticking" exercise, and that actual stakeholder empowerment might be met with resistance from senior management. It was suggested that stakeholder opinions could be diluted or distorted to the point where they had little real impact. One respondent suggested that a possible solution to this problem would to have repeat engagements, allowing stakeholders to evaluate ongoing policy impacts. This was referred to as "closing the loop". This implies that in order to maximise impact (as well as stakeholder satisfaction), engagement should be an ongoing process or "conversation" rather than a one-off activity, echoing the iterative approach found in agile development practices.

4   Future Trends and Conclusion

As we noted at the start of this chapter the discourse on e-government has evolved significantly in recent years. One of the most influential concepts has been that of Digital Era Governance, originally proposed by [44]. A key insight from the authors is that changes in governance are driven not simply by public sector adoption of new technologies, but by changes in society at large. These social changes take many forms—cognitive, behavioural, organizational, political, and cultural—but all can be linked back in some way to the evolution and impact of information technology. Mike Bracken, formerly of GDS, makes a similar point when he says: "Digital means applying the culture, practices, processes and technologies of the internet era to respond to people's raised expectations." [51].

This insight may help to explain why digital transformation is occurring in parallel with the drive towards more citizen-centred government, insofar as low-cost, disintermediated forms of communication enabled by the internet create an expectation that governments will embrace deeper citizen engagement. Dunleavy et al. [44] label this mode of governance "Needs-Based Holism". Citing Hood [52], they point out that "detector" mechanisms (which enable information-seeking) are as important to government functioning as "effectors" (which enable delivery). The *engage* platform may thus be considered a novel "detector mechanism" for government.

It is worth noting how scarce and underdeveloped such tools appear to be given the demand for effective solutions. Even in the case of technology-orientated practitioners and early adopters such as GDS and 18F, non-digital user research methods seem to predominate. It may be that user research data—which is often qualitative, complex and subtle—may not lend itself to digital capture or analysis. Or perhaps it is merely that suitable solutions have yet to be developed. Or perhaps, as Kotamraju and Geest [53] suggest, there is a fundamental tension between user and government needs that creates a barrier to adoption of user-centred methods and tools. Such questions inevitably point to opportunities for further research.

If we speculate about what form such technologies might take, the experience of *engage* suggests that the greatest opportunity lies in unobtrusive user interface design, systems that complement well-established forms of human interaction, and approaches that are tailored towards the capture and analysis of qualitative data. While the *engage* system is undoubtedly an early-stage technology, it perhaps illustrates the potential for digital tools to support a new era of citizen-centred governance.

References

1. Zhang H, Xu X, Xiao J (2014) Diffusion of e-government: a literature review and directions for future directions. Gov Inf Q 31(4):631–636
2. Belanger F, Carter L (2012) Digitizing government interactions with constituents: an historical review of E-Government research in information systems. J Assoc Inf Syst 13(5):1
3. Osman IH, Anouze AL, Irani Z, Al-Ayoubi B, Lee H, Balcı A et al (2014) COBRA framework to evaluate e-government services: a citizen-centric perspective. Gov Inf Q 31(2):243–256
4. Mahmood Z (ed) (2013) E-government implementation and practice in developing countries. IGI Global, Hershey
5. Chen Y-C (2010) Citizen-centric E-government services: understanding integrated citizen service information systems. Soc Sci Comput Rev 28(4):427–442
6. Edmiston KD (2003) State and local e-government: prospects and challenges. Am Rev Public Adm 33(1):20–45
7. Irani Z, Weerakkody V, Kamal M, Mohammed Hindi N, Osman IH, Latef Anouze A, Al-Ayoubi B (2012) An analysis of methodologies utilised in e-government research: a user satisfaction perspective. J Enterprise Inf Manag 25(3):298–313
8. Dwivedi YK (2009) Viewpoint: an analysis of e-government research published in Transforming Government: People, Process and Policy (TGPPP). Transform Gov People Process Policy 3(1):7–15
9. Irani Z, Dwivedi YK (2008) Editorial. Transf Gov People Process Policy 2(4):221–224
10. Welch EW, Hinnant CC, Moon MJ (2004) Linking citizen satisfaction with e-government and trust in government. J Public Adm Res Theory 15(3):371–391

11. Riley TB (2003) Defining e-government and E-governance: staying the course (The Riley Report), eGov Monitor, London
12. Irani Z, Elliman T, Jackson P (2007) Electronic transformation of government in the UK: a research agenda. Eur J Inf Syst 16(4):327–335
13. Hazlett S, Hill F (2003) e-government: the realities of using IT to transform the public sector. Manag Serv Qual 13(6):445–452
14. Sharif A, Irani Z, Weerakkody V (2010) Evaluating and modelling constructs for decision making in e-government. J Oper Res Soc 61(6):929–952
15. Carter L, Weerakkody V (2008) e-government adoption: a cultural comparison. Inf Syst Front 10(4):473–482
16. Layne K, Lee J (2001) Developing fully functional E-government: a four stage model. Gov Inf Q 18(2):122–136
17. Gant J, Chen Y (2001) Transforming local e-government services: the use of application service providers. Gov Inf Q 18(2):343–355
18. Fang Z (2002) e-government in digital era: concept, practice and development. Int J Comput Internet Inf 20:193–213
19. Brandtzæg PB, Heim J, Karahasanovic A (2011) Understanding the new digital divide – a typology of internet users in Europe. Int J Hum Comput Stud 69(3):123–138
20. Saebo O, Rose J, Skiftenes Flak L (2008) The shape of eparticipation: characterizing an emerging research area. Gov Inf Q 25(3):400–428
21. Al Shafi S, Weerakkody V (2007) Implementing and managing e-government in the state of Qatar: a citizens' perspective. Electron Gov 4(4):436–450
22. Coursey D, Norris D (2008) Models of e-government: are they correct? An empirical assessment. Public Adm Rev 48:523–536
23. Norris D, Moon MJ (2005) Advancing e-government at the grassroots: tortoise or Hare? Public Adm Rev 65:64–74
24. West D (2004) E-government and transformation of service delivery and citizen attitudes. Public Adm Rev 64:15–27
25. Scott J (2006) "E" the people: Do U.S. municipal government web sites support public involvement? Public Adm Rev 66:341–353
26. Hiller JS, Belanger F (2001) Privacy strategies for electronic government. IBM Center for the Business of Government, Washington, DC
27. United Nations (2008) UN e-government survey 2008: from e-government to connected governance. United Nations, New York
28. Pardo TA, Tayi GK (2007) Interorganizational information integration: a key enabler for digital government. Gov Inf Q 24:691–715
29. Janowski T (2015) Digital government evolution: from transformation to contextualization. Gov Inf Q 32(3):221–236
30. Teerling ML, Pieterson W (2010) Multichannel marketing: an experiment on guiding citizens to the electronic channels. Gov Inf Q 27(1):98–107
31. Cegarra-Navarro J-G, Garcia-Perez A, Moreno-Cegarra JL (2014) Technology knowledge and governance: empowering citizen engagement and participation. Gov Inf Q 31(4):660–668
32. Pieterson W, Ebbers W, van Dijk J (2007) Personalization in the public sector. Gov Inf Q 24(1):148–164
33. Linders D (2012) From e-government to we-government: defining a typology for citizen coproduction in the age of social media. Gov Inf Q 29(4):446–454
34. Carlitz RD, Gunn RW (2002) Online rulemaking: a step toward E-governance. Gov Inf Q 19(4):389–405
35. Bertot JC, Jaeger PT, Hansen D (2012) The impact of polices on government social media usage: issues, challenges, and recommendations. Gov Inf Q 29(1):30–40
36. McDermott P (2010) Building open government. Gov Inf Q 27(4):401–413. http://doi.org/10.1016/j.giq.2010.07.002
37. Missingham R (2011) E-parliament: opening the door. Gov Inf Q 28(3):426–434

38. Bannister F, Connolly R (2011) The trouble with transparency: a critical review of openness in e-Government. Policy Internet 3(1):1–30
39. Brown MM (2007) Understanding e-government benefits. Am Rev Public Adm 37:178–197
40. Brown AW, Fishenden J, Thompson M (2014) Revolutionising digital public service delivery: a UK government perspective. Retrieved from http://www.blogs.jbs.cam.ac.uk/markthompson/wp-content/uploads/2014/02/Digital-Public-Service-Delivery.pdf
41. GDS (2016) GDS design principles. (n.d.). https://www.gov.uk/design-principles. Accessed 1 Aug 2016
42. Farmer JP, Panchadsaram R (2016) Designing American government. Des Manage Rev 27(1):6–11
43. Mergel I (2015) Open collaboration in the public sector: the case of social coding on GitHub. Gov Inf Q 32(4):464–472. http://doi.org/10.1016/j.giq.2015.09.004
44. Dunleavy P, Margetts H, Bastow S, Tinkler J (2006) New public management is dead—long live digital-era governance. J Public Adm Res Theory 16(3):467–494
45. Von Hippel E (1986) Lead users: a source of novel product concepts. Manage Sci 32(7):791–805
46. Galbraith B, Cleland B, Martin S, Wallace J, Mulvenna M, McAdam R (2013) Engaging user communities with eParticipation technology: findings from a European project. Technol Anal Strateg Manage 25(3):281–294
47. GDS (2016) Welcome to user research methods Wiki. (n.d.). https://userresearchmethods.hackpad.com/Welcome-to-User-Research-Methods-Wiki-S0j1jM7vrcp. Accessed 1 Aug 2016
48. Daae J, Boks C (2015) A classification of user research methods for design for sustainable behaviour. J Clean Prod 106:680–689
49. Preece J, Rogers Y, Sharp H (2002) Interaction design: beyond human-computer interaction. Wiley, New York
50. Cleland B, Mulvenna M, Galbraith B, Wallace JG, Martin S (2012) Innovation of eParticipation strategies using living labs as intermediaries. Electron J E-Gov 10(2):120–132
51. Bracken M (2016) What we mean when we say digital. https://digital.blogs.coop/2016/06/14/what-we-mean-when-we-say-digital/
52. Hood C (1983) The tools of government. Macmillan, Basingstoke
53. Kotamraju NP, van der Geest TM (2012) The tension between user-centred design and e-government services. Behav Inf Technol 31(3):261–273. http://doi.org/10.1080/0144929X.2011.563797

Chapter 12
Play It to Plan It? The Impact of Game Elements on Usage of a Urban Planning App

Sarah-Kristin Thiel and Titiana Ertiö

Abstract Public participation experts and scholars alike are experimenting with gamification in their quest to motivate citizens to participate in urban planning. This chapter investigates the impact specific game elements can have on citizens' motivation in a mobile participation application. We present findings from a long-term field study with a gamified mobile participation prototype where we explored participants' awareness, acceptance, and experiences of using gaming elements in the application. Our results indicate that the effects of gamified participation are limited as it seems to only be an effective strategy to increase participation for those who are affine to games. For others, the majority who is usually already intrinsically motivated, gamification has little to offer. Yet, when gaming elements offer added value to their engagement, our participants approved of these elements. This work contributes to both gamification as well as to the burgeoning field of mobile participation in urban planning by providing insights about the effect of specific game elements and recommendations for the use of gamification in urban planning applications.

1 Introduction

Electronic participation (e-participation) refers to the use of information and communication technologies (ICT) with the goal to reduce traditional barriers of participation such as physical presence at a specific place at a specific time. e-Participation opportunities started out as web-based. Aiming to increase the overall level of their citizenry's participation, municipalities all over the world have developed their own e-participation platforms. As of now, this goal has not been met yet [1, 25, 45]. One could argue that the main reason for these efforts not having fruited yet, is because of their novelty: citizens struggle to keep track of their

S.-K. Thiel (✉)
Technology Experience Center, Austrian Institute of Technology GmbH, Vienna, Austria
e-mail: sarah-kristin.thiel@ait.ac.at

T. Ertiö
Department of Social Research, University of Turku, Turku, Finland

© Springer International Publishing AG 2018
S. Saeed et al. (eds.), *User Centric E-Government*, Integrated Series in Information Systems 39, DOI 10.1007/978-3-319-59442-2_12

governments' "latest" engagement tools [29]. Other evaluations of e-participation tools have shown that merely offering information (a one-way interaction channel) is not engaging enough for people to start using them. To address this situation, several practitioners and researchers have turned to gamification [40]. But can game elements in participation applications actually meet the goal and promote public participation? gamification has proved successful in influencing user behavior (i.e. increase engagement) in several domains [17, 44], including education, business, or health. By introducing gameful aspects potentially tedious tasks have been made more enjoyable (e.g. [14]). In this chapter, we investigate whether such positive effects can be replicated for urban planning mobile applications.

Today, citizens have the opportunity to engage in urban and political affairs using mobile applications, commonly denoted as mobile participation. Undoubtedly, the biggest asset of mobile participation is situated engagement and ubiquity: citizens can participate on-site whenever they transit a planning location [11, 26]. For instance when walking through a park, a citizen could deem that it should include a playground and instantly submit this idea to the city administration. The proliferation of mobile phones coupled with their cost-effectiveness, simplicity, and convenience of using applications has led to unprecedented numbers of urban governance applications [7, 13].

This contribution investigates if and how game elements impact participation with mobile urban planning applications. Based on previous results from gamification studies it could be posited that game elements will boost people's motivation to participate in urban planning applications. Despite an rapidly growing body of literature on the subject, little empirical research yet exists explaining how gamification works. Attempting to shed light on which specific implementations work best (or better) in certain scenarios [30], apart from effects on motivation, we examine the effects of individual game design elements [8]. While youth is commonly assumed to be quite open-minded towards anything game-like, less is known about other generation's attitudes towards game elements, particularly in the context of public participation. Departing from previous findings that "usual suspects" are usually older and the older generation not particularly being in favor of games [43], it is possible that the current users of e-participation systems might not appreciate game elements in this context. On the other hand, this notion is about to change as nowadays elderly start discovering and enjoying games [23]. It is hence relevant to explore citizens' attitudes towards gamefulness in public participation contexts. And in case gamified participation is accepted among (some part of) the population, the next step is to explore which of the mechanics and elements characteristic to games can effectively promote public participation. It is hence relevant to explore citizens' attitudes towards gamefulness in public participation contexts.

We present findings from a 5-months-long field trial conducted with a urban planning application in the city of Turku, Finland. The platform served as an official channel to contact local authorities and it was openly communicated that the trial was part of a research project. The research team repeatedly encouraged officials to provide feedback to citizens' input. The application itself was uniquely designed to respond to issues the municipality wanted to address. Our findings are reflective of the specific conditions under which we tested the application and therefore might only to a limited degree be generalizable to other digital participation tools (i.e. web-based platforms) or to other contexts.

2   Background

Research on e-participation is well established, but gamified electronic participation is yet in its infancy. In contrast, gamification and gaming elements are very common in mobile applications for entertainment, edutainment, health and other disciplines (see [22] for a review). There are few studies that fit the context of our case study; most of which are small-scale trials testing the digital participation tools. We begin this section with a short overview of how gamification and public participation in urban planning can be defined and combined into gamified urban planning apps.

2.1   Adding Game Elements to Influence Motivation to Participate

The most commonly accepted definition describes gamification as the use of "game elements in non-game contexts" [9]. Gamification is most commonly applied to proclaim the usage of services. By adding concepts characteristic to games (achieving mastery or autonomy), gamification attempts to add a gameful layer to a system rather than building an entire new game [20]. The main objective of applying gamification is to influence users' motivations. In that respect gamification differs from persuasive technologies, which aim to change attitude or behavior directly (see [32]).

Gamification can be described as adding a hedonic layer to purely utilitarian systems [21]. Hedonic refers to the entertainment aspect that ought to arise when engaging with the game. As users in that moment are anticipated to forget or suppress the external objectives of the service (utilitarian aspect), the game part plays on users' intrinsic motivation to engage (and keep engaging) with the service.

Before gamifying a system it is important to understand what game aspects exist and how they link with other components of the system. In both games and gamification research, several models and frameworks exist that describe and structure game aspects. While providing a conceptual structure, these frameworks can further be used to examine the effect of individual game elements.

MDA (mechanics, dynamics and aesthetics) framework is among the most popular models for games [24]. The MDA model describes the interactions between the rules of the game (mechanics) and the system (dynamics) to generate the gameful experience (aesthetics). Hunicke et al. describe games as a collection of mechanics and dynamics that together trigger aesthetics in players [24]. Mechanics describe the components of a game on a data and algorithm level, referring to the actions, behaviors and control mechanisms afforded to players (e.g. shuffling and betting in card games). Dynamics are the run-time interactions and player's behaviors that are induced by mechanics (e.g. time pressure, opponent play). Dynamics also evoke specific emotional responses (aesthetics) in players (e.g. fellowship, competition).

The MDA model provides a good starting point for describing what makes a game gameful. At the same time, it lays a foundation for understanding the influence of a particular game element on the gameful experience as well as on the player's behavior. It thus presents a good structure for investigating the effect and effectiveness of specific game elements.

We use the term "game element" to describe visible implementations of a game aspect or component that uses or builds on one or more game mechanics. In short, game elements represent interface-based artifacts with which users can interact either directly (e.g. avatar that can be played with) or indirectly (e.g. earning points awarded for in-app activities). The inclusion of the game element concept extends the MDA model, allowing us to refer to an established theory of game research in order to present the key measurements and link experiences to game mechanics.

2.2 Public Participation in Urban Planning

Traditionally, public servants engaged citizens in urban planning through established face-to-face participation methods like public hearings, citizen panels, and deliberations. With the adoption of ICTs, e-participation became an umbrella term for everything from e-voting, e-petitioning to online budgeting. In urban planning, Geographic Information Systems (GIS) gained traction and finally established themselves as a preferred public engagement method for planners. However, especially early on, electronic tools were highly specialized and citizens lacked the skills to use them effectively. In fact, while the digital divide with the increasing proliferation of digital devices loses significance, lack of sufficient skills to use e-participation tools still remains a major barrier to participation (see second-level digital divide or generational divide).

The jury is still out for what might be considered effective public participation in urban planning. A common understanding is that involving diverse groups of citizens yields better plans [5]. This statement lies on the assumption of crowd intelligence, postulating that large and diverse groups of individuals outperform small groups of experts. Again this implies that e-participation platforms succeed in engaging a broader population, hence going beyond the "usual suspects" of public participation. For this gamification might be a promising approach [3, 39].

Brown and Chin advocate two types of criteria for evaluating the effectiveness of public participation: process and outcome criteria [4]. Process criteria evaluate how a participatory tool has been constructed and implemented; outcome criteria evaluate the results of the public participation process. For example, representativeness (understood as representative sample of the population), involvement in the design of the participation, and convenience are assessed as process criteria. Workable solutions, consensus or participants' satisfaction are, among others, considered outcome criteria. Public participation has been extensively researched in political sciences too. From this perspective, "effectiveness" of participation includes educating citizens, impact on policy, deliberation, and increased trust.

For e-participation tools to make a valuable contribution to public participation they need to effect either process or outcome criteria. When experimenting with gamification in urban planning, the balance between participation and engagement needs attention: the goal is to increase participation (the number of users and contributions) as well as engagement (the quality of the discussion, deliberation and argumentation). In terms of enjoyment and fun, the game elements need to be smoothly integrated so as not distract participants from the "seriousness" of urban planning. As mentioned, citizens' choice of how to participate (which tool, when and where) is also part of evaluating public participation effectiveness. Next, we introduce gamified urban planning and unravel the reasons for gamifying citizen participation.

2.3   Gamified Urban Planning

While gamification itself has not received much attention in the domain of citizen participation, simulation games have a long history in urban planning [16]. Building on the success of commercial simulation game *SimCity*, research dealt with the development and evaluation of serious civic games designed to support and simulate urban planning.

The rationale behind this approach is grounded in the argument that games facilitate learning processes [10]. While playing games that simulate urban planning processes, it is anticipated that citizens learn about planning procedures and instruments as well as about the roles of various stakeholders involved [18]. Civic games are employed to train urban planners but also to support decision-making. In this context civic education refers to the provision of an environment in which citizens can broaden their understanding of urban and political issues, deepen and enrich their substantive knowledge about key actors and the government's role in the planning process [37]. With regards to learning processes, it is further distinguished between collective reflection and collective exploration [10, 18]. Collective reflection refers to citizens improving their civic skills by way of collectively reflecting on spatial issues in their environment. Features allowing for social interaction between participants can support collective reflection.

Drawing on the success of social networking sites, features enabling social interaction are often integrated in participation tools [21]. This practice has become so popular, that social features have almost become an integral part of gamification strategies. The second concept, collective exploration, refers to processes where citizens playfully investigate various options until achieving consensus. While research on simulation games has grown into a research discipline, introducing playful activities into participatory processes and gamified participation are only now starting to be explored. In practice, the norm are so called "reporting apps" (e.g. *FixMyStreet*), allowing citizens to fill in service requests which the city administration then attends to. Gamified urban planning apps are still few and as a consequence, research on the effect of game elements for urban planning is in its infancy.

2.3.1 Notable Examples of Gamified Participation Tools

Albeit not classifying as public participation as we define it (i.e. involving two distinct stakeholders, where one is an public institution), *DoGood* supports civic engagement the mobile application allows sharing and coordination of good deeds. A user study showed that especially the game elements linked to social aspects (e.g. social influence, social recognition) were able to tap into the intrinsic motivation of participants.

Love Your City! [38] is a mobile application that includes game aspects like emoticons, profiles, statistics and a fading date for contributions (i.e. determining when the contribution will be removed from the app). The app facilitates visualizations for urban planning sites by using augmented reality. Other examples resemble the popular simulation game SimCity. Apps like *NextSuisse* and *StreetMix* provide users with online spaces for creativity (addressed in the previous chapter as game aesthetics). *NextSuisse* allows citizens of cities in Switzerland to explore opportunities for a future development of their neighborhood in two phases. In a first phase, citizens can develop their home town by placing assets (e.g. trees, public transportation, housing) from a tool box on the scene representing their home town. In a second phase, citizens can test their design against developments (e.g. population growth) that are based on real-world data as well as calculated factors such as living quality. Shifting to a smaller scale, *StreetMix* focuses on one street at a time. The app allows users to design a street by adding or removing lanes for public transport, bike lanes or widening sidewalks. To the best of our knowledge, the gaming aspects of these apps haven't been evaluated.

On the contrary, Poplin evaluated how serious games could be used as means for solving complex urban planning issues. Among her findings of the evaluation of *NextCampus* [33] was the critique of the game being too complex; therefore, she suggested to reduce the number of game elements, which would provide a clearer structure to the game. With *NextCampus* essentially being a game, Poplin was confronted with the question of whether results from this system can be considered serious opinions from players or just results of the game-play. In a notable example, *B3-Design your marketplace* was evaluated by two user groups [34]. Both university students and the elderly appreciated the game aspects and were enthusiastic in learning about their environment. However, the elderly did not comment directly on the integrated game elements, which raises the question whether this group had actually taken note of the game aspects.

Thiel and Lehner evaluated a first version of the present prototype [41]. In contrast to the study presented here, the study only lasted one afternoon and took place without the municipality's involvement in the trial. The study did not investigate the effect of individual game elements but rather looked at the gamification strategy as a whole. Participants' reaction towards gamified participation were explored and whether adding gamification to a participation platform yields in different usage patterns and topics/themes addressed. No significant differences were found regarding posted contributions and thematic focus. Some participants raised concerns that game aspects might devaluate the process as some people might attempt to "play" the system. Overall, game elements were regarded as a sideshow to voicing their opinion.

Detailed evaluations of the effects of gamification on planning apps are scarce [40]. As noted, the majority of previous work has focused on the development of serious games or civic games, which were then evaluated with regards to the general acceptance of game aspects. In summary, the evaluation of specific game elements for civic participation is missing in both research and practice. This study addresses this research gap.

3   Examining Game Elements in Täsä

In order to gain insights into the potential impact of game elements that were incorporated in urban planning apps, we analyzed the results of a long-term field trial. In close cooperation with the local municipality of Turku in Finland, a sophisticated mobile participation prototype was introduced as an official communication channel for the duration of 5 months. During that time, the application (named Täsä) was available for download from all major app stores (Android, Apple, Windows). Instructions for using the application were provided on a separate website.

3.1   Data Collection and Assessment

Our methodology to collect data from this user study consists of three parts: (1) an in-app pre-survey, (2) usage of the app logged in the backend and (3) a post-survey distributed via e-mail. To keep the registration process light-weight, we did not inquire any demographics upon registration. Users could voluntarily answer an in-app questionnaire (1), which consisted of socio-economic background variables (age, education, gender, mobile phone skills, etc.) as well as a set of political questions (trust in institutions and efficacy). It was mainly modeled after questions asked in the ESS (European Social Survey). 185 users completed this pre-survey, giving us some indication about our user base. After the trial, we send all registered users a post-survey (3) to which 129 out of our 800 registered users answered. This questionnaire contained some 30 questions evaluating user experiences with the app: motivation, social interaction, technical features of the app, desired improvements. Each question in the survey was optional as a measure to counter-fight general low response rates of questionnaires. This resulted in some of the responses in the survey being incomplete (17%). Some participants skipped all closed questions and only answered the open-ended questions that asked for additional feedback and comments. This suggests that our users truly reflected on the opportunity of mobile participation for urban planning. We asked app users directly to rate their perception of the influence of game elements. In doing so, we believe that the responses are more reliable than asking indirectly.

This study reports on a batch of questions (i.e. blocks) that evaluate participants' awareness, perception and experiences with the game aspects included in the application. The first block inquired whether certain game-related aspects in the application influenced participants' motivation to use the participation platform. Looking into this is of great relevance as it provides us insights on what aspects (e.g. elements of the technical realization or the nature of the participatory process) make people participate. There is yet a lack of studies on e-participation that evaluate the user experience. We argue that taking the user perspective into account is at least equally than focusing conceptual aspects of participation methods such as their connection to policy implementation. Therefore we added two more user experience relevant aspects to our investigation. Apart from asking about the influence of (all) game elements in general, we further asked about the effect of the aesthetic competition and achievement (see Table 12.2). If not stated otherwise, responses were measured on a five point Likert-scale from 1= "not at all" to 5= "very much". A second block assessed participants' awareness and appreciation of the included game elements and mechanics. Here answers were measured based on four items combining the factors awareness and appreciation (4-point Likert scale from "I did not notice" to "I noticed and liked"). The third block inquired how the game aspects affected participants' usage behavior (dynamics). We measured this block using Boolean values (yes or no; see Table 12.5). Towards the end of the trial we further conducted semi-structured interviews with 12 participants, who had up to this point not become active in the participation app.

3.2 Täsä: The Mobile Participation Application

The prototype had been developed in an iterative user-centered process and hence was tested in various smaller scale studies (e.g. [41, 42]). It builds on the participatory sourcing approach, where citizens' voluntary input is used for deliberation, ideation and feedback processes. Central to the concept are contributions, which are geo-referenced pieces of content. Ideally, a contribution would include all possible fields in the template: location; classification (Idea, Issue, or Poll); picture; title and description; tag (infrastructure, transportation, architecture, urban planning, recycling, innovation); emoticons; attached to (name of mission).

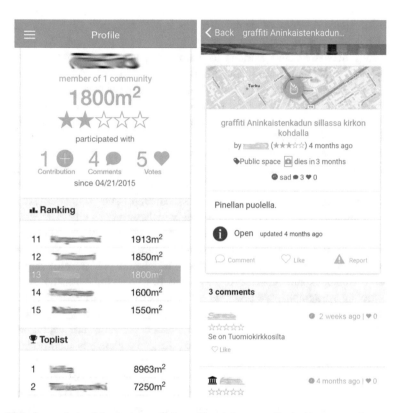

Fig. 12.1 Screenshots of the prototype (*left*: profile; *right*: a contribution)

The image on the right side of Fig. 12.1 shows an example of a contribution. Contributions are publicly visible on both a map and as a list. They can be commented and voted upon by other users. The detailed contents of contributions are outside the scope of this chapter. In short, contributions belong to three categories: urban environment (river banks, market square, service requests), transportation in the city (public and private transportation, parking, biking, including safe areas to cross streets), and leisure activities (green areas, public spaces, sports and events). Civil servants responded to those contributions, discussing suggestions with citizens who uploaded contributions and providing status updates. The servants requested feedback on upcoming plans or controversial topics themselves, known as missions in the Täsä app.

This form of communication between a city and its citizens shall not only give city administration a better understanding of citizens' wishes and opinions, but also give citizens the opportunity to become involved in processes and decision-making regarding plans that affect their life. Participation therefore holds benefits for both parties. People are more likely to be supportive of the implementation of related policies, projects as well as collective efforts if they have been involved in the planning process [19, 35].

We integrated a series of game elements in the Täsä prototype with the goal to cast a wider net of participants as well as increase its usage. We started by identifying mechanics characteristic for games that served as a pool for designing the gamified elements in Täsä. The final selection of game elements was based on (1) interviews with users of location-based and pervasive games, where we explored the motivations to engage with such systems [27]; (2) experience reports of participatory processes from practitioners; (3) review of existing gamified public participation platforms [40].

A first version of the prototype was evaluated in two user studies, where the first was an internal test focusing on usability and technical problems [42]. The second study was designed as a 1-day field trial in which the general concept and the acceptance of the game elements were evaluated [41]. In the context of that study, ten participants were instructed to freely walk through a city district and post about anything they came across and found worth suggesting or reporting to the city administration (e.g. opportunity to turn an abandoned park into a playground; fix a broken street lamp) using the application. Participants of this study appreciated the game elements and reported to have had fun engaging with the system. In the following paragraphs, we describe the game elements (all caps) integrated in the final version of Täsä detailing their implementation and the associated game aesthetics. In order to enhance readability, game elements are capitalized and aesthetics italicized. Table 12.1 summarizes the game elements incorporated into the mobile participation platform.

As mentioned, contributions are the core of Täsä. The danger of being spammed is omnipresent, particularly when allowing for social interaction (i.e. commenting other people's posts). We therefore developed a mechanism that automatically controls the quantity of input while at the same time taking quality into account: the LIFETIME element. Upon creation, all contributions start with an initial LIFETIME, which decreases over time. In-app activities such as commenting and voting prolong the LIFETIME of a contribution. Without such activities, a

Table 12.1 Summary of game elements included in the Täsä prototype

Element	Description	Aesthetic
Lifetime	Each contribution has a limited lifetime that can be prolonged by commenting or voting on it	Challenge
Points	In-app activities (e.g. comments, votes) are rewarded with points	Achievement and competition
Profile	Overview of a users' in-app activities and status	Expression
Progress overview	Overview of for which in-app activities a user has been awarded points	Progress
Missions	In-app tasks relating to a specific topic that can be answered by assigning contributions to them	Challenge
Reputation system	Number of stars awarded reflects the prominence of content	Achievement

contribution dies, meaning they disappear from the system (i.e. the post becomes invisible to users but is archived in the backend). The LIFETIME element is a form of *challenge* with the goal to keep contributions alive over time. The mechanics behind this aesthetic is further known as time constraint or as subordinate concept scarcity. Our implementation is based on the assumption that people are more likely to be interested in and hence interact with contributions that they consider relevant and ignore those irrelevant.

All in-app interactions earn users POINTS, which are displayed in individual PROFILES. These POINTS are measured in square meter and symbolize a user's area of influence that he or she has gained through active participation. Different activities earn users a varying amount of POINTS. Posting a contribution for instance as active and deliberative activity is awarded with more points than expressing one's interest by voting on a comment or contribution. This further reflects recent arguments rating voting as a "watered-down form of participation" [15], equal to slacktivism. POINTS are characteristic for *achievement* systems, where users are rewarded with either virtual or physical artifacts. Apart from personal satisfaction of having achieved a certain amount of POINTS or receiving visual and quantifiable feedback for their participation, POINTS are not connected to a universal meaning. They do however allow for *comparison* and *competition* among users. This is facilitated through a HIGHSCORE list and a LEADERBOARD, both displayed in a user's PROFILE. We decided to include two distinct visualizations of user-rankings with the aim to (1) engage those who have been active in the application for a long time and those over-achieving, and (2) encourage those who have recently joined the platform. New users might not have seen their names on the HIGHSCORE list, but users ranked above and below their own achievement. They could still set themselves the goal to overthrow the user ranking directly above him or her. In this case, the competition between users could turn into mini-challenges. The PROFILE further contains an overview of a user's past ACTIVITIES, detailing when and for what activities he or she has received POINTS. This allows users to reflect on their PROGRESS (also referred to as progression).

Posting contributions, thereby proposing own ideas is essentially a bottom-up process, where citizens make use of their democratic rights by starting their own initiative. The prototype further allowed for top-down initiatives. By creating in-app tasks (so called MISSIONS), the municipality and urban planners could receive targeted feedback from citizens. In such missions, the city administration but also citizens may ask for input on specific topics. For instance, inquiring suggestions regarding the placement of further bike racks across the city or for suggesting temporary uses of buildings and urban areas. We argue that these missions represent *challenges* when formulated in a way requiring users to provide suggestions or solutions regarding a particular topic. Missions can be responded to by assigning contributions to them. We aimed at creating a balanced app, part of which was enabling citizens to create Missions in the same way public servants did. Findings from an earlier evaluation showed that users appreciated MISSIONS, as they gave the application and discussions a certain focus [41].

The REPUTATION system is a game-related feature that was only introduced near the end of the trial. Instead of being based on quantity (i.e. number of in-app activities such as POINTS), this game element reflects the (perceived) quality of participation/posts. The more valuable the community rates a user's generated content (user's comments and contributions), the more stars this user is awarded. The REPUTATION level is determined by the total number of votes a user has received for his or her content. Contributions are richer in content than comments. Thus votes for contributions are counted double in the computation of a user's REPUTATION level. Whenever a user performs an activity her REPUTATION level is displayed alongside his/her username. The amount of stars (zero to five stars) indicates the relevance of the content posted by the respective user. As such, it can be seen as status symbol. Further, a PROGRESS bar in the user PROFILE informs how many votes a user has yet to receive until receiving another star. In that respect, the REPUTATION system also implements the game aesthetic *achievement*.

Social aspects have become common for games and gamification [20]. Yet, it is still debated among game researchers and also other scholars about whether social interaction actually qualifies as game element or even belongs to the game context. Magerkurth et al. note that particularly for pervasive gaming, social interaction is an important component [28]. Social aspects include social interaction, social influence and social relationships (i.e. teamwork, fellowship). Although the application did not allow users to send each other private messages, it still enabled social interaction through commenting features. Social influence of a user could be dependent on a user's REPUTATION level and social relationships be formed through taking part in discussions (from which *collaborations* could arise). Following this argument, we argue that Täsä was built for social interaction or provides opportunity for socializing on urban planning topics.

3.3 Overview of Täsä Usage

From June 2015 to October 2015, 780 people registered with the Täsä app, which was free to download from three major app stores (i.e. Apple App Store, Google Play and Windows Phone Store). We informed the citizens about the existence of the app as an official communication channel with the municipality and local newspaper and flyers. As part of the marketing campaign, posters with QR codes were physically placed at locations that asked questions (MISSIONS) by the city authorities. With the having been accessible only in the Finnish, Swedish and Austrian[1] app stores, in theory only smartphones linked to these app stores could download the app. This entails that also people not living in Turku (= the trial site) could interact with Täsä (e.g. tourists). We had no way of ensuring that the app was exclusively used by residents of the City of Turku—neither did we want to

---

[1]Institutions from these countries formed the consortium of the respective research project.

exclude temporary visitors to Turku as they might introduce different perspectives. Unless they filled in the questionnaire, we have no way of knowing where they were residing. Our sampling method can hence be described as voluntary sampling. While this self-selection can result in the sample not being representative it does reflect a real-world scenario of how other e-participation systems acquire their user base.

According to the in-app survey data, most of the respondents who participated in the trial were young professionals (20–30: 36%, 31–40: 34%), highly educated (62% had an academic degree) who were both curious about testing the app as well as interested in urban planning (see [12]). The gender distribution was balanced even though men participated slightly more than women (f: 41%; m: 59%). Participants indicated a relative high interest in politics and a very high interest in urban planning. A third of the participants stated affinity to games, another 28% reported to play games often or constantly. More detailed insights on who participated and what motivated them as well as the influence of attitudes towards politics on participation are summarized in other papers [2, 12].

We did not use any monetary incentives to compensate for participation. Participant data was generated voluntarily by active participants of the app, who agreed to be part of this study (i.e. accepting a disclaimer in the app). Participation varied significantly over the 5 months (see Fig. 12.2). The participation pattern exhibits a long-tail of activity distributed until the end of the trial without changes after the introduction of the reputation system. As it happens with most digital tools, the vast majority of registered users were lurkers, people who only read the content without contributing (cf. [31]).

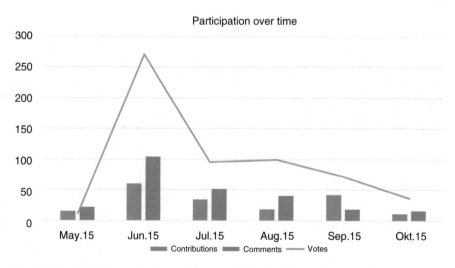

Fig. 12.2 Participation reached its peak in June 2015. Overall, most in-app activities were votes on content

4 Results

We structure our results around the game aspects components identified in the Mechanics-Dynamics-Aesthetics model [24]. In the mechanics section, we report on users' awareness of integrated game aspects. In the dynamics section, we provide insights as to how participants interacted with these game aspects. The aesthetics section describes how participants perceived the influence of the game aspects on their experience of using the mobile participation platform.

Without specifying specific aspects or elements, we asked participants whether the inclusion of game elements impacted their motivation (see Table 12.2). The results show that the game elements did not influence (hence neither increased nor decreased) participants' motivation to take part ($M^2 = 1.63$). About 60% of the respondents replied that game elements did not affect their motivation at all. Only seven participants (6%) indicated that the game elements had some or a considerable amount of impact.

4.1 Mechanics

One question asked participants to state to which extent the possibility to earn points impacted their motivation to use the mobile participation platform (cf. Table 12.2). Similar to the overall impact of game elements, collecting points had close to no influence on motivation for 60% of the respondents. Again, merely four users (3%) said the points motivated them "much" or "very much" to be active in the application.

Apart from inquiring about the impacts on people's motivation, we were further interested in the awareness and acceptance of individual game elements (cf. Table 12.5). From interviews during the trial, we had learned that some game elements had not been noticed as such by participants. We therefore wanted to investigate how many participants were unaware of some or even all game-related elements. A post-survey question thus asked on a multivariate scale whether users were aware of the respective elements and in case they were, whether they liked them (see Table 12.3). This scale was used for the elements LIFETIME,

Table 12.2 Influence of game aspects on users' motivation (1 = "not at all", 5 = "very much")

To what extent did the following influence your motivation to use Täsä?	M	SD
Game elements of the app influenced my motivation	1.63	0.90
Possibility to earn points when using the application	1.66	0.93
Ability to compete with other users for points	1.41	0.75

---

[2]In this chapter "M" refers to the mean values of assessed measures.

Table 12.3 Awareness and acceptance of game elements included (1 = "I did not notice", 2 = "I noticed, but did not like", 3 ="I noticed, but was indifferent", 4 = "I noticed and liked")

Game element	1	2	3	4
Contributions disappeared from the app when their"life" ended	68%	7%	18%	7%
Lifetime of contributions increased by voting and commenting on them	71%	4%	11%	14%
Earning reputation stars when others liked content you created	53%	7%	24%	16%
Being able to judge the relevance of content based on reputation stars	54%	9%	30%	7%
Being able to browse own and others' profiles	48%	11%	30%	11%
Keeping track of one's progress in the game	62%	14%	21%	2%

REPUTATION SYSTEM, PROFILE and PROGRESS. For the game elements LIFETIME and REPUTATION SYSTEM, we inquired two aspects. For LIFETIME, whether users noticed (1) that contributions disappeared from the application when they had run out of lifetime and (2) the possibility to prolong contributions' lifetime by voting or commenting on them. The two aspects of the REPUTATION SYSTEM asked participants' awareness regarding (1) earning reputation stars by receiving votes for their content and (2) judging the relevance of other users' input based on their respective reputation level.

Across all four elements, 62% of respondents to the post-survey noted that they had not taken notice of at least one of the elements. In fact, 36 users indicated that they had not noticed any of the listed game elements. The most noticed element (51% of our respondents) was the PROFILE. The element that had been overlooked by most users was the LIFETIME and to be more concrete, the fact that the lifetime of contributions could be prolonged by voting or commenting on them. In case they had been aware of the features/game elements, participants were asked to state on a three point Likert-scale (1 = "did not like"; 2 = "indifferent"; 3 = "did like") whether they had liked the respective feature. The feature rated negative the most was the PROGRESS information (16%). The game element, which got the most positive votes was the ability to earn REPUTATION STARS (13%). The possibility to prolong the LIFETIME of contributions was noticed least among all game elements (25%). 5% of respondents noticed the LIFETIME but did not like the element, 10% noticed it but were indifferent and 15% noticed and like it. Hence, the limited effects of the LIFETIME effect are partially due to the elements' design, which should have been more clear.

We further asked those participants who used our gamified participation tool to rate the appropriateness of including game elements in the domain of citizen participation. We measured the responses again on a five point Likert scale (1 = "Not appropriate at all" to 5 = "Very appropriate"). Slightly more than half of the respondents did not view it appropriate to add game elements to public participation ($M = 2.57$, $SD = 1.08$). 21% of these respondents believed that gamification and public participation shouldn't be merged. Only 16% rated gamifying participation as somewhat appropriate. As few as 4% perceived it as very appropriate. Another third (32%) reported to be indifferent.

Table 12.4 Correlations between selected game mechanics and level of participation

Variable 1	Variable 2	r	p
Appropriateness	Game affinity	0.346*	0.000
Appropriateness	Interest in urban planning	0.056	0.697
Appropriateness	motivation by game elements	0.468*	0.000
Game affinity	motivation by game elements	0.338*	0.000
Activity count	Appropriateness	−0.601	0.509
Activity count	Game affinity	0.058	0.525
Activity count	Interest in urban planning	−0.265*	0.000

*$p < 0.001$

In order to investigate how the three aspects (motivation, acceptance and experience) as well as attitudes are connected and might determine a citizen's engagement within a digitally mediated participation process, we calculated correlation indexes (= r, see Table 12.4). We found a moderate, positive correlation between perceived appropriateness of gamified participation and game affinity ($r(120) = 0.346$, $p = 0.000$) suggesting that those liking games in general were also in favor of adding game elements to public participation. The latter was not found to hold when conducting the test with interest in urban planning. While perceived appropriateness of gamified participation did not associate with liking individual game elements included in the app, perceived appropriateness did correlate with being motivated by them, $r(121) = 0.468$, $p = 0.000$. Moreover, being affine to games correlates with being motivated by the included game elements, $r(121) = 0.338$, $p = 0.000$. Controversially, neither game affinity nor being motivated by these game elements did yield in participants liking them. Being able to increase the lifetimes of contributions is the only exception here, as those motivated by it also liked this feature $r(120) = 0.240$, $p = 0.000$. Summarizing, these findings suggest that gamefulness in this context can motivate people that have an intrinsic interest in games to engage in public participation. This group was also found to be in favor of the concept of gamified participation.

Previous studies found that hedonic aspects drive actual use [21], yet our data cannot confirm this tendency for game-related attitudes. For instance, the belief that gamified participation is appropriate did not lead to increased participation ($r(121) = −0.601$, $p = 0.509$). Conversely, interest in urban planning positively correlated with the level of participation ($r(180) = 0.265$, $p = 0.000$). This finding supports Hamari and Koivisto's claim that attitudes do not directly affect actual use but that utilitarian and social aspects have an effect on use intentions through attitude [21].

We further analyzed whether liking individual game elements led to an increased participation. Our results show that in this trial, appreciating specific game elements can lead to increased participation. Liking the mechanic of slowly dying contributions positively correlated with activity counts' of participants, $r(122) = 0.367$, $p = 0.000$, resulting in more contributions, comments and votes. In contrast, being aware and liking the opportunity to prolong the lifetime of contributions merely resulted in more comments, $r(120) = 0.255$, $p = 0.005$. This suggests that implementing a method that controls the quantity of content posted (here the LIFETIME element), leads to more content being posted. For gaining reputation stars, we could not find any correlation with the level of participation, $r(122) = 0.175$, $p = 0.054$. Yet, being able to judge the relevance of posts based on reputation stars awarded to users yielded in more comments, $r(122) = 0.195$, $p = 0.032$. It remains unclear whether participants commented more because they wanted to improve their own reputation or whether the fact that the relevance the community attributed to a specific user increased their motivation to reply to this user's posts.

4.2   Dynamics

According to Hunicke et al., dynamics define the player's behavior and how these work to create aesthetic experiences [24]. As these dynamics describe how users react to game elements, third block of questions in the post-survey asked participants to rate items on a list of statements that applied to their experience of using Täsä.

One common critique of gamification is that users might "game" the application, that is either manipulate the system or cheat in the game. With regards to gamification, we argue that there is a difference in manipulating and cheating. While "manipulating" refers to acts that are motivated by the objective to achieve something in the non-game context, "cheating" is an approach to progress in the game. In the context of our gamified application, the LIFETIME of the contributions can be tampered with. Voting and commenting on relevant contributions in order to keep them "alive" is an encouraged activity within Täsä, one that is rewarded with points. Keeping irrelevant or one's own contributions alive is not encouraged, particularly if the only motivation is to gain more points. 93% of participants indicated that they have not actively tried to keep contributions alive, 9% tried to do so by voting and commenting. These findings serve as indication that the majority of participants neither tried to manipulate nor cheat the system.

Another point of critique assumes that gamification might increase usage of a system by only encouraging participation (reach) but not engagement (depth of participation). In this field study, neither participation nor engagement was directly rewarded (e.g. no vouchers as compensation). Indirect or emotional rewards such as feelings of altruism and having a say in how the city is planned, were subject to the individual participants. Given the lack of incentives for participating, the only motivations to become an active contributor can be associated with genuine interest in urban affairs or with voicing one's opinion, gaining social influence or recognition within a community and, finally, the fun of playing a game.

Table 12.5 Participants' experiences of succeeding in the game while using Täsä

Statement	No	Yes
I actively tried to keep posts in the application alive	93%	7%
I tried to keep contributions alive by posting and voting on them	91%	9%
Sometimes I posted content only in order to succeed in the game	99%	1%
I tried to get more points by posting content	98%	2%
I repeatedly checked my points	98%	2%
I was aware of other users' points	93%	7%
I felt a competition between the users	94%	6%
I attributed more relevance to posts from people with a higher reputation level	86%	14%
I felt discouraged by seeing how many points other users had already gained	97%	3%
Seeing other users' progress encouraged me to become active as well	95%	5%

We asked participants if they sometimes posted content only to succeed in the game (binary scale, see Table 12.5) to find out how prevalent the motivation of advancing in the game was. With 99% of participants denying having done so, we are confident that the percentage of people who took part only because of the game, is vanishingly small. As an inference, we can also claim that participation came from motivations beyond playing the game. At this point, it is important to remember that these results are based on self-reported data, meaning that a considerable amount of participants might have still tried to game the system but did not want to admit in doing so.

The question as to whether participants tried to gain more points through in-app activities such as posting content and voting yielded in a 98% negative response rate. Keeping track of one's points was an activity that only 2% of the participants pursued. Although participants seemed disinterested in their own profiles, 7% of all participants indicated to have been aware of other users' points.

4.3 Aesthetics

Another block in the post-survey aimed to address the aesthetics of the participation platform. Aesthetics are brought about by the integrated game elements. In contrast to game elements which can be "used" by interact with them (e.g. writing contributions to earn points), aesthetics arise when interacting with a gamified system (or playing a game). They aim to evoke emotional responses in users and players [24]. Table 12.1 lists the aesthetics in Täsä and matches them with the respective game elements that brings them about.

We asked participants to what extent the ability to compete with other users for points had an influence on their overall motivation to participate. Our goal was to investigate how allowing for and creating *competition* between participants was in increasing engagement in public affairs. As with the other measurements, we used a five point Likert scale (1 = "not at all"; 5 = "very much"). Responses showed that *competition* with fellow users did not affect participants' motivation at all ($M = 1.41$, $SD = 0.75$). 22% said that being able to compete for points only had a minor impact on their motivation. This shows that participants were not out to compete with their fellow citizens. In fact, only 9% of the participants felt some kind of competition between the users.

We further explored whether the *achievement* system (here points) had a positive (encouraging) or negative (discouraging) effect on users (see Table 12.5). 97% participants responded that they did not feel discouraged by seeing how many points other users had already gained. The same magnitude (95%) disagreed with the statement that seeing other users' progress encouraged them to become active as well. 87% of participants were indifferent to keeping points (e.g. neither discouraged or encouraged).

We inquired what role the opportunity to interact and exchange ideas with other users had on engaging in public affairs because we were interested in the effect of social interaction among participants. For over one third of our participants, the ability to socially interact with others somewhat impacted their motivation to use Täsä ($M = 2.69$, $SD = 1.06$). Almost half (45%) indicated that social interaction had little or no influence, whereas for 20% of participants being able to interact with others did at least impacted their motivation to a great extent.

Apart from direct social interaction (e.g. communication with other participants), there are also other behaviors and experiences that are evoked by being exposed to a community (i.e. publicly posting one's opinion). As participants of Täsä could stay completely anonymous by choosing a pseudonym instead of their real names, the application offers few possibilities to people's personalities and attitudes. The REPUTATION SYSTEM was introduced as a way to give participants an indication of another user's reputation by summarizing the overall quality of his or her previous posts (e.g. star level). The idea was that users would attribute more relevance to posts from users with a higher reputation level and therefore be inclined to also engage in discussions this user was involved in or initiated him/herself. 14% of the participants confirmed this tendency (see Table 12.5).

5   Discussion

Based on the results of our case study, we discuss the effectiveness of game elements in mobile urban planning applications structured around three themes: motivation, participation, and appropriateness. As our results are based on the evaluation of a specific mobile application with a distinct selection of game elements, results should be considered carefully and with this context in mind. Where we deem it appropriate, we try to generalize aspects beyond the scope of our field trial and draw conclusions for the design of future participation applications.

In the Täsä Trial, Game Elements Contributed Little to Motivate Citizen Participation

Our results show that the game elements we included in our mobile participation prototype did not succeed in raising participants' motivation to engage in discussions about urban planning.[3] Particular elements (e.g. points) supporting competition do not seem to stimulate engagement in the context of public participation.

Information and feedback are commonly considered very important elements in applications, particularly so in games. Therefore it is somewhat surprising that most of those users who had been aware of the progress information (i.e. activities they had gained points for), had been either indifferent (17%) or did not like this display (16%). Hardly any of the participants repeatedly checked their score, which further indicates an indifference to points in general. With almost none of the participants being interested in gaining points, we conclude that points were not an effective method for increasing the motivation to participate in our trial. Moreover, the aesthetic of competition, which can be stimulated by the comparison of points, seemed to have little impact on the vast majority of users. In fact, only very few actually felt a competition between users. Even if there had been competition going on, responses to the post-survey indicate that participants would not have been influenced by it. This suggests that competition as an aesthetic is rather ineffective in motivating people to participate in urban planning. A reason for this might be that democratic principles (e.g. every opinion should carry the same weight) do not align with mechanics such as competition. On the other hand, being able to contact fellow citizens is not a strong motivation either. It seems that when engaging in urban affairs, people are not looking for opportunities to interact or compare themselves with others. While introducing the point system almost had no encouraging effect on participants in terms of group dynamics, seeing other users' progress did not discourage them either. For the vast majority keeping track of users' success or failure (e.g. in leaderboards or highscore lists) had no impact on their participation. This leads us to conclude that point systems are at least not harmful in the context of public participation. Overall, public participation can be described as an individualistic activity, which is supported by the idea of democratic actions that should also not be influenced by others.

A finding that mitigates the statements above concerning the effectiveness of gamification in mobile urban planning applications, is that over 70% of our participants indicated to be at least somewhat interested in politics (71%) and 94% in how the city of Turku (trial location) is physically planned. This supports our argument that our participants were already enough intrinsically motivated and thus did not need or care for another motivational aspect. The lack of support for gamification in the trial may be the result of citizens' perception of urban planning being a "serious matter" (35% were primarily interested in urban planning). It appears that for the citizens in our trial, matching the seriousness of urban planning with the fun of game elements eluded. We had no way of anticipating who

---

[3] Here participation refers to activities in the application (i.e. posting contributions or comments).

the users would be and what they would find interesting. We planed for gamification as an aid to boost participation. If anything, our findings suggest that when prior motivation is in place gamifying a participation app (except for lifetime and reputation) has little effects on participation. The question then becomes: why were citizens in our trial unresponsive to game elements? Perhaps game aspects are still a hot topic for researchers that citizens are unknowledgeable about. Furthermore, gathering points in our trial was not associated with any incentives and merely showed how active a user was. This lack of meaning of collecting points might have been the reason for the ineffectiveness of motivating users to engage more. On the other hand, incentivizing and hence encouraging citizens' participation for monetary gain in the context of urban planning might not be very sustainable nor leading to truthful or thought-through contributions (i.e. gaming the system in the quest for points).

LIFETIME Increased Participation and REPUTATION Was the Most Meaningful Game Element

Täsä participants have not realized that contributions can be revived by actively engaging with the content, commenting and voting. We interviewed participants half-way through the trial, and they seemed confused and surprised when asked about the lifetime feature. They did not seem to know what (game element) we were referring to. From these discussion, we also learned that some participants (who had taken note of the specific design of the contribution icons) mistook these icons as loading bars, signaling that the data for that particular contribution was still being loaded. Only when we showed them the interface element and explained its purpose, did they understand and noted that this mechanic was actually a good idea to avoid irrelevant content and spam. Contrary to these opinions, results from the post-survey suggest that even if they did notice the lifetime feature, only a few users (5) indicated that they liked both aspects of the lifetime element, namely contributions disappearing as well as the possibility to prolong lifetime with in-app activities.

The lifetime mechanic, albeit overlooked by most, was the most effective in terms of increasing participation. Those participants who liked the lifetime mechanic contributed more than those who indicated that they have not noticed nor liked this element. This result shows that the lifetime mechanic can be a powerful tool both for auto-regulating the content of the application and also encouraging participation. In addition, it shows that this game element should have been explained in more detail (e.g. make the design more explicit). Based on our findings, we argue that lifetime—or in broader terms scarcity—is an element that can potentially promote citizen engagement.

In contrast to the other gaming elements, the reputation system was introduced rather late in the trial (1 month before end) and therefore participants had less time to grow accustomed with the feature. Nevertheless, the reputation system was the third most noticed element in the application. In light of the late deployment, its positive ranking by 12% of participants is remarkable. Furthermore, 12% of the participants indicated to have responded to particular posts because of the reputation system, making reputation—or in broader terms social status—by far the most effective game element.

Compared to other gaming elements, the profile received good ratings from participants. In contrast to the reputation system, the high rating of the profile stems from many users being indifferent about the profile. The profile mainly provided information about a user's game progress (number of contributions and comments posted, points gained) but no personal information. As such it would appeal to those participants affine to competition or curious about other users' activities and let those inspire their level of participation. Our conclusion is supported by the fact that social interaction was not an important aspect of the application.

In summary, our findings illustrate that presenting users with an opportunity to see the achievements of other users can be an effective aspect in the quest to entice people to become active as well. It is noteworthy that this interest in others' progress is not induced from a competitive mindset, but more to orient oneself around others, their ideas and maybe also to find one's place in a community. In this respect, our conclusions reflect previous results noting that people do not want to directly compete in the context of doing good deeds [36]. According to our results, the same holds true for public participation in urban planning applications.

Albeit Skeptical, People Are Not Adverse Towards Imbuing Public Participation with Game Elements

Concerning the perceived appropriateness of using game elements in the context of public participation, participants were divided. Most saw the integration of game aspects as neutral; others had a more critical stand. In the context of public participation, reward-based gamification might not be a viable choice as participants ignored earning points and were not interested in competing with fellow citizens. Whenever game elements provided added value in relation to their engagement (e.g. relevance of other posts, star level and increased lifetime), participants were in favor of those elements. Our findings further showed that none of the elements was distinctly disliked by participants. Instead the vast majority was indifferent to them. These results (liking/disliking of game elements) are obviously overshadowed by the vast majority of post-survey respondents not having been aware of the respective elements.

Overall, our findings concerning the appropriateness of applying gamification in urban planning context suggest the existence of at least three user groups: (1) one that disapproves of the use of game elements, (2) one that is indifferent to them and (3) one that values them in retrospect for facilitating their own participation. With slightly more than half of the participants believing the inclusion of game elements in urban planning apps to be inappropriate, we believe that gamification in this context does alienate a large user group. A practical implication of this finding would be that using gamification should only be the last resort in trying to increase participation. Moreover, if applied, the choice of game elements and how they are integrated needs to be considered very carefully. One suggestion could be to let users decide whether they want to augment their participation with a gameful experience as advised by self-determination theory: providing users autonomy of their actions and activities in an application will have a positive effect on their intrinsic motivation [6].

6   Limitations

One limitation of this research ties in with the self-reported data from users who responded to the post-trial survey (120; i.e. 15% of the 800 total users). While these respondents reflect quite closely the application's population in terms of activity and demographics, the representativeness of our users is skewed when compared to the population of Turku overall. Täsä attracted young professionals with high educational attainment (see [12]). Given these findings, we caution when attempting to generalize our findings. Even with such a sample, we position ourself at the top-end of mainstream HCI research who test technologies with under 50 participants.

Another factor that limits our findings is the fact that we did not explicitly inform Täsä users of the existence of game elements and therefore did not follow the example of commercial apps. It could be argued that especially for applications that aim to engage users in democratic processes and activities ("democracy apps"), the design should be more transparent and inform citizens about the concepts used in the application itself (e.g. gamification to boost motivation). We did not actively encourage competition between users (i.e. rewarding points) in an attempt to not alienate those not in favor of games. Our results taught us that gamification might indeed have supported the recruiting/onboarding phase. The question of whether points without explicit competition or incentives motivate participation and activity within apps is something we encourage gaming experts to explore further.

We deliberately chose to not conduct a more experimental design, meaning to create two different versions of the application—one with and one without gaming elements. In this research project, given constraints of time and uncertainty about who would use the app, we opted for a single application design. Reasons further included that we wanted to avoid confusing and displeasing citizens by giving away two apps. We feared that we would need to explain this setup and why as well as how we chose who received what versions. In our opinion, employing two different methods for voicing one's opinion would go against democratic principles. Moreover, our reasoning included a quite practical fact. As the apps were free to download from the app stores, it would have been difficult for us researchers to control who downloaded what version.

7   Conclusion

We presented results from the Täsä field trial, in which a mobile participation prototype including a selection of game elements was tested by both citizens and authorities in Turku, Finland over 5 months. We investigated the effects specific game elements can have on participation when incorporated into mobile urban planning applications by inquiring participants' awareness, acceptance and experiences regarding their use of the Täsä app.

In contrast to previous work on gamification, which has primarily focused on evaluating the acceptance of gamification in general in various domains, the objective of this research was to get insights into which game elements have what kind of impact on users' motivation and hence likelihood to engage with a system. In the context of e-participation, earlier work has mostly concentrated on the design of full-fledged games rather than applying gamification or analyzing the impact of specific elements.

The main result found is that the positive impact of game elements in this case study was very limited. Merely those affine to games reported to be motivated by game elements as well as approved of the concept of gamified participation. Rating gamified participation as appropriate also correlated with being motivated by game elements. However, the majority, which was highly genuinely interested in urban topics and might not need further reasons to engage, was not motivated by the included game aspects. As such, they were also not particularly responsive to nor interested in game elements.

Participants were not looking for opportunities to socially interact with fellow citizens or competing with them, but rather just wanted to voice their opinion. Applying gamification to public participation is a tight-rope walk, as it seems to only reach and be effective for a specific group: those interested in games. Yet, even this group does not approve of all game elements. On the other hand, those unmotivated by game elements do not approve of the concept of gamified participation. While we would not argue that our findings draw the entire gamification approach into question, we recommend to integrate game aspects in such a way that the engagement itself is supported. For instance, we found that when game aspects provide added value to their political engagement, people welcomed these elements and led to increased participation. This was the case for the lifetime elements and the reputation system as it allowed users to rate the relevance and the quality of contributions. Future studies should investigate how and why people notice or neglect gaming elements in participation processes and whether our results would have been different for other game elements. From a methodological perspective, we found that the MDA framework provided a good model to describe different aspects in user experience with gamified applications.

This research contributes to gamification research as it advances insights on how specific game elements can affect people's behaviors and motivations in different contexts. Additionally, we contribute to e-participation engagement as it provides useful insights about what strategies might be effective to increase the level of participation.

Acknowledgements This research was supported by a grant received from Urban Europe in context of the project "Building Pervasive Participation". The authors also thank the City of Turku for their support during the Täsä field trial.

References

1. Åström J, Grönlund Å (2012) Online consultations in local government: What works, when, and why. In: Connecting democracy: online consultation and the flow of political communication. MIT Press, Cambridge, Massachussetts, pp 75–96
2. Åström J, Karlsson M (2016) Will e-participation bring critical citizens back in? In: International conference on electronic participation. Springer, Berlin, pp 83–93
3. Bowser A, Hansen D, Preece J, He Y, Boston C, Hammock J (2014) Gamifying citizen science: a study of two user groups. In: Proceedings of the companion publication of the 17th ACM conference on computer supported cooperative work and social computing. ACM, New York, pp 137–140
4. Brown G, Chin SYW (2013) Assessing the effectiveness of public participation in neighbourhood planning. Plan Pract Res 28(5):563–588
5. Burby RJ (2003) Making plans that matter: citizen involvement and government action. J Am Plan Assoc 69(1):33–49
6. Deci EL, Ryan RM (1985) Intrinsic motivation and self-determination in human behavior. Plenum, New York, London
7. Desouza KC, Bhagwatwar A (2012) Citizen apps to solve complex urban problems. J Urban Technol 19(3):107–136
8. Deterding S (2011) Situated motivational affordances of game elements: a conceptual model. In: Gamification: using game design elements in non-gaming contexts, a workshop at CHI
9. Deterding S, Dixon D, Khaled R, Nacke L (2011) From game design elements to gamefulness: defining gamification. In: Proceedings of the 15th international academic MindTrek conference: envisioning future media environments. ACM, New York, pp 9–15
10. Devisch O, Poplin A, Sofronie S (2016) The gamification of civic participation: two experiments in improving the skills of citizens to reflect collectively on spatial issues. J Urban Technol 1–22
11. Ertiö TP (2015) Participatory apps for urban planning – space for improvement. Plan Pract Res 30(3):303–321
12. Ertiö TP, Ruoppila S, Thiel SK (2016) Motivations to use a mobile participation application. In: International conference on electronic participation. Springer, Berlin, pp 138–150
13. Evans-Cowley JS (2012) There's an app for that: mobile applications for urban planning. Int J E-Plan Res 1(2):79–87
14. Eveleigh A, Jennett C, Lynn S, Cox AL (2013) "I want to be a captain! i want to be a captain!": gamification in the old weather citizen science project. In: Proceedings of the first international conference on gameful design, research, and applications. ACM, New York, pp 79–82
15. Foth M, Brynskov M (2016) Participatory action research for civic engagement. In Civic media: technology, design, practice. MIT Press, pp 563–580
16. Glenn EH (2012) Playing games with the budget: ideas for emphasizing the legislative elements of budget-making through an online multiplayer toy. Available at SSRN 2171435
17. Goh DH, Lee CS (2011) Perceptions, quality and motivational needs in image tagging human computation games. J Inf Sci. doi:10.1177/0165551511417786
18. Gordon E, Baldwin-Philippi J (2014) Playful civic learning: enabling lateral trust and reflection in game-based public participation. Int J Commun 8:28
19. Grant J, Manuel P, Joudrey D (1996) A framework for planning sustainable residential landscapes. J Am Plan Assoc 62(3):331–344
20. Hamari J, Koivisto J (2013) Social motivations to use gamification: an empirical study of gamifying exercise. In: ECIS, p 105
21. Hamari J, Koivisto J (2015) Why do people use gamification services? Int J Inf Manag 35(4):419–431
22. Hamari J, Koivisto J, Sarsa H (2014) Does gamification work?–a literature review of empirical studies on gamification. In: 2014 47th Hawaii international conference on system sciences. IEEE, New York, pp 3025–3034

23. Hill TJ (2016) Gaming among seniors is on the rise around the world. [Online] (Jan 2016). Available http://www.bigfishgames.com/blog/gaming-among-seniors-is-on-the-rise-around-the-world/
24. Hunicke R, LeBlanc M, Zubek R (2004) Mda: a formal approach to game design and game research. In: Proceedings of the AAAI workshop on challenges in game AI, vol 4, p 1
25. Komito L (2005) e-participation and governance: widening the net. Electron J e-gov 3(1): 39–48
26. Korn M (2013) Situating engagement: ubiquitous infrastructures for in-situ civic engagement. Ph.D. thesis, Department of Computer Science, Aarhus University, Science and Technology
27. Lehner U, Baldauf M, Eranti V, Reitberger W, Fröhlich P (2014) Civic engagement meets pervasive gaming: towards long-term mobile participation. In: Proceedings of the extended abstracts of the 32nd annual ACM conference on human factors in computing systems. ACM, New York, pp 1483–1488
28. Magerkurth C, Cheok AD, Mandryk RL, Nilsen T (2005) Pervasive games: bringing computer entertainment back to the real world. Comput Entertain 3(3):4
29. McAleer SR, Panopoulou E, Glidden J, Tambouris E, Tarabanis K (2016) Augmenting social talk: the# ask project. In: Conference for E-democracy and open government, p 61
30. Morschheuser B, Hamari J, Koivisto J (2016) Gamification in crowdsourcing: a review. In: 2016 49th Hawaii international conference on system sciences (HICSS). IEEE, New York, pp 4375–4384
31. Nonnecke B, Preece J (1999) Shedding light on lurkers in online communities. In: Ethnographic studies in real and virtual environments: inhabited information spaces and connected communities, Edinburgh, pp 123–128
32. Oinas-Kukkonen H, Harjumaa M (2009) Persuasive systems design: key issues, process model, and system features. Commun Assoc Inf Syst 24(1):28
33. Poplin A (2012) Playful public participation in urban planning: a case study for online serious games. Comput Environ Urban Syst 36(3):195–206
34. Poplin A (2014) Digital serious game for urban planning:"b3–design your marketplace!". Environ Plan B: Plan Des 41(3):493–511
35. Potapchuk WR (1996) Building sustainable community politics: synergizing participatory, institutional, and representative democracy. Natl Civ Rev 85(3):54–59
36. Rehm S (2015) DoGood: a gamified mobile app to promote civic engagement. Ph.D. thesis, Ludwig-Maximilians-Universität München
37. Shkabatur J (2011) Cities@ crossroads: digital technology and local democracy in America. Brooklyn Law Rev 76(4):11
38. Stembert N, Mulder IJ (2013) Love your city! an interactive platform empowering citizens to turn the public domain into a participatory domain. In: International conference using ICT, social media and mobile technologies to foster self-organisation in urban and neighbourhood governance, Delft, 16–17 May 2013
39. Sumner A (2011) Getting started with gamification. In: Proceedings of the SIDLIT conference. JCCC
40. Thiel SK (2016) A review of introducing game elements to e-participation. In: Proceedings of CeDEM16: conference for E-democracy and open government, July 2016. IEEE, New York, pp 3–9
41. Thiel SK, Lehner U (2015) Exploring the effects of game elements in m-participation. In: Proceedings of the 2015 British HCI conference. British HCI '15. ACM, New York, NY, pp 65–73
42. Thiel SK, Lehner U, Stürmer T, Gospodarek J (2015) Insights from a m-participation prototype in the wild. In: 2015 IEEE international conference on pervasive computing and communication workshops (PerCom Workshops). IEEE, New York, pp 166–171
43. Thiel, SK, Reisinger M, Rderer K (2016) I'm too old for this!: Influence of age on perception of gamified public participation. In: Proceedings of the 15th international conference on mobile and ubiquitous multimedia. ACM, pp 343–346

44. Thom J, Millen D, DiMicco J (2012) Removing gamification from an enterprise SNS. In: Proceedings of the ACM 2012 conference on computer supported cooperative work. ACM, New York, pp 1067–1070
45. Toots M, Kalvet T, Krimmer R (2016) Success in eVoting–success in eDemocracy? The Estonian paradox. In: International conference on electronic participation. Springer, pp 55–66

Chapter 13
Usability Evaluation of the Mobile Application of Centralized Hospital Appointment System (CHAS)

Buket Taşkın, Hüsna İrem Coşkun, and Hakan Tüzün

Abstract The aim of this study is to evaluate the usability of the mobile application of Centralized Hospital Appointment System (CHAS) developed by the Ministry of Health in 2012, as part of e-government efforts in Turkey. A study group was formed consisting of 16 people, 8 females and 8 males between the ages of 18 and 55, and selected for their CHAS experience. Qualitative and quantitative methods were used as part of a mixed research design. Qualitative data sources for the study consisted of observation notes taken while performing authentic tasks that were selected through field research, notes generated by the think-aloud method and meeting notes taken after the process. Quantitative data were collected with a performance evaluation form and questionnaire. Researchers analyzed the data using SPSS 21 program for the quantitative data, and using Microsoft Word and Excel for the qualitative data derived from the participant group. Descriptive analysis, nonparametric chi-square test (single sample with two variables) and Kruskal-Wallis H Tests were used for the quantitative analysis of the data. Moreover, a content analysis method was used for the qualitative analysis of the data. Results of the data analysis indicated that participants of both male and younger groups performed better than others, which was significantly distinctive and matched other literature related to the usability of technology in the many tasks performed by the application. In addition, participants who had experience of using touch-screen devices and were of higher educational status were found to be statistically significantly more successful than other participants. Findings derived from the study indicate that the general specifications and interface of the CHAS mobile application are beneficial and necessary for accessing the medical services. Conclusions also suggest that the application would be easier and more effective to use after the suggested revisions have been made.

B. Taşkın • H. Tüzün (✉)
Hacettepe University, Ankara, Turkey
e-mail: htuzun@hacettepe.edu.tr

H.İ. Coşkun
Turkish Airlines, İstanbul, Turkey

© Springer International Publishing AG 2018   231
S. Saeed et al. (eds.), *User Centric E-Government*, Integrated Series in Information Systems 39, DOI 10.1007/978-3-319-59442-2_13

Keywords Mobile application • Usability • Think-aloud • CHAS • Centralized Hospital Appointment System • Survey • Turkey

1 Introduction

Information and Communication Technologies (ICTs) have been widely used for many domains such as government, health, and some others [1]. Governments take advantage of ICTs to complete the e-government strategies in order to provide better service for the citizens and to eliminate existing bureaucracy, therefore achieving significant economic and operational efficiencies [2]. The Internet, delivering information and enabling online transactions, has been a convenient and cost-saving channel for governments. E-government systems can help with planning the government departments and harness the right technology and networks that are critical in facilitating agile, secure, reliable, and compliant Information Management Systems [1]. Different e-government services, which are used on various platforms, have emerged in parallel to the e-government efforts.

With the rapid developments in ICTs, new types of technological devices emerge and make our lives easier. Mobile devices can be regarded as the most important ones among these. Mobile devices accompany users in different environments all day long. Unlike desktop devices, mobile devices are very light and can be carried by users. Cultural environments in which users live and life's necessities shape the use of mobile devices [3]. The first devices that come to mind when we speak of mobile devices are smartphones, tablets, laptops, and palmtop computers. Smartphones, owned by almost everybody in every section of modern society, are the indicators of the improvement in the mobile market. Although they were regarded as great innovations a couple of years ago [4], smartphones became a necessity for many people and gained an important place in their daily lives since they provide freedom, enable one to access information and provide immediate feedback for communication. The fact that these devices, which make it possible to access information anytime and anywhere, are continually developing new features is inevitable [5].

The most recent evolution of cellphones is that they can be accessed and used easily to suit the needs of a person through the applications developed on these platforms. Human-Computer Interaction examines the relationship between humans and machines. Studies conducted to examine the usability of mobile applications in Human-Computer Interaction increased in number as mobile devices were developed, and many new applications emerged. New competition arises with these technological innovations and various companies launch mobile devices with various specifications. While these specifications include various screen sizes, resolutions, and operating systems, a more important factor is the usability of the mobile technology [6]. Among the characteristics that are related to usability are: adapting to the mobile devices, the ability to continue using them, the elimination of hardware and software problems, and enabling user interaction [7].

It is now possible to perform daily routines, such as shopping or making reservations at any time and from anywhere, with the latest mobile devices and infrastructure. A user can access many services with his/her mobile device from wherever he or she is. Usage rates for mobile technologies in the healthcare industry have increased in recent years and applications have been enhanced in terms of usability and popularity [8, 9]. For example, Apple had 13,000 mobile applications related to healthcare in 2012 [10]. Improving health services in Turkey and the world is gaining importance, and significant studies related to health practices based on technology are being conducted [11].

In this context, the Ministry of Health of the Republic of Turkey took the first steps of e-government towards a Centralized Hospital Appointment System (CHAS), bringing medical institutions and citizens together under the "Health Transformation Program" in 2009, to present citizens with the opportunities that time and technology allow. Following the pilot studies in 2012, patients were provided with the opportunity to choose a doctor from second- or third-grade medical institutions using the ALO 182 call center, the web site, and the mobile application [12]. With this system available to all citizens, patients could make appointments for any time at any hospital in accordance with their healthcare needs, the working hours of the doctors, and their workload.

Studies highlighted that mobile applications used in the healthcare industry have certain limitations and need to be developed in terms of their interaction [13]. In this context, this study aims to analyze the usability of the CHAS mobile application— where the target audience is any citizen—in terms of the authentic tasks assigned to the participants. After performing these tasks, participants highlighted the issues affecting its usability and made suggestions for solutions to these issues. Figures 13.1 and 13.2 show user interface of the CHAS mobile application.

Fig. 13.1 Main screen CHAS Mobile application

Fig. 13.2 Appointment
screen of CHAS Mobile
application

1.1 Usability

Usability has various definitions in academic and commercial studies [14]. These
definitions include the following:

- Target audience's ability to use the system effectively and easily after being
  supported or trained to perform certain tasks [14],
- The ability the user shows in helping him or her perform a task using a tool in an
  environment,
- Usability is an indicator of how well technology has been adapted in the
  applications [15].

What these definitions have in common is related to how easily people will adapt
to the technology [6]. Usability tests are conducted with the think-aloud method
and this method is based on the studies of Ericsson and Simon [16]. Process of
conducting the usability test is as follows:

- Tasks are set,
- Tasks are assigned to the users in a task environment—specified as a laboratory
  or field study—and the participants are asked to think aloud while exploring the
  application interface,
- Information necessary for usability is collected as the participants think naturally
  (aloud). The researcher can either record these or take notes [16].

The usability tests are typically aimed at observing the users while they are using
the software, or hardware, and detecting any problems arising as a result of the
interactions, thereby indicating the areas to be improved [17]. The usability test
method is based on evaluating the ease of use by observing the users perform certain
tasks.

1.2 Research Methods for the Usability Test of Mobile Applications

Two methods (field and laboratory experiments conducted in accordance with the targets and usability) are used in researching mobile applications, and these methods have their positive and negative aspects [18]. A field study with selected, authentic tasks was conducted to obtain results relating to the daily use of the application in real life.

1.2.1 Laboratory Experiments

Laboratory experiments in usability test environments can be easily performed, because there are few elements that can distract the participants. The participants feel comfortable, and they can be easily employed by the researcher. Factors such as noise, interference, or actions that can affect the performance of the researchers and participants are not present in these environments [19]. If the participants are aware that they are in a foreign environment and being tested, they may be negatively affected, and that may give rise to outcomes that affect the results [18].

1.2.2 Field Experiments

Field experiments are the research methods based on the experiences of the participants in authentic environments and are considered to be more reliable than experiments in the laboratory environment, yielding more realistic results. The challenge in this method is that external factors cannot be strictly controlled. If the application is created in the usual environment of the participant, the risk of distracting factors, such as noise or interference, is high. These factors were eliminated as much as possible in this study. Authentic environmental conditions were protected, and issues such as noise, light, or Internet connections that could jeopardize the validity of the study were largely controlled by the precautions taken. Spare mobile devices with Internet connection were present in case of any hardware or connection issues that might have arisen during the process. The direction followed in this study is summarized by the flow diagram in Fig. 13.3, which was put forward in [18].

As this study is related to authentic usability, it was conducted as a field study. Modern and traditional tools were used for data collection, such as think-aloud, observational, and questionnaire methods [20]. Reviewing the literature for improving applications related to health, evaluating users' comments and conducting pilot implementations and usability studies are considered important [21]. When evaluated for their usability, mobile applications' specifications, such

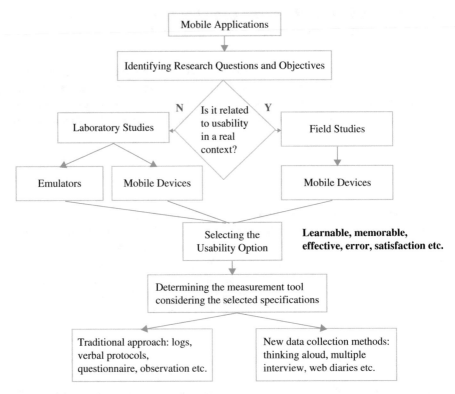

Fig. 13.3 A framework for designing and applying the usability test in mobile applications (adopted from [18])

as enabling users to integrate into the system, its functionality, its guidance, quality of information, interface specifications, and graphics quality should all be considered [22].

2 Literature Review

Even though studies related to usability are conducted in the design and development stages, they are often used for improving completed applications. Developing e-government applications need more usability studies for their improvement, validity, and reliability. Karahoca [23] researched the usability of a mobile emergency service application developed by them to access the patient records of a hospital in a fast, accurate, and efficient way on tablets [23]. Researchers were provided with feedback from nurses and doctors while they were designing the application and they completed their study in two stages. Various tasks related to certain scenarios were assigned to six nurses and four doctors. Times spent performing these tasks were recorded. Moreover, a motivation questionnaire was developed by the researchers, which was used to support the data. As a result of the review, it was found that those who had a high motivation used the interface on a tablet PC effectively. It was also realized that buttons and font sizes should be changed as a result of the usability test.

In another study conducted by Vélez [24], the usability of an application developed to find a solution to the issue of accessing the services in rural areas of Ghana was researched. With the usability tests performed for the application, called mClinic, various goals, such as making it easier for nurse midwives to access the information and reduce the workload in reporting were set, and these goals were set in accordance with a needs analysis. The data in the usability analysis were collected through participant observation, contextual questioning, and interviewing methods. With the data, the application was evaluated with heuristic evaluation, field experiment, and usability questionnaires in the second development stage. As a result of this study, issues in selecting the hardware were detected with the heuristic evaluation. In addition, usability questionnaires indicated that nurse midwives found the application easy to use, but their self-efficacy in using the technology was low [24].

In the study conducted by Hashim [25], a questionnaire related to the usability of a mobile learning application was taken by 66 university students and 12 of them were investigated with participant observation. A significant relationship was found between the usability questionnaire's sub-sections on topics of consistency, flexibility, learnability, least action and most memory load—and participant observation. The usability test was used in this study to evaluate an application previously developed [25].

A prototype edition and usability tests conducted in both an experimental environment and on site were used for improving the myMytileneCity mobile application, an electronic tourist guide. Twenty participants taking part in the experimental environment test—conducted with emulators—were asked to perform the tasks set before them. These participants used the mobile application with authentic devices in a field test. Following these tests, participants were interviewed and their opinions were noted. Many improvement suggestions were made at the end of the tests, and participant satisfaction was found to be high [26]. The literature review indicates that applications were improved in accordance with the results and suggestions from the usability tests.

3 Method

A usability field study and mixed research design was conducted in which quantitative and qualitative data collection methods were used together. Details follow.

Table 13.1 Age and gender distributions of the participants

	18–25 years old	26–35 years old	36–45 years old	Over 45 years old	Total
Female	2	2	2	2	8
Male	2	2	2	2	8
Total	4	4	4	4	16

3.1 Participants

Participants were selected by considering age criteria, gender, and CHAS experience. Those who have used the CHAS mobile application before were not included in the study. Characteristics of the participants are shown in Table 13.1.

3.2 Data Collection Tools

To collect data for the study, notes were taken while the participants performed their tasks and thought out aloud. This was combined with observational and interview notes, questionnaire results, and evaluation forms (filled in by the researchers) displaying how the participants performed their tasks.

3.3 Data Collection Process

First, users were asked whether they had used CHAS on a mobile platform before. The purpose of the study was explained by the researchers and the participants were asked to fill in the questionnaire containing demographic information. The participants were asked to perform the selected tasks with their smartphones or any other mobile device (if available). If they did not have their smartphones, they were asked to perform them with the mobile devices provided by the researchers. The tasks the participants were asked to perform are listed in Table 13.2.

While the tasks were being performed, researchers helped the participants when needed. Task completion rates were specified by considering how the participants perform the tasks with the support from the researchers. Moreover, participants' start and finish times were recorded with completed durations measured in seconds.

4 Data Analysis and Findings

With the codes determined by the researchers, analysis of the data were completed using the SPSS 21 program for the quantitative data and using Microsoft Word

Table 13.2 Tasks participants were asked to perform in the study

Tasks
1. Download and install the Centralized Hospital Appointment System software on the mobile device
2. Log into the system
3. Make an appointment for the city, county, hospital, clinic, polyclinic, and the doctor indicated by the researchers
4. Cancel the appointment
5. Change your e-mail in the system
6. Change your password in the system

Table 13.3 Demographic variable distribution of the participant group

	Gender	Age	Educational status	Computer literacy	Experience of using touch-screen device	Experience of using CHAS
Mean	1.50	2.50	2.13	2.13	2.19	3.31
Min.	1.00	1.00	1.00	1.00	1.00	1.00
Max.	2.00	4.00	4.00	3.00	3.00	4.00

and Excel for the qualitative data derived from the participating group. Descriptive analysis, nonparametric chi-square test (single sample and two variables) and Kruskal-Wallis H Tests were used for the quantitative analysis of the data.

4.1   Quantitative Data Analysis

Descriptive statistics, nonparametric chi-square test, and Kruskal-Wallis H Tests (as the study group was lower than 30) were used for the analysis of the quantitative data in this study [27].

4.1.1   Demographic Data Analysis

In this study, demographic data were collected for the participants relating to their gender, age, educational status, computer literacy, experience of using a touch-screen device, and CHAS. The demographic variable distribution of the participant group consisting of 16 people is shown in Table 13.3.

4.1.2   Analysis of Participant Evaluation Data

How the participant group was made up in terms of the demographic data is explained in Table 13.4 with frequency and percentage values.

Table 13.4 Participant group's demographic distribution by frequency and percentage

Demographic variables		Frequency	Percentage
Gender	Female	8	50.0
	Male	8	50.0
Age	18–25 years old	4	25.0
	26–35 years old	4	25.0
	36–45 years old	4	25.0
	Over 45 years old	4	25.0
Educational status	High school	7	43.8
	Associate degree	1	6.3
	Bachelor's degree	7	43.8
	Master's degree	1	6.3
Computer literacy	Low	4	25.0
	Medium	6	37.5
	High	6	37.5
Experience of using touch-screen device	Low	3	18.8
	Medium	7	43.8
	High	6	37.5
Experience of using CHAS	I do not have a membership	2	12.5
	I have just heard/seen	2	12.5
	I have a membership but I have not used it yet	1	6.3
	I have only used ALO 182 line	11	68.8

Table 13.5 Participant groups' system evaluation

	Interface	Frequency of getting lost	Ease of use	Usability level
Mean	3.88	2.44	2.69	4.13
Minimum	2.00	1.00	1.00	2.00
Maximum	5.00	5.00	5.00	5.00

Once having collected the study data and completed the tasks, participants were asked to evaluate the CHAS interface, frequency of getting lost, ease of use, and usability levels. Evaluation data were collected as five-point Likert items. Mean, minimum, and maximum values from the participants' evaluations are presented in Table 13.5.

4.1.3 Results of the Single Sample Chi-Square Analysis

Results of the analyses and participant group's system evaluation scores (interface, frequency of getting lost, ease of use and usability level) indicated that no significant

Table 13.6 Chi-square analysis results related to the task completion degrees of the participant group

	Task 1	Task 2	Task 3	Task 4	Task 5	Task 6
Chi-square	10.88	2.38	0.88	7.50	7.63	6.13
sd	4	2	2	3	2	2
p	0.028	0.305	0.646	0.058	0.022	0.047

Table 13.7 Changes in group's rates of completing Task 2 (gender)

Group	N	Mean rank	Total rank	U	p
Female	8	5.88	47.00	11.00	0.016
Male	8	11.13	89.00		

difference was found. Considering the task completion degrees, the results of the chi-square analysis are presented in Table 13.6.

The participant group showed a significant difference within itself in terms of the score distribution of Tasks 1, 5 and 6. The significant difference in Task 1 and Task 6 indicated task completion. However, the difference in Task 5 indicates non-completion of the task. In other words, the participant group was significantly successful in downloading and installing the application, and changing their password. The group was unsuccessful in changing their e-mail in the system. The fact that the e-mail section was optional in the signing up process and that many users only provided the obligatory information are considered to be the reasons for this failure.

4.1.4   Results of Bivariate Chi-Square Analysis

The chi-square analysis of the distribution (by gender) of the participants' task scores indicated that there was a significant difference in Task 2 scores: X^2 (sd $= 2$, n $= 16$) $= 7.33$ (p < 0.05), p $= 0.016$. Table 13.7 shows that this difference favors the males.

According to the results of chi-square test—performed to study the relationship between CHAS experiences of the participant group and the task scores—a significant relationship was found between Task 5 completion rates and system experience. For X^2, it was found that the significant difference (sd $= 6$, n $= 16$) $= 16.73$ (p < 0.05), p $= 0.010$ arose from the fact that the majority of those who used ALO 182 line could not complete the task. A comparison between the user evaluation rates and task scores revealed a relationship between the interface evaluation and Task 6 scores. Users who evaluated the interface positively had higher scores in Task 6: X^2 (sd $= 6$, n $= 16$) $= 13.93$ (p $= 0.030 < 0.05$). It was also found that users who evaluated the application's ease of use negatively had higher scores in Task 5: X^2 (sd $= 8$, n $= 16$) $= 16.40$ (p $= 0.037 < 0.05$).

Table 13.8 Changes in the completion rates of Task 1 (by age)

Group	n	Mean rank	sd	X^2	p
18–25 years old	4	12.50	3	8.103	0.044
26–35 years old	4	10.00			
36–45 years old	4	7.50			
Over 45 years old	4	4.00			

Table 13.9 Changes in the completion rates of Task 5 (by age)

Group	n	Mean rank	sd	X^2	p
18–25 years old	4	11.88	3	8.795	0.032
26–35 years old	4	11.13			
36–45 years old	4	5.50			
Over 45 years old	4	5.50			

Table 13.10 Changes in the completion durations of Task 6 (by age)

Group	n	Mean rank	Sd	X^2	p
18–25 years old	4	11.25	3	8.50	0.037
26–35 years old	4	11.75			
36–45 years old	4	5.50			
Over 45 years old	4	5.50			

4.1.5 Results of Kruskal-Wallis H Test Analysis

The task performance of the demographic variables (excluding gender) and their relationship was analyzed with the Kruskal-Wallis H test. A significant relationship was found between the age variable and completion rate of the performance of Tasks 1 and 5 (completion rate and duration). Changes in the completion rates of Task 1 (by age) are presented in Table 13.8 ($p = 0.044 < 0.05$). Younger participants were found to be more successful in downloading and installing the application.

Changes in the completion rates of Task 5 (by age) are presented in Table 13.9 ($p = 0.032 < 0.05$). Younger participants were found to be more successful in changing their e-mail in the system.

Changes in the completion durations of Task 6 (by age) are presented in Table 13.10 ($p = 0.037 < 0.05$). Younger participants were found to be faster in changing their password in the system.

Mean changes in task scores (by age) were found to be at the limit of significance, favoring the younger users ($p = 0.053$). Changes (by age groups) in the mean scores obtained from all the tasks to be performed on the mobile application and the greater success of the younger age groups were some of the expected findings. A significant relationship was found between the educational status variable and the completion rates of Task 2 and Task 3. As the education level got higher, completion rates of Task 2 and Task 3 were found to get higher. Changes in the completion rates of Task 2 (by educational status variable) are presented in Table 13.11 ($p = 0.023 < 0.05$) with users becoming more successful in logging in to the system as their educational status got higher.

Table 13.11 Changes in the completion rates of Task 2 (by educational status variable)

Group	n	Mean rank	sd	X^2	p
High school	7	5.50	3	9.523	0.023
Associate degree	1	3.00			
Bachelor's degree	7	11.71			
Master's degree	1	12.50			

Table 13.12 Changes in the completion rates of Task 3 (by educational status variable)

Group	n	Mean rank	sd	X^2	p
High school	7	5.57	3	8.326	0.040
Associate degree	1	4.00			
Bachelor's degree	7	11.29			
Master's degree	1	14.00			

Table 13.13 Changes in the completion rates of Task 1 (by experience of touch-screen device use)

Group	n	Mean rank	sd	X^2	p
Low	3	3.50	2	6.861	0.032
Medium	7	8.00			
High	6	11.58			

Table 13.14 Changes in the completion rates of Task 2 (by experience of touch-screen device use variable)

Group	n	Mean rank	sd	X^2	P
Low	3	4.33	3	8.326	0.040
Medium	7	7.64			
High	6	11.58			

Changes in the completion rates of Task 3 (by educational status variable) are presented in Table 13.12 (p = 0.040 < 0.05). A rise in educational status also increased the rate of success in making an appointment.

Task 1 and Task 2 completion rates and the mean task scores were found to change in accordance with the experience in the use of touch-screen devices. Changes in the completion rates of Task 1 (with the experience in the use of touch-screen devices) are presented in Table 13.13 (p = 0.032 < 0.05). Those who have more experience of using touch-screen devices are more successful in downloading the application.

Changes in the completion rates of Task 2 (by experience of touch-screen device use *variable*) are presented in Table 13.14 (p = 0.040 < 0.05). Those who have more experience of using touch-screen devices are more successful in logging in to the system.

Changes in the mean task completion scores (by experience of touch-screen device use variable) are presented in Table 13.15 (p = 0.027 < 0.05). This result indicates that being experienced in using touch-screen devices is an effective factor for the completion rates of all tasks and a factor boosting success.

No significant difference (in terms of task completion scores) was found between computer literacy level and task performance.

Table 13.15 Changes in the
mean task completion scores
(by experience of
touch-screen device use)

Group	n	Mean rank	sd	X^2	P
Low	3	4.33	2	7.217	0.027
Medium	7	6.93			
High	6	12.42			

Table 13.16 Analysis of the participant group's system evaluation.

Questions	Subjects	Frequency
Most beneficial specifications	Speed	7
	Being a mobile application	2
	No necessity to talk with someone	3
	No necessity to wait like in ALO 182 line	2
Least beneficial specifications	Other identification info can be obtained from e-government with the id no	7
	Asking landline number	2
Specifications that can be added to make the application more useful	Detailed info about the doctors (résumé, workload etc.)	5
	Automatically filling the location info by location detection	2
	Searching all doctors of a certain department in all hospitals	1
Improvements to the interface to make the application more satisfying	Using different and vivid colors	3
	Bigger fonts and buttons	5
	Birth date selection section should be changed	6
General suggestions and comments	It is beneficial from all aspects but only young people can use it	3
	Deficiencies in directing the user	5
	Crashing issues in certain sections (especially in selecting the county) should be solved	5

4.2   Qualitative Data Analysis

The observational, interview-based, and think-aloud notes collected qualitatively
were analyzed using Microsoft Word and Excel in accordance with the codes
specified by the researchers [28]. The participant group was asked to answer
open-ended questions and evaluate the system. Evaluations were categorized in
accordance with the subject titles in Table 13.16 and the frequency of subjects
mentioned.

   In the data collection stage of the study, participants were asked to think aloud
while performing their tasks and participants were observed by the researchers.
According to the observation and think-aloud notes and analysis results, the issues

Table 13.17 Analysis of think-aloud and observational notes

Issues	Frequency	Details
Connection issue	4	
Touch-screen issue	3	
Getting lost	8	Guidance deficiencies (5)
Unnecessary specifications	15	Landline (5)
		e-mail (6)
Specifications that should be added	5	Other identification to be obtained from e-gov with id no (2)
		Detailed info about the doctors (2)
		Warning about how many characters a password must have (1)
Usability (+)	1	Listing the hospitals
Usability (−)	39	Crashing issues in county selection section
		Entering the date of birth (10)
Ease of use/understanding (+)	2	Selection in accordance with the appropriate criteria
Ease of use/understanding (−)	33	Appointment cancellation (8)
		Downloading mobile application (7)
		Guidance deficiencies (5)
Interface (+)	2	
Interface (−)	12	Entering the date of birth (6)
		Appointment cancellation (5)

in Table 13.17 were found to be mentioned frequently. Issues presented in the table were selected in accordance with the general observations of the researchers and the + and − symbols were used to indicate the positive and negative statements. The frequency of mentioning the issue details was presented in the details section in the parenthesis.

5 Results

The usability of the CHAS mobile application developed by the Turkish Ministry of Health was tested by the participants in specific gender and age groups. Issues were detected in the application interface and its operation when critical tasks were performed, and suggestions to improve the usability of the application were provided by the participants.

Findings indicated that the majority of the participants used the ALO 182 appointment service. The results of the visual interface evaluation indicated that the majority of the participants were satisfied with the application. While using the application and examining the frequency of getting lost, it was found that participants had getting lost issues occasionally. It was concluded that the participants rated the system's ease of use as medium-level. In terms of usability, the majority of the participants stated that they found the CHAS mobile application easy to use.

Findings proved that the participants who got high scores in evaluating the interface also had high scores in changing the password. Participants whose educational statuses were high did not have any difficulties in logging in and making an appointment. It was found that users who had previous experience of touch-screen devices used the application easily and their rates of completing the tasks were high.

Task completion rates for the male participants were found to be higher than those of the female participants. Results of this study correspond to similar studies in this field. In the usability study of Sonderegger and Sauer [29], females had slightly more difficulties than males in completing the tasks and higher mistake rates [29]. The difference in inclination (to use technology) between the females and males favors the male participants, which is in line with the findings of Venkatesh and Morris [30]. In terms of the age groups, younger participants had higher rates of completing the tasks. Results related to the gender and age group variables correspond to the general inclination of the field.

Younger users demonstrated better performance in the web usability test [31]. The fact that younger participants had higher figures in task completion rates is thought to result from their exposure to technology at an early age, as stated by Morris and Venkatesh [32]. One of the interesting results of the study is that the participants' computer literacy level did not affect their task performance, contrary to similar studies [11] in which the participants who had higher computer literacy completed the tasks in a shorter time period.

6   Suggestions and Recommendations

Improvements made by considering the suggestions provided by participants will help users access the healthcare services easily. Following the improvements, new usability studies may be conducted using different methods with bigger participant groups.

Participants stated that they found it helpful using CHAS via a mobile application. However, they indicated that it was unnecessary for the system to ask too much personal information. Some participants stated that certain personal data could be obtained from the e-government system. Moreover, some participants emphasized that detailed information about the doctors should be added to make the application more efficient.

Automatic location entry using location detection technology is among the suggestions made by participants. Sections that challenged the participants most were signing up, putting in the date of birth, date of appointment, and appointment cancellation. Some participants had to log in a couple of times in this section.

Some participants stated that the application has deficiencies in guiding the users. Suggestions have been made for the signing up and information entry sections in general. The fact that the application fails and displays a white screen without responding to the participant interactions in the county selection section highlights the necessity to improve its performance. Some users thought vivid colors should be used in the application. Bigger and clearer buttons for critical operations, such as appointment cancellation that directly affect interaction, and fonts, are among the primary suggestions of the participants. The CHAS mobile application is regarded as a helpful and necessary application for accessing healthcare services and it is thought the suggested improvements will make the application easier to use.

References

1. Bouguettaya A, Rezgui A, Medjahed B, Ouzzani M (2004) Internet computing support for digital government. In: Singh MP (ed) Practical handbook of internet computing. CRC Press, Boca Raton
2. Cao J, Chc Z (2007) Applications of lCT Services for E-Government. In: Xu L, Tjoa A, Chaudhry S (eds) IFIP International Federation for Information Processing, vol 254: Research and practical issues of enterprise information systems II Volume I. Springer, Roston, pp 689–694
3. Namlı Ç (2010) Mobil Uygulama Kullanılabilirliğinin Değerlendirilmesi. Master dissertation. İstanbul University
4. Taner N (2013) Kullanıcılarının akıllı telefonları değerlendirmeleri: Kastamonu şehir merkezinde bir uygulama. Uluslararası İşletme ve Yönetim Dergisi 1(2):127–140
5. INNOVA (2014) http://www.innova.com.tr/en/centralized-hospital-appointment-system.asp
6. Coursaris CK, Kim D (2006) A qualitative review of empirical mobile usability studies. In: AMCIS, p 352
7. Mazman SG, Tüzün H, Akbal S, Yeniad M (2010) Bölüm web sitelerinin kullanılabilirlik testi: otantik kullanıcılarla ve otantik görevlerle bir durum çalışması. In: Proceedings of the international conference of education, research and innovation (ICERI 2010), Madrid, 15–17 Nov 2010
8. Patrick K, Griswold WG, Raab F, Intille SS (2008) Health and the mobile phone. Am J Prev Med 35(2):177–181
9. Tarcan M, Hikmet N, Tarcan GY, Top M, Sapaz B (2013) An investigation on implementation of Central Hospital Appointment System (Chas) in Turkey. In: Proceedings for the Northeast Region Decision Sciences Institute, p 1016
10. William B, Po-Yin Y, Marlene R, Rebecca S, Brown W (2013) Assessment of the Health IT Usability Evaluation Model (Health-ITUEM) for evaluating Mobile Health (mHealth) technology. J Biomed Inform 46:1080–1087
11. Gökay G, Erçil Y, Tokdemir G, Çağıltay N, Aykaç YE (2015) Kişisel Sağlık Kaydı Sistemleri Kullanılabilirlik Durum Çalışması. Tıp Teknolojileri Ulusal Kongresi. Vogue 15(18)
12. The Ministry of Health in Turkey. CHAS website https://www.mhrs.gov.tr/Vatandas/. Accessed 2014
13. Boulos MNK, Brewer AC, Karimkhani C, Buller DB, Dellavalle RP (2014) Mobile medical and health apps: state of the art, concerns, regulatory control and certification. J Public Health Inform 5(3):e229. doi:10.5210/ojphi.v5i3.4814
14. Shackel B (2009) Usability-context, framework, definition, design and evaluation. Interact Comput 21(5–6):339–346

15. Carayon P, Cartmill R, Blosky MA, Brown R, Hackenberg M, Hoonakker P, Walker JM (2011) ICU nurses' acceptance of electronic health records. J Am Med Inform Assoc 18(6):812–819. doi:10.1136/amiajnl-2010-000018.

16. Kaikkonen A, Kallio T, Kekakainen A, Kankainen A, Cankar M (2005) Usability testing of mobile applications: a comparison between laboratory and field testing. J Usability Stud 1(1):4–16

17. Davies DJ (2007) Improving the usability of mobile applications through context-awareness. Doctoral dissertation, University of Oregon

18. Zhang D, Adipat B (2005) Challenges, methodologies, and issues in the usability testing of mobile applications. Int J Hum Comput Interact 18(3):293–308

19. Tamminen S, Oulasvirta A, Toiskallio K, Kankainen A (2004) Understanding mobile contexts. J Pers Ubiquitous Comput 8:135–143

20. Beck ET, Christiansen MK, Kjeldskov J, Kolbe N, Stage J (2003) Experimental evaluation of techniques for usability testing of mobile systems in a laboratory setting. In: Proceedings of Ozchi, pp 106–115

21. Boudreaux ED, Waring ME, Hayes RB, Sadasivam RS, Mullen S, Pagoto S (2014) Evaluating and selecting mobile health apps: strategies for healthcare providers and healthcare organizations. Behav Med Pract Policy Res 4:363. doi:10.1007/s13142-014-0293-9

22. Stoyanov SR, Hides L, Kavanagh DJ, Zelenko O, Tjondronegoro D, Mani M (2015) Mobile app rating scale: a new tool for assessing the quality of health mobile apps. JMIR mHealth uHealth 3(1):e27. doi:10.2196/mhealth.3422

23. Karahoca A, Karahoca D, Pınar İ, Yalçın Ş (2008) Mobil Acil Servis Yazılımı İçin Tablet PC Kullanılabilirlik Analizi. 2. Ulusal Sistem Mühendisliği Kongresi, İstanbul

24. Vélez O (2011) Design and usability testing of an mHealth application for midwives in rural Ghana. Doctoral dissertation, Columbia University

25. Hashim AS, Ahmad WFW, Ahmad R (2011) Usability study of mobile learning course content application as a revision tool. In: Visual informatics: sustaining research and innovations. Springer, Berlin, pp 23–32

26. Kenteris M, Gavalas D, Economou D (2009) An innovative mobile electronic tourist guide application. Personal Ubiquitous Comput 13(2):103–118

27. Büyüköztürk Ş (2004) Sosyal bilimler için veri analizi el kitabı: İstatistik, Araştırma Deseni, SPSS uygulamaları ve yorum. (Press 11). Pegem Publications, Ankara

28. Yıldırım A, Şimşek H (1999) Sosyal Bilimlerde Nitel Araştırma Yöntemleri. (Press 9). Seçkin Publications, Ankara

29. Sonderegger A, Sauer J (2010) The influence of design aesthetics in usability testing: effects on user performance and perceived usability. Appl Ergon 41(3):403–410

30. Venkatesh V, Morris MG (2000) Why don't men ever stop to ask for directions? Gender, social influence, and their role in technology acceptance and usage behavior. MIS Q 24:115–139

31. Chadwick-Dias A, McNulty M, Tullis T (2003) Web usability and age: how design changes can improve performance. ACM SIGCAPH Computers and the Physically Handicapped, vol 73–74, pp 30–37

32. Morris MG, Venkatesh V (2000) Age differences in technology adoption decisions: implications for a changing work force. Pers Psychol 53(2):375–403

Index

© Springer International Publishing AG 2018
S. Saeed et al. (eds.), *User Centric E-Government*, Integrated Series in Information
Systems 39, DOI 10.1007/978-3-319-59442-2

Printed in the United States
By Bookmasters